ociology for Social Work

Also by Lena Dominelli

Community Action: Organising Marginalised Groups

Love and Wages: The Impact of Imperialism, State intervention and Women's Domestic Labour on Workers' Control in Algeria, 1962–1972

Anti-Racist Social Work

Feminist Social Work

Women and Community Action

Women Across Continents: Feminist Comparative Social Policy

Gender, Sex Offenders and Probation Practice

Getting Advice in Urdu

Anti-Racist Social Work Education: Models for Practice

Anti-Racist Probation Practice

Sociology for Social Work

Lena Dominelli

Consultant editor: Jo Campling

palgrave

Published by
PALGRAVE
Houndmills, Basingstoke, Hampshire RG21 6XS and
175 Fifth Avenue, New York, N. Y. 10010
Companies and representatives throughout the world

PALGRAVE is the new global academic imprint of
St. Martin's Press LLC Scholarly and Reference Division and
Palgrave Publishers Ltd (formerly Macmillan Press Ltd).

ISBN 0–333–61521–2

This book is printed on paper suitable for recycling and
made from fully managed and sustained forest sources.

A catalogue record for this book is available
from the British Library.

10   9   8   7   6   5   4
06   05   04   03   02   01   00

Editing and origination by
Aardvark Editorial, Suffolk

Printed in China

To Nazareno, Salvatore, Nicola, David and Nicholas

Contents

CHAPTER THREE
**A Sociology of Social Work and Feminist
Sociological Social Work**

CHAPTER FOUR
The Institutional Parameters of Social Work

CHAPTER FIVE
Care and Control Dynamics in Caring Relationships

CHAPTER SIX
Professionalism and Training

CHAPTER SEVEN
**Education or Training? Power Struggles for
the Heart of a Profession**

Contents

Acknowledgements

Writing a book draws on the ideas, observations, philosophies and life experiences of many. Every encounter I have had has shaped the way I perceive the world, making it difficult to acknowledge all those who have assisted me in the process. I am grateful to all of you for sharing your knowledge with me in the hopes that I would both speak your truths and become wiser. I would want to identify the students and kind workers who let me watch them struggle with difficult dilemmas, facilitate the empowerment of others, laugh with them in joy at their successes and weep with them over their failures. But this is not possible. Nonetheless, you know who you are and whether I have approximated your visions for social work.

More specifically, I would want to mention the readers who gave me their comments and insights. They have made me ask myself probing questions in responding to their views. In particular, I would like to thank my colleagues, David Phillips, Tim Robinson and Glynis Jones for their helpful criticisms. Also, I am grateful to Sue Boldock for her secretarial assistance.

To my family, especially my mother and father, I owe thanks for providing the loving care that freed up my time to work on this book day and night. Finally, to David and Nicholas, I express my humblest appreciation of their good humour in surviving without me for months on end while I got on with writing. This is not a new experience for them, but they do live in hope that, someday, I will have time to participate more fully in mundane activities that mean a lot to us.

Lena Dominelli

Introduction

Social work is currently in a crisis, which has generated much controversy as its legitimacy as a state activity, financial sustainability, professional probity and methodologies have come under public scrutiny. Its failure to resolve social problems in the terms set by either policy makers or users has undermined its status and existence. The high costs of service delivery through centralised state provisions which fail to achieve their objectives of either alleviating personal distress or controlling problematic individuals have fuelled its unpopularity. Highly publicised examples of poor practice, particularly in the child protection field and the abuse of vulnerable individuals by those caring for them have dented public confidence in practitioners' professionalism. Those seeking to create new methodologies for social work practice which are more in keeping with its commitment to serving humanity and enhancing individual wellbeing have been castigated for their idealism and failure to address the nastiness evident in personal behaviour by setting up false expectations about liberation amongst users.

In this climate of charge and counter-charge between two sides, which may be characterised roughly as those wishing to accentuate the controlling elements of social work by focusing on individual responsibility and those favouring the empowerment of users individually and collectively through a progressive structurally oriented social work, there is a need for a calm analysis that enables us to evaluate what is happening in social work practice and make decisions about its future direction. This book makes a contribution to the debate which resolving this controversy requires by arguing that sociological social work from an anti-racist feminist perspective provides us with the tools for making sense of the predicaments

1

facing social work education and practice and giving us a way forward that can meet the aspirations of individual users while, at the same time, taking account of society's concern that the best possible use is made of the limited public resources which are made available to social workers. In short, sociological social work aims to identify and disentangle the politics of practice, thereby enabling us to take more rational decisions about social work activities from a humanistic position which is concerned with facilitating an individual's capacity to develop his or her full potential for growth in a society which acknowledges interdependence as part of the covenant between the individual and the state. Sociology, as an academic discipline, provides us with a firm intellectual foundation on which to build sociological social work.

A sociological connection

Sociology, along with psychology and social policy is one of the cognate disciplines in social work (CCETSW, 1976). Its importance to the discipline of social work was recognised early in the history of the profession. Indeed, the Charity Organisation Society (COS) began training British social workers in the School of Sociology as early as 1903 (Younghusband, 1964). Yet, the relationship between sociology and social work has been an uneasy one, veering from being supportive (Leonard, 1966) to outright hostility (see Davies, 1981, 1985). At times, sociology has advanced understanding in the profession by clarifying its epistemological (knowledge) base (Heraud, 1970). On other occasions, it has provided the theoretical framework within which practice paradigms have developed, for example integrated methods and systems theory (Pincus and Minahan, 1973).

There have also been periods when social work has barely acknowledged the presence of sociology, for example, in the heyday of psychological approaches to the profession when psychodynamic casework ruled (Bailey, 1982). Moreover, sociologists from within social work and outside it, have mounted swingeing critiques about the nature of professional practice, emphasising its control dimensions, (Corrigan and Leonard, 1978; Day, 1981, 1987; Parry *et al.*, 1975; McLeod and Dominelli, 1982). As antagonistic critics, sociologists have challenged the 'wooliness' in social work practice (Davies, 1985; Davies and Wright, 1989; Sibeon, 1989). On the helpful side, sociology has been considered a handmaiden of social work, able to deliver to it a better, more scientific form of practice (Younghusband, 1964). Leonard (1966) anticipated a renewal of its influence in social work.

Social work educators and practitioners have also been concerned at the colonising aspects of sociology. The nature of this colonisation has meant that, at times, social work and sociology have been considered synonymous with each other because they both deal with similar social issues and problems. Indeed, social work has been referred to as 'applied sociology' (Heraud, 1979). However, in this relationship, it is social work rather than sociology which loses its discipline status.

At some points, the social work agenda has been defined through sociological analyses, which have left practitioners and educators feeling that others have been setting the agendas within which they have to operate and have done so in ways which indicate that they have neither understanding nor sympathy for the complexities of practice (Sainsbury, 1982; 1985). Then there are sociologists who have made their reputations through close examinations of social work practice, but have done so without having to either get their hands dirty in the realities of practice, or draw out the implications of their theoretical perspectives and critiques for practitioners (Heraud, 1979). In other words, their work has been theory rather than practice led and has not been practice-relevant in consequence. The expectation that sociology should provide practice-relevant materials is hotly contested by sociologists who feel that sociology's claim to scientific status precludes sociologists from setting prescriptions for practice (Giddens, 1982).

What is sociology?

Dame Eileen Younghusband, the doyenne of social work, has defined sociology as the 'study of society'. For her, this:

> includes the social structure of society, its social institutions, and how people live... (And) culture... (which) deals with the ways in which... individual behaviour, values and attitudes are culturally conditioned; and how different peoples handle the great life experiences of courtship, marriage, birth, growing up, work, old age, death (Younghusband, 1964:124).

This definition will be recognisable to social workers whose life work is the task of intervening in the institutions and situations that Younghusband identifies. It underscores the close connection between the two disciplines.

What is social work?

Social workers work with people who live in society and have difficulty in handling life crises, so the study of society is relevant to them. For Younghusband (1964:39), social work is 'centred around social problems arising from the interrelation between man (sic) and his (sic) social environment'. Consequently, social workers deal with the 'person-in-their-situation' and seek to bring together both social and personal causes in the problems individuals display.[1]

Social work, therefore, responds to unmet human needs that arise as people go about their daily lives. It is carried out in a variety of settings – social services, voluntary organisations, probation, community agencies. Social work is an area of human activity firmly located within the *social domain*, and a suitable subject for sociological study. Additionally, its concern with the fit between individuals and their social circumstances, is a 'distinctive characteristic of social work' and provides its foundation as a *discipline in its own right*. Katherine Kendall (1978:43) argues that the uniqueness of social work as a distinct professional activity rests on its capacity to:

> assess the nature of the need and the problem, to estimate the capacity of the person to handle the problem, to foster every inner strength of the person toward the goal of finding his (sic) own solution, and to utilise all the outer resources of the environment and the community which might be of value in this problem-solving endeavour.

This way of conceptualising social work covers the bulk of activities undertaken in the statutory sector, but it fails to take on board the 'preventative' dimensions of social work. Although this element has recently been squeezed in state-supported social work as the economic imperatives of reducing national budget deficits have highlighted public expenditure cuts in welfare services in, for example, Britain, Canada and the United States (see Walker and Walker, 1987; Armitage, 1975; Mullaly, 1993; Sidel, 1986), it remains an important part of the whole picture in welfare provision.

Many innovative services which have arisen in the voluntary sector have focused on preventative work (Dominelli, 1989; Lowe, 1993; George, 1995). Sociological insights from organisational sociology can help us understand why opportunities for particular types of social work are more easily fostered in one type of organisation than another and in any given epoch.

Sociology's relevance to social work

Is sociology, therefore, relevant to social work practice? And if the answer is 'yes', in what ways? This book argues for an affirmative response. Sociological analyses provide theoretical perspectives that can subject policies and the work which practitioners do to systematic analysis, thereby enhancing our understanding of what is done and why. Sociology can be used to illuminate structures, processes and social relationships in social work and contribute to the development of more appropriate forms of practice.

Many of social work's most recent postwar developments have been underpinned by sociological rather than psychological approaches to the discipline (Bailey, 1982; Sainsbury, 1985). But, the relationship has not been one-way. Social work theory and practice has impacted on sociology's theoretical base as well as being influenced by the sociological insights that academics and practitioners have brought with them. The links between the two are particularly evident in the work of symbolic interactionists and ethnomethodologists who have focused on delinquency and youth sub-cultures, for example, Becker (1966), Whyte (1961) and Matza (1964). There remains much more which can be gained through a deeper cross-fertilisation between the two disciplines. In this text, I utilise critical sociology focusing on anti-racist and feminist perspectives to demonstrate this point. A more detailed consideration of traditional sociology and its impact on social work will contribute to my task.

The structure of the book

Chapter One examines sociological concepts and their contribution to social work theory and practice. Chapter Two focuses on sociological social work as it exists in practice. Chapter Three considers a sociology of social work drawing on feminist and anti-racist perspec-

tives. Using their insights, I go on to examine the institutional base
of social work in Chapter Four. Chapter Five concentrates on how a
sociological approach can shed light on care and control dynamics in
caring relationships. Chapter Six uses sociological analysis to
examine how particular visions of social work are elaborated to
specify practice tasks and identify those key players involved in
defining and redefining its activities. Power is at the heart of the
definitional process. It is considered in Chapter Seven in terms of
power struggles to determine what the profession stands for as well as
the socialisation process whereby particular types of social work
professionals are produced. Chapter Eight explores how professional
ethics and ideologies shape the realities of practice and the changes
the profession has undergone as it struggles to free itself from the
voluntaristic 'anybody can do it model' to a more restrictive scientific
model with a professional remit. Chapter Nine examines strategies
which shift the power axis from the 'bureau-professionals', as Parry
et al. (1979) have called social workers ensconced in state welfare
organisations, to the techno-managers. Chapter Ten attempts to
establish new paradigms for social work practice rooted in a feminist,
anti-racist sociological analysis.

Sociological theories

Sociology helps us to understand social interactions between
ourselves and others by subjecting such interactions to critical
scrutiny. Questioning perceived wisdoms and superficial analyses of
social life is the substance of sociological theory. That sociology has
an investigative role has been apparent since its 'founding fathers'
laid the basis of the discipline in the last century. Comte (1838), who
is credited with inventing the term 'sociology', made a critical
understanding of society in order to influence human activities the
centrepiece of his concept '*prevoir pour pouvoir*' (which I translate as
'knowledge empowers'). Durkheim's writings (1964a, 1964b) also
portray a commitment to moving human society in progressive
directions through a consideration of how it works. Hall *et al.* (1992)
argue that this concern with the perfectability of human institutions
has been a major theme in sociological thought to the present day. A
product of the 'Enlightment', this progressive thrust emanates from
the transformative nature of industrialisation on society's political,
cultural and social institutions and has been termed 'modernity'. Its

key features are: a 'nation-state' characterised by large-scale adminis-trative and bureaucratic structures; a secular society; the spread of rational (scientific) thought; the goal of controlling nature; and a specific division of labour. Social work, deeply implicated in the administrative and bureaucratic structures of the nation-state, is part of 'modernity'.

Theories are the linchpin of any sociological analysis and are crucial in determining the subject matter of an investigation and its methodology. There are a number of levels at which theory operates. These range from poorly theorised commonsense to sophisticated intellectual formulations at the highest level of abstraction and cover both microlevel and macrolevel phenomena. Howe (1987) argues *all* social work practice contains theory, regardless of whether a practi-tioner acknowledges it or not. However, to merit the appellation of theory for the purposes of enhancing our understanding of society, a theory should contain the following elements:

- descriptive powers
- explanatory powers
- predictive powers (Coulshed, 1988; Worsley, 1987).

Theories operate at a number of levels of abstraction ranging from 'grand theories' which operate at macrolevel analyses of society, for example monetarism, Marxism, functionalism, to microlevel analyses, which are involved in detailed investigations of a particular situation, for example symbolic interactionism in a case study (see Whyte, 1961; Becker, 1966; Nicholson, 1990). Additionally, there are theories of the 'middle range' (Merton, 1957), which deal with social phenomena in less reified manner than 'grand' theories. Focusing largely on the organisational and institutional level, these are less concerned with the 'laws' which govern society than were Comte, Durkheim or Marx.

In this book I argue that social work has been influenced by theories at all levels in the abstraction continuum. Moreover, social work as a discipline in its own right is interdisciplinary, that is, it draws from many other disciplines. The uniqueness of social work, however, is its focus:

on the *interplay* of social, cultural, economic, physical and psychological factors. Such an emphasis is a necessary concomitant of our (social

workers') service to man (sic) in his environment and an outgrowth of
our goals, which incorporate both individual well-being and social
betterment (Kendall, 1978:46).

The breadth and depth of the social work task makes it difficult to
draw tight boundaries around its remit, but it highlights the fact that
practitioners must encompass all levels of analysis within their work.
Although different theories have prospered at various points in time,
key ones have been: Social Darwinism, functionalism and Marxism
which draw on 'grand theories'; psychodynamic casework and
systems theories, which focus on 'middle range' theories; symbolic
interactionism, and postmodernism, which set their sights on
microlevel considerations.

The view that social workers should draw on different levels of
theories for different purposes is not an uncontested one. Edwina
Currie, a recent Minister of Health, deemed sociology 'left-wing
rubbish' and therefore unnecessary for social workers. Her fears of
the subversive potential of sociology, or indeed the social sciences
more generally, has been echoed through the corridors of time. Back
in the days of the COS, some of its key personnel had labelled
sociology 'contaminating knowledge' and were keen to take it out of
the curriculum, even though British social work training was located
in a School of Sociology (Jones, 1983, 1994b). Heraud (1979) is
concerned that including the social sciences in the social work
curriculum gives a spurious legitimacy to the profession and an
undeserved status. More recently, Davies (1985:220) has maintained
that the social sciences serve no useful role in social work practice.
Some sociologists, for example Sibeon (1989; 1991), argue that
social work should only deal with 'middle range' theories. Curnock
and Hardiker (1979) suggest that practitioners need to develop
'practice theories', a concept which encompasses the 'practice
wisdoms' espoused by Davies (1985). This idea has also been
advocated by Richards (1987), Phillipson *et al.* (1988) and Lishman
(1991). The debate about the role of sociological theory in general
and in social work practice in particular is likely to run and run, as
long as the range of stakeholders with an interest in social work
remain divided. It reflects one of social work's 'contemporary and
perennial problems' (Lee, 1982).

Note

1 I use the third person plural when referring to an individual to avoid using the male first person singular pronoun to stand for both men and women and thereby exclude women through language. This convention will be adhered to throughout the book. In addition, I use the term 'women' to focus on sexist dynamics; 'black people' to highlight racist ones. My doing so does *not* imply that their experiences are homogeneous.

1

An Exploration of Sociological Concepts

Sociological perspectives

Sociology is a vast discipline characterised by a variety of theoretical approaches and perspectives. In this chapter, I have space to consider only a few which have had an important impact on social work education, research and practice. My handling of these will draw on the notion of 'ideal types' – itself a construct taken from Weberian sociology (Gerth and Mills, 1948). An *ideal type* is an abstract tool which highlights features of a phenomenon which are sociologically significant, that is, help us better understand social reality. Although I cover a number of theoretical perspectives, those I examine in greater depth are positivism, Marxism, feminism and postmodernism.

Positivism

Characteristics of positivist theories

The nineteenth-century sociologists Emile Durkheim (1964a, 1964b, 1969) and Auguste Comte (1838) are credited with the initial development of positivist theories. Positivism has been crucial in legitimating sociology's claim to scientific status and has drawn highly on paradigms prevailing in the natural sciences (see Kulin, 1970; Barnes, 1985).

The key assumption positivists make is that the methods of the natural sciences are relevant to sociological studies. This requires human behaviour to be quantified as demonstrable or empirically testable 'facts' which can be used to establish social laws which explain present behaviour and predict future trends. Positivist methodologies carefully record observable events and have little patience with the unobservable dimensions of human behaviour, for example, the unconscious, or intuition (Barnes, 1974). The scientist, as a person, is removed from the object(s) of study and engages in neutral and value-free enquiry. Traditional ideologies of professionalism in social work draw on the notions of the objectivity of the observer from the events being observed inherent in this scientific paradigm. Positivists' concern with identifying the distinctive features of the phenomena under consideration gives rise to dichotomous thinking – the 'either-or' categories which feminists have heavily criticised (Collins, 1991; Abbot and Wallace, 1990). Dichotomous thinking encourages people to divide the social world into separate and unrelated events.

Positivists have a consensus view of society in which the principles of rationality, equality and freewill guide individual action. These principles, associated with the Enlightenment, have been grouped together as the modernist project firmly rooted in the industrialisation process (Hall *et al.*, 1992; Giddens, 1990). In a positivist framework, socialisation is the mechanism whereby each person acquires the appropriate value system of society. Within the scientific community, socialisation provides the means through which cognitive and procedural continuity of thought is maintained over time and space (Barnes, 1985). The training of scientific personnel and the recording of developments in written form become key methods through which this objective is achieved in scientific practice (Barnes, 1985).

Socialisation also ensures conformity to recognised principles and modes of conduct. This theory is problematic in that it cannot explain why a 'socialisation' process fails in certain individuals. Those deviating from its key tenets may find themselves penalised and ostracised by their peers, although their ideas may in the long run prove more accurate, for example the controversies around whether the earth was flat. This illustration reveals the impact of non-scientific considerations in the scientific arena. The political, economic, social or personal objectives of individuals and groups can, and do, intervene in scientific investigations. In other words, 'science' is not neutral. Transposed on to the social arena, the scientific community's paradigms and values can lead to the labelling of individuals critical of its tenets as eccentric, pathological or socially inadequate.

Positivism has played an influential role in the development of social work's practice paradigms and professional ethics, despite social workers' claims to using intuition and insights in their practice. The works of Spencer (1877), particularly his espousal of Social Darwinism, played a key role in the activities of the COS in both Britain and the United States. Social Darwinism, with its emphasis on the 'survival of the fittest', had a more extensive impact on the United States' pioneer society. In Britain, the situation was tempered by the struggle the COS had to mount for control of the social work curriculum against the advocates of social reform (Walton, 1975).

Positivist parameters are also enshrined in the works of major theorists such as Talcott Parsons (1957, 1968) – the acknowledged 'father' of the functionalist school in sociology. Parsons's theories have been useful in elucidating concepts which have found resonance in social work practice. The most important of these are:

● social stratification
● sex role differentiation
● institutional relationships.

These concepts will be examined in greater detail subsequently. While Parsonian sociology has declined in favour recently (Bailey, 1982; Sainsbury, 1985), its modern variant in social work is represented by the competency-based approach currently being promoted by the Central Council for Education and Training (CCETSW), the government and employers in Britain (Mainframe, 1994; Dominelli, 1995).

At this point, I will consider the methodology which underpins positivism as its general parameters have impacted on the procedures social workers use in carrying out their assessments of individual needs and the resources available to meet them. The method which positivists have utilised in explaining various forms of human behaviour begins with observing a phenomenon and then setting up a *hypothesis* which is tested against *empirical* or observable reality. The factors utilised to do this testing are called *variables*. Variables can be *dependent* (that is, those that rely on other factors for their impact and therefore are considered secondary) or *independent* (that is, those that are primary or fundamental). The *assumption* that is made is that if a consistent relationship emerges between variables, one causes the other. Relationships between variables are analysed through statistical procedures. The findings obtained from such an investigation are then used to test the hypothesis.

A hypothesis is the *tentative statement* which is set up for examination. The test takes the form of seeing whether or not the hypothesis can be rejected rather than accepted. The hypothesis is subsequently revised as necessary to take account of the empirical facts which have emerged. A new hypothesis based on these is then postulated and the process of verification begins again. Thus, positivism has a methodology which can be replicated by others wishing to study the same social phenomenon. The examination of social phenomena in this way is believed to be neutral, objective and scientific. That is, positivism has claimed that the identity of the researcher and the methodology used are independent of what is being researched. This framework has been challenged by a variety of sociologists including ethnomethodologists, symbolic interactionists, Marxists, feminists and postmodernists.

The uses of positivism in social work

Positivist research can help social workers make sense of 'clients'' behaviour and establish plans of action for future work with them by providing 'hard' data.[1] It has been employed in investigating the causes of problems and evaluating the effectiveness of interventions. Positivism's evaluative framework has enhanced its credibility among social workers whose main concern is working with individuals in one-to-one or casework relationships. By focusing on the person, social workers address change at the personal level and can more easily examine defects in the character of the individual caused by inadequate parenting, without worrying about structural considerations. The example below illustrates a positivist approach to social work.

EXAMPLE

Social workers monitoring service useage use a positivist approach to discover whether working-class people have recourse to their home help provisions more frequently than middle-class people.

They proceed as follows. First, they observe useage patterns. From their observations they formulate a fairly precise, that is, testable hypothesis. This takes the form that working-class people are twice as likely as middle-class people to use home helps.

Social class becomes the variable applied to test the relationship on which the hypothesis stands or falls. Social class is operationalised: defined quantitatively to make it amenable to testing. They settle on the last occupation held prior to receiving the service for doing this. The social workers then devise a way for collecting the relevant data over a period (a month) recording the frequency of useage by both working-class and middle-class people.

Their findings reveal that out of 100 users during that period, 21 were middle class and 79 were working class. Their hypothesis has not been verified. Working-class people are five times as likely to call upon this service – a higher frequency of service useage than anticipated.

Note that the hypothesis can only be corroborated, not proven. Full verification is an unachievable goal in positivistic paradigms. In considering this outcome, the social workers have a number of possible options. One would be to terminate the research, having acquired the 'hard' information they sought. Or, they might seek to verify their findings by rerunning the survey. If the subsequent investigation confirms their previous findings, they might decide the hypothesis was inadequate and could alter it to the higher frequency. If the survey, run again with this alteration, is corroborated, they might conclude the hypothesis is firm enough for taking action.

Taking action based on their findings becomes a matter of how these are *interpreted*, and not on the positivistic theoretical framework used in the investigation. Its adherents claim scientists eschew making practical decisions because, unlike their theoretical considerations, these are political matters (Barnes, 1974, 1985; Kulin, 1970). Social workers, on the other hand, are in the business of following interventionist methodologies to make decisions. Research could, and should, guide their work. The values held by the decision-makers and the variables which researchers deem worthy of study are more relevant to the research decision-making process. These shape the research design, influence the outcome and undermine the alleged neutrality of their research approach.

In the case study presented above, the social workers have more than one option open to them. Positivism assumes but does not uncover causal connections between variables. Class could indicate other factors at play: poverty preventing people purchasing private services in the open market; lack of alternatives to state provisions.

Ability to pay, or income status, might be a more significant variable than class. While income is dependent on class, it is not wholly determined by it.

Overuse of home help services provided by the state could be taken to indicate a number of conflicting possibilities: higher levels of poverty experienced by working-class claimants; eagerness among working-class people to use this service; lack of access to its provisions by middle-class people; or the unwillingness of middle-class people to use services if these are deemed residual and stigmatised. Social workers might, therefore, postulate that the working-class group receive so few services through the market that their overuse of state provisions is acceptable and no other changes need to be initiated. Social workers valuing participation and casting themselves in more enabling roles might use similar information to increase service take-up by disadvantaged groups on whose behalf they advocate.

The uses to which research may be put are varied. Positivism's failure to engage with the political nature of knowledge provides a contradiction at its heart and has caused it to lose favour among critical theorists, for example Marxists from the Frankfort School (Marcuse, 1968; Habermas, 1963, 1987) and feminists (Stanley and Wise, 1983; Tong, 1989; Reinharz, 1992). Positivism provides a method for recording events rather than explaining them.

Thus, groups identified as 'overusing' welfare provisions have been subjected to more stringent criteria for eligibility. This punitive scenario has been imposed on social workers in both Britain and the United States by the New Right. Its agenda during the 1980s and 90s has been dominated by crudely theorised positivist research aiming to cut welfare provisions. Rightwing ideologues' preoccupation with the 'underclass', that part of the working class they allege abuses and depends on publicly funded welfare, has justified axing benefits previously available as of right for residual services restricted to selectively targeted groups for a limited period (Murray, 1984, 1990, 1994; Glazer, 1988; Minford, 1984). The New Right has utilised empiricist studies to pathologise working-class people for failing to deal adequately with their welfare needs (Morris, 1994). In the process, they have drawn on dichotomous thinking which simultaneously focuses attention on poor people's behaviour and ignores the privileged 'givens' such as access to social resources and power confirmed upon elites by the positions they hold. Indeed, their advantages are defended as personal strengths which contrast with the individual weaknesses of the proclaimed 'underclass'. Structural forms of discrimination and oppression are downplayed along with the structural benefits which shape the *unlevel* playing fields in which people's roles as active agents are enacted.

Positivist research sustains a harmonious view of society in which each individual performs their allotted role(s) to the best of their ability. It is amenable to individualistic explanations which emphasise personal responsibility rather than systemic shortcomings when things go wrong.

Positivism as a methodology may be perceived as neutral (Barnes, 1985) but the value system and ideological orientation of those who use its findings load it with bias. Its alleged neutrality can be and has been challenged on more fundamental grounds: the nature of the questions being asked and the ways in which answers sought are dependent on the value system and objectives of those undertaking the research (Abbott and Wallace, 1990; Smith, 1979; Adamson *et al.*, 1988).

Critiques of positivism

Positivism has been criticised from a number of perspectives. Its assumption of societal consensus has been questioned by conflict theorists who claim discord characterises modern society. Positivism can also be faulted on logical grounds. There is no necessary causal relationship between one variable and another. In the case study considered earlier, we could argue that service useage is unrelated to class – it could be the location of the office, the times during which the office is open, accessibility to other alternatives, and a host of other reasons. Also, there is no logical reason why a particular constellation of factors which resulted in a particular pattern at one point in time will repeat itself in another. It may be that if the office were moved to a different location, or another office is examined using the same methodology, a different pattern of useage would emerge. Moreover, there is no logical reason why the social sciences should follow the paradigm of the natural sciences (Giddens, 1982, 1987, 1984).

Many research activities possible in the natural sciences cannot be replicated in work with human beings. 'Social facts' are not easy either to define or establish except arbitrarily. It is difficult to specify the relationship between variables when our knowledge of social situations is limited and partial. It is impossible to quantify quality without damaging the nature of the interactions being reduced to numerical form (Smith, 1987). Researchers cannot insist that people act in particular ways unless they want to become dictators. Finally, the assumptions and connections that researchers make, or find acceptable, depend on their belief systems. Their morality and ethics guide both the question to be examined and the use to which findings are put (Reinharz, 1992). Therefore, positivism cannot be raised above the level of any other 'scientific', that is, systematic analysis of social phenomena.

Other weaknesses emerge when examining positivism from other perspectives. Certain Marxists, for example Nicolaus (1966, 1973), have criticised positivism for maintaining the interests of the ruling classes by exposing the dynamics of life for the underprivileged. Meanwhile, the beneficiaries of the status quo remain unsubjected to critical appraisal. Hence, positivism provides a useful methodology for those interested in maintaining social control over potentially dissident populations (Flaherty, 1995). Social work, as a discipline concerned with both care and control issues, has to exercise caution in how far it takes positivism to its bosom without considering its impact on interpersonal relationships and the power that is enacted through them. For, if social work takes positivism's methodology for granted, it will fail to acknowledge its potential use in perpetuating inequality and injustice (Parry *et al.*, 1979; Corrigan and Leonard, 1978; Leonard, 1975b).

Feminists have taken this argument further by examining how positivism has enabled the gender-blindness inherent in mainstream sociological thought to render women's experience of the world invisible (Roberts, 1981; Stanley and Wise, 1983; Adamson *et al.*, 1988; Collins, 1991). Women are the main group of 'clients' with whom social workers work (Wilson, 1977). Much of their work takes sex and gender roles as given (Dominelli, 1984; Marchant and Wearing, 1986). Those writing from anti-racist and black perspectives[2] have argued that positivism has endorsed white cultural hegemony in the scientific field by accepting as legitimate only those explanations of social reality which have confirmed white ideological positions (Collins, 1991; Small, S, 1994). Hence, black people have been poorly served by social workers and probation officers (ADSS, 1978; Dominelli, 1988; Devore and Schlesinger, 1981; Dominelli *et al.*, 1995; Denney 1992).

The 'facts' which have been investigated, how these have been examined, and how the findings have been evaluated have been highly influenced by the subjective context within which the research has taken place. In challenging positivism's epistemology – the methods through which it acquires knowledge, and ontology – the assumptions underpinning its theoretical base, feminists and black activists have exposed the hollowness of its claims to a 'scientific, objective, neutrality' (Bryant *et al.*, 1985; Stanley and Wise, 1983). They have demanded that their voices be heard. And, their critique has included alternative paradigms which can provide a more accurate rendition of reality.

Initially, their challenge took the form of 'adding on' women's and black people's experience by including gender and 'race' as variables in the research (Eichler, 1980, 1988; Davis, 1982). Feminists subsequently went on to question the very basis of positivist paradigms – its allegedly neutral and objective scientificism (Smith, 1979; Roberts, 1981; Stanley and Wise, 1983; Collins, 1991; Thomas Bernard, 1994). In doing so, they undermined both the edifice on which positivism had been constructed and its 'normative standards'. Finally, their critiques unleashed new forms of sociology which locate the subject of study more centrally in the research framework.

Their new paradigms have influenced the development of sociological knowledge, begun breaking down the hegemonic position of positivism, and questioned the process whereby sociologists have been socialised as researchers. The impact of feminist research methodologies in universities has been significant in limiting the dominance of positivism as *the* methodology for the social sciences. However, their success in both exposing the inadequacies of positivism and elaborating viable solutions to them is now subject to a fierce backlash which fails to address the weaknesses they have highlighted. Instead of seeking the development of less oppressive forms of human knowledge and understandings of the social relationships people create through the research process, the counterattack in Britain and the United States has sought to reassert the hegemony of more traditional views. Orchestrated by opinion formers in the mass media and strongly endorsed by government ministers on behalf of the state, the backlash is powerful and sets the scene for further conflict (Dunant, 1994; Murray, 1994). Such actions, reactions followed by further action and reaction in a dialogical process indicate the contested and political nature of knowledge itself.

Marxism

Characteristics of Marxist theories

Marxism is a body of sociological thought classified as 'grand theory'. It is credited to Karl Marx (Bottomore, 1964). His contribution to theoretical knowledge was to develop a paradigm which revealed the conflictual nature of society, the structures through which conflict is mediated and the mechanisms whereby new social orders are created. Marx drew on the works of others, for example the classical economist Adam Smith, radical economist David Ricardo and radical philosopher Pierre-Joseph Proudhon. However, Marx's unique contribution covered the transformation of societies through social action underpinned by an understanding of the laws of history and the dynamics through which the environment could be controlled.

Rejecting the Hegelian notion of history being created through a contest of ideas, Marx proposed a *materialist* view of it rooted in empirical study (Lowith, 1964; Bottomore, 1964). This formed the basis of the scientific method which he used to unravel the hidden secrets of historical developments. Marx's work produced the remarkable insight that economic forces drove social development in a structural and systematic manner. For him, history progressed through epochs ranging from the early communalistic to communistic society (Marx, 1965; Marx and Engels, 1985) Different groups would compete for power to determine the shape of the social formation prevailing in each historical stage. Changes from one *social formation* to another occurred as a result of revolutionary convulsions which would shake society to its foundations. Moreover, each social formation contained within itself the seeds of its own destruction. The world, currently in the capitalist social formation, would become a socialist one through class struggle initiated by the proletariat, which would ultimately create the classless communist society.

Under capitalism, the struggle for hegemony would be conducted between two antagonistic classes – the *proletariat* or working class who sold its labour power and the *bourgeoisie* or capitalists who owned the means of production, which enabled it to purchase and exploit the labour of the working class. The lack of property would enable the proletariat, the anticipated revolutionary agent, to install the socialist order as a transitionary stage to full communism when the means of production would be collectively rather than individually owned and the exploitation of 'man by man' (sic) cease. In

Marxist analyses, the state has been portrayed as the instrument of class rule, thereby emphasising its social control function.

This simplified synopsis of the key features of Marxism is partial. There are a number of different schools of thought which have flourished under the Marxist banner. These have encompassed orthodox Marxism with highly tyrannical overtones, as depicted by Stalinism in the former Soviet Union (George and Manning, 1980), the democratic centralism of Lenin (1961), the more libertarian views of Kollantai (1971), and the more complex expositions of Trotsky (1963), Luxembourg (1951), and Gramsci (1971). The arguments about what Marxist thought represented were evident in his own day, and Marx is reported to have said 'I am not a Marxist', as a way of signalling his dissent from much of what was being done in his name (Bottomore, 1964). Nonetheless, Marxists posited a progressive view of history. As it unfolded, industrial and technological inventions would be harnessed to give man (sic) increasing control over nature. Ultimately, his greater capacity for good would triumph.

A key element of Marxist thought relevant to social work is its insights into the state. The orthodox view of its role as the 'instrument of the ruling class' is deterministic and functionalist (Anderson, 1976). This variant has been challenged and reshaped in a less vulgarised form in which the class struggle becomes terrain that is fought over (Gough, 1979; Corrigan, 1977). Although the outcome of the power struggle between the bourgeoisie and the proletariat is not a foregone conclusion, how the victory of the proletariat is assured remains unclear.

Marxism has been important in raising questions about the nature of social work. Having located social work within the state apparatus, Marxists have exposed the primacy of its control functions over its caring functions (Corrigan and Leonard, 1978; Bailey and Brake, 1975; Moreau, 1979; Beaumont and Walker, 1981; Bolger *et al.*, 1981). They have also highlighted the significance of class relations within social work, particularly in the 'client'–worker and employer–employee relationships (Moreau, 1979, Mullaly, 1993; Corrigan and Leonard, 1978; Joyce *et al.*, 1987). Also, of vital importance has been the Marxist view that the poverty in which the majority of social work 'clients' live is structural (Corrigan and Leonard, 1978; Beaumont and Walker, 1981).

Poverty, as a systemic and integral feature of capitalism, requires the immiseration of the masses so that the privileged few can enjoy their lifestyles of luxury (Offe, 1984; Marx, 1965). Poverty, Marxists claim, is not caused by the pathology of indigent people as bourgeois intellectuals would have us believe (Glazer, 1988 and Murray, 1984, 1990, 1994; Minford, 1984), but is a predictable product of the system itself (Cloward and Piven, 1972, 1977, 1982; CDP, 1977a, b, 1978).

Marxist thought has given rise to 'structural social work', currently popular in Canadian schools of social work (see Moreau, 1979; Mullaly, 1993) where Carleton University in Ottawa leads the field in this direction. In Britain, a leading exponent of Marxism as a major form of social work in the mid 1970s was Peter Leonard when he held the Chair of Applied Social Studies at Warwick University (Corrigan and Leonard, 1978). However, the diversity Marxism provided among British schools of social work was contested and shortlived (Jones, 1983, 1994a).

The uses of Marxism in social work

Despite its aspirations, Marxist thought has had a fairly limited impact on social work practice. Its preoccupation with class as the sole determiner of oppression led to the neglect of other needs important to social workers' clientele. The exclusion of 'race' and gender from its remit led black people and feminists respectively to create their own theoretical perspectives for practice (Ahmad, 1990; Dominelli, 1988; Brook and Davis, 1985; Marchant and Wearing, 1986; Hanmer and Statham, 1988; Dominelli and McLeod, 1989; Wilson, 1977). Although the charge has been overly exaggerated, Marxism has also been castigated for being too abstract to be relevant to practitioners in their daily tasks (Sibeon, 1991).

Marxist theory had a major input into the 'rediscovery of poverty' in the late 1960s and the responses to it in both Britain and the USA. The community action initiatives under the War on Poverty Programme in the United States and the Community Development Projects in Britain are the key sites in which structural explanations of poverty gave rise to important examples of practice (Loney, 1983; Cloward and Piven, 1972), including becoming embroiled in a debate as to whether community action constituted a part of social work (Popplestone, 1971; Dearlove, 1974). Many perceived Marxism not as wholly irrelevant but as a threat (Gould, 1977). Its opponents in British social work education and practice took its challenge seriously enough to organise against its spread and legitimacy

(Pinker, 1979, 1984, 1993, 1994; Davies, 1981; Wright, 1977; Harbart, 1985a, b).

Sadly, the initiatives for eradicating poverty were shortlived. Community activists in Britain (Loney, 1983; Dominelli, 1982) and the United States (Cloward and Piven, 1972, 1977, 1982) implicated not only private entrepreneurs but the state in creating and reproducing the conditions of poverty. Their indictment included the way in which state organisations controlled subject populations, such as working-class people and black people, to prepare the conditions for the accumulation of capital and their greater exploitation as workers (Offe, 1984; Dearlove, 1974; Bridges, 1975; Sivanandan, 1976).

In Britain, 80 per cent of problems for which social work assistance has been sought are income related. This figure has been consistent over time (Seebohm, 1968; Cohen *et al.*, 1992; Becker, 1991). This insight has spurred people committed to tackling social inequalities to continue with an influential theory which has promised solutions to intractable problems. British academics, for example Corrigan and Leonard (1978), Jones (1979, 1983, 1989) and those steeped in practice, such as Beaumont and Walker (1981), have sought to make connections between Marxist thought and social work and probation practice.

Politicians and rightwing commentators seeking to undermine their arguments and reject the injection of public funds into projects tackling economic deprivation, educational underperformance, poor housing and inadequate training schemes, began to attack structural analyses and solutions to poverty by deploring the moral lassitude of poor people and their chronic unwillingness to work their way out of poverty (Murray, 1984; Glazer, 1988; Minford, 1984). These theorists also deprecated the state for encouraging dependency on public largesse among claimants. Tax revolts such as Proposition 13 in California, the rise of Reaganism in the United States and Thatcherism in Britain, have both fuelled and responded to demands for the withdrawal of the state from the welfare arena so that individual and family responsibility for welfare needs could be realised through provisions purchased in the marketplace.

These reactions, and the theories underpinning them, eschew structural analyses of social interaction. Statistics reflecting the high rates of unemployment and poverty affecting working-class people, particularly women and black people, became manipulated to highlight the intransigent nature of poor people and their unwillingness to 'fend for themselves'. The concept of 'welfare dependency', formulated to describe the New Right's version of events, focused public attention on gains made in relieving *absolute poverty* rather than *relative poverty* (Glazer, 1988; Murray, 1984, 1990, 1994; Minford, 1984), thereby ignoring widening disparities in wealth and opportunities. The concept 'welfare dependency' suggests a self-generating sub-culture among a stable population of claimants. However, the shifting composition of the welfare 'client' group precludes this possibility (Morris, 1994). Meanwhile, the numbers of people in poverty are rising significantly. Fortunately, some social work academics have continued to explore the implications of Marxist analyses for their work with poor people (Moreau, 1979; Jones, 1983; Mullaly, 1993).

Despite its attractiveness, Marxism has not met expectations about developing more appropriate social work practice. Even academics and practitioners sympathetic to its general thrust have criticised it for taking people as cardboard characters rather than addressing the complexities of their relationships with both the state and others (Dominelli, 1977). The strengths and limitations of intervention made by Marxist-oriented practitioners are revealed in the example below.

CASE STUDY

Caroline, a black woman of Afro-Caribbean descent, was a lone parent with two small children. She was due to appear in court for defrauding the Department of Health and Social Security[3] of £4340 by holding an undeclared part-time job for ten hours a week. In trying to mitigate the severity of the offence and guide the magistrates in their sentencing, the white male probation officer's Social Enquiry Report (SER) emphasised the low income on which the woman and children were trying to survive as an important factor leading to the offence. He recommended a one-year probation order. The magistrates made it two to give Caroline time to 'sort out her life'.[4]

The Marxist insights of this probation officer have led him to argue in mitigation for what he considered an appropriate sentence. His arguments for leniency were accepted by the magistrates and interacted with their views that women need 'welfare' intervention. The portrayal of women as needing 'welfare support' and caring rehabilitation emerges as a common theme in the way those administering justice treat women (Worrall, 1990). Such approaches reinforce stereotypes of women as incapable of managing their own affairs. However, women offenders do not deem probation an easy option. They prefer community service orders and fines as less intrusive disposals (Dominelli, 1983). Focusing on structurally caused poverty without addressing the relevance of gender dynamics in this illustration resulted in an individual woman offender receiving a harsher punishment. Classism and sexism have intersected to produce a more undesirable outcome from the woman's point of view.

Critiques of Marxism

Marxism has been criticised from a number of standpoints. New Right theorists would criticise the probation officer in this example for not making the woman responsible for her actions. Arguing that a considerable number of poor single-parent women do not commit offences, they would condem this intervention as 'do-gooding' which minimises the harmful consequences of the woman's actions on others – 'the victims'. This would include the taxpayers who foot the bill for the criminal justice system (Glazer, 1988). A concern over the demise of traditional family life also prompts New Right theorists to argue that the woman should provide for her family by getting maintenance from her (ex)husband if she has one, finding a male partner who could support her by marrying him, or seeking employment (Minford, 1984: Gilder, 1981). Punishment is their order for the day, not plea bargaining for breaking the law.

Although ignored by New Right critics, structural constraints guide how an individual woman will evaluate the choices open to her. The jobs available to women in Caroline's position rarely provide sufficient income for paying living expenses and wages for childcare (Morris, 1994). Taking a low-paid, dead-end job would not extricate her from poverty and she would lose social security benefits in the process (Cohen, *et al.*, 1992). Nor is enforced dependency on a man conducive to good family relations. As ethnomethodologists and symbolic interactionists have demonstrated, breaking the law may be a rational response in debilitating circumstances (see Becker, 1966; Matza, 1964). It represents a mobilising of resources in the woman's own favour.

Max Weber (1968, 1949, 1978) was a major critic of Marxist understandings of society. He argued that class, though important in the unfolding of social events, is not their sole determiner. The state, ideology and organisations are also significant. Weber's conceptual framework is relevant to social workers. Social work is a state activity situated within its organisational structures. Ideologies influence how images of 'poor people' who become 'clients' are constructed and the professionalism of social workers understood. Weber's ideas about power, roles and status are also useful. But, they fail to take account of gender differentials and other social divisions.

Feminists commenting on Caroline's case would criticise Marxists' failure to examine the gendered nature of justice and poverty which trap proportionately more women than men (Scott, 1984; Worrall, 1990; Morris, 1994). Feminists would want probation officers to address the issue of what social resources women need to transcend their situation. They would highlight the intrusive nature of probation orders on women who are constantly in the limelight for their parenting abilities, making women's experience of probation orders a more punitive ordeal than for men (Dominelli, 1983). They would expect probation officers to explore individual women's concerns about possible sentencing options and recommendations through dialogue during interviews when data are collected for their Report. Checking out the appropriateness of a particular sentence for any given individual rather than responding on the basis of stereotypes about women (Worrall, 1990) produces better practice. Taking a gendered approach enables probation officers to consider other disposals, for example fines and conditional discharges. Feminists have also criticised Marxists for failing to consider the gendered nature of class (Barrett, 1981; Beechey, 1980) and 'race' (Dominelli, 1988; Ahmad, 1990). Various social divisions, therefore, make women social workers' and women 'clients'' relationships with the state different from men's (Dominelli and McLeod, 1989; Collins, 1991).

Black activists would criticise the work done by this probation officer for failing to identify the woman's racially structured experience of both poverty and the criminal justice system (Dominelli, 1983; Cook and Hudson, 1993). Black women work in some of the lowest paid jobs in society (Bruegal, 1989). Their resources for purchasing childcare would be even more limited than white women's. Moreover, white social institutions, including those charged with meting out justice, stereotypically portray black women as 'dangerous' (Carby, 1982; Cook and Hudson, 1993; Dominelli *et al.*, 1995). Lengthening the probation order above that recommended can be interpreted as a stereotypical response to that perception. The two-year probation order therefore, becomes the outcome of 'race', class and gender interacting with each other to produce a worse outcome for black women. These dynamics also result in black women being disproportionately represented in prison (Home Office, 1986; Alfred, 1992).

Feminism

Characteristics of feminist theories

Feminists have mounted a major critique of sociology as a discipline, criticising all major schools of thought for falsely presenting their claims as gender neutral and of universal validity (Tong, 1989; Smith, 1979, 1987; Eichler, 1980; Stanley and Wise, 1983; Roberts, 1981). Feminist scholars have demonstrated that gender is a key element in the framing of knowledge. Unless gender differences are identified, the specificity of women's encounters with social institutions is lost. Beginning by 'adding' women on to existing theoretical foundations, feminists moved on to formulate more profound analyses of our own. These have transformed the concepts we use to make sense of the world. Moreover, feminist research focuses on how social relations are organised to oppress women and carries with it a demand for transforming them. More recently, the extensive diversity of women's experiences of oppression has been recognised and feminists have begun to address its significance (Collins, 1991; Reinharz, 1992; Tong, 1989).

Feminists have created feminist sociologies (Smith, 1987; Abbott and Wallace, 1990; Stanley 1990) which develop feminist epistemology (knowledge base) and ontology (methods of knowing). This has included forming specific subdivisions of sociology, for example feminist criminology (see Smart, 1976, 1984; Faith, 1994).

The entry of feminist sociologists into the intellectual arena produced uncomfortable moments for traditional sociologists. Highlighting the significance of gender exposed the falseness of their claims to accurately describe reality. For example, the assumption that heads of households are male does not reflect actuality. Large numbers of women are in this position either because they are the breadwinners or head families without male partners through death, divorce, separation or choice. Those of us training in sociological research in the late 1960s to early 1970s recall amusing anecdotes used to justify the status quo. In my own case, a professor told me that 'Women distort the findings and make the analysis much harder', when I queried why I couldn't add 'sex' as a variable to the questionnaire we were developing for a sophisticated social survey. The invisibility of the gendered dynamics driving research before feminists began challenging them was confusing given the popularity of C Wright Mills' (1970) *The Sociological Imagination*. For this text emphasises a constantly reflective and critical appreciation of the research subject and respondents.

As a lowly research assistant, and in the days before my own feminist consciousness had been developed, I found the reply strange, but didn't know what to do with it. However, I felt it made a mockery of women's lives. Why was it unacceptable to say 'This piece of research looks at male heads of households'? Sadly, such attitudes continue. While undertaking research for this book, a woman primary teacher undergoing gynaecological treatment told me how men are used as research subjects to test the effects of oestrogen in breast cancer. She wondered how men would feel if women were to be used when studying the role of testosterone in cancer of the prostate glands. The universality of men's experience remains valid in 'scientific' thought!

These types of experiences convinced women who later developed feminist research frameworks, the centrality of asking:

● 'Who was doing the research?'
● 'Why were they doing it?'
● 'What did they hope to demonstrate by it?'
● 'Who was going to use its findings?'

Understanding how power relations affected the research process enabled feminists to transcend the preoccupation with administrative power beloved by Weberian sociologists.

Feminists' main contributions to sociological knowledge include:

● identifying gender as an important sociological concept which pervades all of our understandings
● highlighting the importance of power in research relationships
● arguing for research subjects to actively particpate in framing the research questions, designing methodologies, carrying out the research and analysing its findings
● exploring group processes whenever possible

- holding researchers accountable for their work
- adding a commitment to improving social relations for women to the research outcomes.

This list is by no means exhaustive. But it highlights substantive areas of difference between feminist and mainstream research (Roberts, 1981; Stanley and Wise, 1983; Eichler, 1980; Smith, 1979, 1987; Gamarnikov *et al.*, 1983; Reinharz, 1992). Moreover, as I indicate below, additional points are raised by each variant in feminist thought and the new directions feminists constantly devise, for example using feminist insights to unpack men's experiences (Festeau, 1975; Dominelli and McLeod, 1989; Dominelli, 1991b; Hearn, 1987; Brittan, 1989; Bowl, 1985; Tolson, 1977). These developments are relevant to social workers who are committed to engaging with 'clients' on an empathetic and empowering basis.

Diversity in feminist thought

Feminism encompasses a variety of schools of thought (Banks, 1981). These revolve around significant differences in theorising the causes of women's oppression and the forms of action proposed for ending it. However, the following features are included in all feminist approaches:

- women as the starting point for feminist analysis and work
- the liberation of women
- working with women in non-oppressive ways:
  - women speaking for themselves, that is, their right to their own voice
  - women controlling the development of the work that is being done
- working collectively with other women
- being accountable to women
- linking the life experiences of individual women to their social situations
- making (and drawing on) connections between women
- acknowledging the political nature of interpersonal relationships or the power relations embedded in them
- recognising the importance of process in feminist activities

- integrating theory and practice by having each contribute to the other's development
- respecting and recognising differences between women
- being self-critical and responsive to criticisms
- respecting and valuing women
- developing alternative visions of the world which can be put into practice in the here and now.

The main schools of feminist thought which have been identified are explored. There are overlaps between them. Hence, they are presented as 'ideal types' (Weber, 1949) or theoretical constructs which have been simplified to their key characteristics for use in analysing social interaction. Some forms of feminism have developed out of women's critique of the offerings presented by other feminists. The capacity to address criticisms, particularly those made by other women seeking to voice their own experiences, has given feminism its dynamism and ability to be non-dogmatic.

The main schools of feminist thought have been classified (Banks, 1981; Tong, 1989) as:

- Liberal feminism
- Radical feminism
- Socialist feminism
- Marxist feminism
- Black feminism
- Postmodern feminism.

I find these categories problematic for black feminists also share liberal, radical, socialist or Marxist understandings of feminism. Women have multiple identities. This is apparent when an individual fits into several categories. Incorporating this reality means revising these groupings in more inclusive directions.

I would want to add anti-racist feminism to the list and have both white and black feminism as the key dimensions within each grouping. Thus, we would have white liberal feminists, black liberal feminists, and so on. It is important to note that black feminism arose out of black women's critique of white feminists' work because it ignored the specificity of their experience and made false assumptions about the universality of white middle-class women's lives (hooks, 1982, 1984).[5] Similar charges have been made by working-class women, older women and disabled women (Gavron, 1966; Hughes and Mtezuka, 1989; Morris, 1991).

Responding to these concerns has been defined as the 'problem of relativism versus universalism'. Casting the debate in these terms, I fear, bogs it down in dichotomous thinking which defines a woman as being *either* 'x' *or* 'y'. This conceptualisation of women ignores the complexity of social life, the multiple identities women hold and the interconnectedness between people and things and among people. I prefer to think of the issue using the *both/and* perspective in feminist thought (Brandwein, 1991; Gottlieb, 1980). The problem to be addressed then becomes that of accounting for both the differences in women's experience of oppressions and the commonalties found within it. This means recognising differences without submerging them in an *assumed* universality of sisterhood, valuing them, and embracing their relevance to women's lives *as these are lived* (see hooks, 1982, 1984; Lorde, 1984; Sibeon, 1991; Ramazanoglu, 1989). Feminists are now seeking to both preserve the unique perspectives developed by different groups of women from their highly specific life experiences and unearth their similarities.

In the sections that follow, I describe key features of each of the schools of thought mentioned above.

Liberal feminism

Liberal feminists are women-centred women who focus on improving women's condition within the existing framework of society. Many of them have been prominent white upper- and middle-class women whose prime concern has been to ensure that women have the same opportunities to fulfil their potential as men. Their analysis consists largely of 'adding' women on to existing social relations (see Friedan, 1963). They are willing to work alongside men to improve conditions for women.

In the past, white liberal feminists would have also accepted uncritically the presence of racism in both their work and mainstream society and reproduced taken-for-granted racist sentiments. Black liberal feminists would have been very aware of this dimension. Speaking from their experience as *black* women, their work would have included an understanding of racism as a social force shaping their life chances. Alongside other activities, liberal feminists, black and white, have led campaigns to get women the vote, child benefits or family allowances paid to women and equal pay for women. The struggles which led to the realisations of their demands reveal their contested and threatening nature (Dominelli, 1991c; Pascall, 1986: Dale and Foster, 1986).

An uneasy relationship with other feminisms

Liberal feminists' position within feminism is problematic for those who feel that feminism is a term that should be used primarily to refer to the transformation of existing social relations (Tong, 1989). This view is a restrictive one which ignores the specific social realities under which women make demands. In the days of the Suffragette Movement, although electoral relations were not in themselves being challenged, their actual interpretation was. Within their historical context, existing privileged social relations were being undermined by women who were fighting for women's rights.

Giddens (1982, 1984) argues that taking on board such realities requires the recognition of 'reflexivity' and 'contingent reality'. This means that people, as actors initiating and responding to social situations, act from their consciousness of the impact of their behaviour on themselves and others, while at the same time being affected by the very process of embarking on such action. Thus, history occurs as people become involved in the process of making it and is located in both time and space. It is not an independent, abstract entity which exists in and of itself. That, in Giddens's opinion, would be a teleological view of history, which would not increase our understanding of social phenomena. It would also be essentialist in that a disembodied 'history' rather than people taking action becomes the motor force of social development.

Sibeon (1991) asserts that theories which fail to recognise people's ability to take decisions for themselves are reductionist, that is, carry illogical consequences by denying human beings the right to make their own choices based on their understandings of reality. Instead, they are portrayed as one-dimensional puppets who act in ways determined by others, including the impersonal forces of history. He castigates both Marxism and feminism for falling into what he calls the 'reductionist trap'. This is an ironic criticism to make about feminism, given that a key purpose of its actions, philosophical orientation and value base is to expand the range of choices available to women and to empower women to take action for themselves

(Stanley, 1990; Abbott and Wallace, 1990). Sibeon's comments are perhaps more indicative of his failure to examine the range of feminist theory and appreciate the complexities and controversies evident in it. These have been crucial in developing and extending feminist theory and practice beyond its original limits as an oppositional voice insisting that it was a part of the intellectual firmament.

Moreover, Sibeon (1991) treats the term 'woman' as a reductionist category by relating to it as if it had a reality in and of itself. His approach denies patterns of structured inequality which affect women as a group at macrolevels of abstraction but which can be further sub-divided into more definitively differentiated groups at microlevels of abstraction to reveal the complex multiplicity of oppressions which particular groups of women encounter. One of the dangers in feminist identity politics is the fragmentation of sexual politics down to the level of the individual, thereby negating the concept of politics which implies at least two actors in every interaction. This happens because focusing on the detailed specificity of experiences reduces the numbers of women who share any particular set of characteristics, as postmodern feminism indicates (Nicholson, 1990; Kristeva, 1984; Irigary, 1985; Cixous, 1981).

Moreover, structured patterns of domination impacting on women are empirically demonstrable as has been evidenced by countless examples of feminist research. The presence of structured inequalities and their ability to endure, albeit in altered form, over space and time needs to be explained, not asserted away as Sibeon does. Their persistence indicates that men acting individually and in groups, have succeeded in organising social interaction by using what Giddens (1982, 1987) calls 'allocative' and 'authoritative' resources in ways which enhance their power to control social developments in their favour over the centuries and across geographical terrain.

Moving across levels of abstraction – from the concrete level of individual experience to the theoretical context in which 'facts' are analysed in depth and back to the concrete again where new forms of practice are created – is how people come to understand themselves and their realities more clearly (Freire, 1972, 1973). Movement across these levels also connects macro and microlevels of analysis in non-dichotomous feminist thought.

Radical feminism

Radical feminists have an analysis of patriarchy or the rule of men as the fundamental cause of the oppression of women. White radical feminists (Firestone, 1971) consider men and women as separate *sex classes*. Relationships between the two are considered antagonistic (see Firestone, 1971; Millett, 1970; Daly, 1973, 1978; Chodorow, 1978; Dinnerstein, 1977). Moreover, the development of women as a sex class is believed to be rooted in the control men exercise over women's reproductive capacities and sexuality (Dworkin, 1981; Brownmiller, 1976; MacKinnon, 1977, 1983).

Others (Rich, 1976), do not subscribe to the separate sex class analysis but continue to be woman-centred while espousing limited, if any, contact with men. Reducing contact with men and demanding separate facilities for women does not necessarily endorse an anti-men position. Although there has been a group of feminists who have espoused hostility to men (Solanas, 1971), their views have held little attraction for feminists generally. Lesbians have been too busy working with women and developing autonomous facilities to expend their energies on men, whom they feel have collared more than their share of women's time and resources (Lederer, 1980). Heterosexual women have little desire to see their relationships with men sundered, although they have wanted them altered radically in egalitarian directions (Jagger, 1983).

White radical feminists have aimed their activities primarily at asserting women's control over their reproductive abilities. They have also argued that women should develop their own independent facilities and have very little to do with men, favouring a path of separate and parallel development. White radical feminists have also been at the forefront of struggles over access to abortion facilities, campaigns demanding an end to male violence against women and campaigns against pornography (Lederer, 1980; Brownmiller, 1976; Dworkin, 1981).

While retaining their woman-centredness, black radical feminists (Lorde, 1984) accept that black women must fight together with black men to end racial oppression. Black radical feminists have also been at the forefront in criticising the racism evident in white radical feminists' analyses. Audre Lorde's (1984) letter to Mary Daly is a famous example of a black American woman taking a white one to task. In Britain, Hazel Carby's (1982) and Pratiba Parmar's (1982,

1986) critiques offer more generalised illustrations. Important elements in white radical feminists' repertoire which black feminists have challenged are: 'abortion on demand' for failing to tackle the atrocities of enforced abortions and sterilisations white doctors practised upon black women; hostile relations between men and women, for these deny the less antagonistic gender relations racism has engendered within and among black families; and marches through black neighbourhoods during 'Reclaim the Night' demonstrations for intensifying media personifications of black men as rapists and muggers (Collins, 1991; Bryant *et al.*, 1985).

Black women's critique of radical white feminism has been acknowledged, albeit imperfectly by white feminists becoming more sensitive to black women's experiences and trying to be inclusive of these in their writings and social action (see Bourne, 1984, 1987; Barrett and McIntosh, 1985). Consequently, white feminists have altered their demands on abortion to encompass women's reproductive rights and control over their bodies. In addition, both black and white radical feminists have focused on the prevalence of homophobia in society at large as well as within feminist groupings. As a result, both black and white heterosexual women have attempted to address heterosexism. Moreover, radical black feminists have taken on board the existence of homophobia within black communities (Parmar, 1986; Lorde, 1984). The references cited also indicate the multiplicity of women's roles and responses to oppressions. That women have begun to respond to each other's critiques gives feminism a capacity for 'reflexive monitoring' (see Giddens, 1990) which makes it dynamic and non-dogmatic in constantly developing theory and practice (Dominelli, 1992a).

Socialist feminism

Socialist feminists take the view that, while women are oppressed by patriarchy – a term of continued controversy, both men and women are oppressed by capitalism (Eisenstein, 1979). Hence, they are interested in tackling issues in ways that enable men to take up feminist struggles. They have been at the forefront of demands that men take equal roles in housework and childcare, raise employment-based issues such as equal pay and ask for legislation promoting sexual equality (Martin, 1978). Some socialist feminists have also been concerned to develop facilities which address men's needs in promoting anti-sexist social relations, for example, work that is being done with violent men and sex offenders (Fagg, 1993; Dominelli, 1991b) More recently, socialist feminists have begun to look for ways in which theories can account for the great diversity in women's experience of gender oppression without losing the common dimensions within it. Jagger (1983), for example, has attempted to rework the concept of 'alienation' to overcome both the problem of relativism and dichotomous thinking, particularly with regard to the division between the private and the public sides of life, production and reproduction. It is yet unclear how successful her attempt will be, but Tong (1989) gives an optimistic evaluation of its potential.

White socialist feminists (Barrett, 1981; Barrett and McIntosh, 1982, 1985) have failed to acknowledge the importance of racism in structuring both class relations and patriarchal relations. Black socialist feminists (Davis, 1982, 1989; Bhavani, 1993; Bhavani and Coulson, 1986; hooks, 1982, 1984; Lorde, 1984; Collins, 1991) have highlighted the different ways in which class and gender are experienced by black women because racism has such a profound impact on their lives. Their experiences of work, family relations, sexuality, childcare and relationships with each other are all influenced by racism. White socialist feminists have begun to respond to this criticism, for example Bourne (1984, 1987), Barrett (1981), Barrett and McIntosh (1985). Moreover, black feminists have made the point that they are not, and never have been, passive victims in the face of racist onslaughts on them as individuals, families and communities.

Black feminists have traced the tracks of their proud history in resisting 'race', class and gender oppressions (Collins 1991; hooks, 1982, 1984, 1993), both alongside black men and independently as women, individually and collectively. They have also identified the wide range of activities they have undertaken in advancing women's liberation more generally by working with both white women and men holding similar aims and objectives (Collins, 1991; Davis, 1989).

Marxist feminists hold a slightly different position from socialist feminists because they have traditionally focused on the alleged dominance of class by challenging the primacy of waged work and production issues (Beechey, 1980; Adamson *et al.*, 1976). Their writings have highlighted the neglect of 'women's work' in Marxist thought, identified how class issues have impacted on women and raised the question of the importance of housework and reproductive work for capitalism (Delphy, 1984; Dalla Costa and James, 1972).

While white Marxist feminists highlighted the specificity of women's experience of oppression under capitalism by thrusting the significance of women's waged and domestic labour into the public domain (Barrett, 1981; Benston, 1969; Coulson *et al.*, 1975), black Marxist feminists, (see Davis, 1982, 1989; Collins, 1991; hooks, 1989) demonstrated the importance of racism in enabling capitalist exploitation to take place on a massive scale. Black women have, therefore, carried the burden of doing the housework of the world. This included working as domestic servants for white middle-class women (Collins, 1991; Moraga and Azaldna, 1981). Consequently, black women's oppression is not the same as white women's, even if they share the same gender and class. More recently, the distinction between Marxist feminists and socialist feminists has become blurred. Women have moved from one category to another, thereby demonstrating both the fluidity of feminist thought and the ability of women to alter their perceptions of reality as their understanding of social relations increases.

Black feminism

Black women have had to organise as black feminists in defence of their own specific interests because white feminists have ignored the impact of racism on their experience as women. Challenging the assumed universality of women's oppression, they have demonstrated that the oppression of black women, whether in the West or in Third World countries, is shaped by racism, whether intended or not. Racism consumes energies which could have been devoted to purposes more in keeping with their aspirations and calls forth different forms of resistance to those favoured by white women (Collins, 1991). At times, racism may make their demands different as well. Thus, black feminists have rejected white radical feminists' calls for access to abortion on demand. For black women in the West were forced to have abortions as part of a eugenicist drive against them (Sidel, 1986). Women in Third World countries have been made the objects of population control initiatives in which Western powers have assumed significant roles (Jayawardna, 1986). Black feminists have also demonstrated how their sexuality has been both compromised by racism and used by white men to exercise control over the sexual expression of both black and white women (Collins, 1991; hooks, 1989). Moreover, most black women in Western societies are located within the ranks of the working class. Many of their struggles have revolved around class oppression too. This resistance has provided another dimension on which black women and men have fought together.

Both American and British black feminists have signalled the inappropriateness of white middle-class feminists' attacks on family structures. Extended black families in Britain and America have provided a safe haven in a dangerous racist world (Ramazanoglu, 1989; Davis, 1982, 1989; hooks, 1989; Collins, 1991). Encompassing a deepened notion of community, black families have created the space where black women can recharge their energies, despite the endless demands others make upon them. In many situations, black women have more in common with black men than white women (Collins, 1991).

In Britain, the issue has been further complicated by seemingly respectable immigration laws. State policies have assumed that white women have a 'right' to family life and constrain them within it, while black women have been denied equal access to it. Immigration legislation, particularly that passed since the 1960s, has divided black families and often made it impossible for them to be reunited in Britain (Bryant *et al.*, 1985; Wilson, 1977). Other Western countries have similar restrictions on immigration from Third World countries (Gordon, 1992; Cohen, 1992). In 1994, the Canadian government proposed to enact legislation denying dependants the right to follow providers who had emigrated to Canada. Furthermore, First Nations peoples in North America had their rights to family life obliterated when their children were forcefully removed from them to attend residential schools where white language and culture were inculcated into them (Haigh-Brown, 1988).

Additionally, black feminists have questioned the ways in which white middle-class women have captured feminism's agenda for their own purposes and ignored black women's struggles against the oppression of women over centuries because these have focused on issues of little interest to them (Collins, 1991). The white media has played a critical role in extending and perpetuating a monolithic image of feminism by portraying it as the preserve of white middle-class women. In doing so, it renders invisible the struggles of a great many other women – white working-class women, older women and disabled women, black and white. Hence, black feminists have protested about being treated as a homogeneous group by white feminists who seek to respond to their critiques. Like white women, black women are culturally, ethnically, religiously and linguistically diverse (Collins, 1991).

Being excluded by white feminists has prompted black feminists to organise autonomously in pursuit of their own interests and talk about black perspectives in feminism (Carby, 1982; hooks, 1982, 1984; Collins, 1991). Some have eschewed the label 'feminist' altogether and chosen to be 'womanist' instead (hooks, 1989, 1990; Phillipson, 1992). Thus, black feminists have sought to make visible black women's contribution to developing feminist theory and practice and creating services capable of meeting the specific needs of black women, for example refuges (Collins, 1991; Guru, 1987). Furthermore, black feminists have refused to prioritise one form of oppression over another, demanding instead the elimination of all of them (hooks, 1982; Murray, 1970; Jordan, 1981; Asante, 1987). This gives black feminism a deep humanism which focuses on empathy for all humankind (Collins, 1991).

Black British women (Grant, 1992; Ahmad, 1990) use the term black perspectives to describe their own particular analyses and experiences of life in racist white societies and signal their desire for ending racist social relations. Black perspectives are rooted in black people's life histories and are not the same as anti-racist perspectives (Dominelli *et al.*, 1995).

Anti-racist feminism

Among white women, anti-racist feminism has developed largely in response to black women's critique of their failure to address the specificity of their position (Bourne, 1984, 1987; Bhavani, 1993; Bhavani and Coulson, 1986). The term is used by both black and white feminists who wish to incorporate struggles against both racism and sexism in their work. Their analyses tend to incorporate several other social divisions, notably class, age, sexual orientation and/or disability (see Langan and Day, 1989). Many of the insights of white anti-racist feminists parallel those of black feminists (see Dominelli, 1991b, c).

Postmodern feminism

Postmodern feminists have criticised the tendency of other schools of critical social thought, including other feminist ones to strive for 'grand theories' which provide the definitive law explaining oppression, the dynamism of history or any other universalising form of discourse (Irigary, 1985; Kristeva, 1984; Cixous, 1981). Focusing on words, and the power relations inherent in them, postmodern feminists have chosen to deconstruct the ways in which people communicate with each other and convey their taken-for-granted assumptions through them. There are a number of different perspectives amongst postmodernists, although the features identified below are common among them (Tong, 1989).

Dealing with microlevel phenomena, they have been able to paint detailed portraits of human activity at the level of interpersonal interaction. They have celebrated the uniqueness of the individual and revealed the multiplicity of identities that each holds. They have also highlighted the fluidity of people's characters and argued for a dialectical approach to social interaction. Postmodernism posits that people are affected by their interaction with others and influence both the interaction and others in turn. Thus, people are constantly in the fluid process of becoming rather than getting bogged down in fixed identities that come out of a particular social formation. Postmodern feminism, therefore, offers a stringent critique of Marxism even though it shares many concepts derived from Marxist thought, particularly Habermas (1987). It also relies on the works of other thinkers such as Lacan (1977), Foucault (1980) and Derrida (1987).

Postmodern perspectives have much to commend them in terms of:

- achieving greater freedoms for individuals
- uncovering hidden nuances and power relations within language
- transcending dichotomous thinking and binary oppositions (Cixous, 1981).

However, their focus is likely to destroy solidaristic sentiments between peoples unless they are very closely matched in terms of their multiple identities. This approach runs the risk of encouraging either fragmentation of social entities formed through collective action or the isolation of self. In the hands of anti-collectivists, postmodern perspectives could lead to extremely conservative politics. Thus, postmodernism has an 'uneasy relationship' with feminism (Tong, 1989). However, many postmodern emphases are evident in early feminist thought, for example a concern with power relations in language (Spender, 1980) and the individual person in their social context (Friedan, 1963; De Beauvoir, 1974).

In summary, the different schools of feminism are fluid. They change over time and overlap. Many women will claim they belong to more than one. This characteristic and a non-monolithic approach to issues, are typical features of feminism. While this is a strength in many situations, the fragmentation it gives rise to can be a serious liability when taking action over specific issues. For example, many white women have felt incapacitated in their desire to address racism because they fear 'making mistakes which will compound the difficulties they create for black women' (McIntosh, 1989; Sawyer, 1989). Many black women are tired of being used as 'tools for educating white women working on their racism' (Narayan, 1988).

Fragmentation also carries the danger of letting different groups focus primarily on 'identity politics'. This may make it difficult to establish the commonalities they share with others experiencing similar forms of oppressions. They may, therefore, lose the capacity to form alliances through which their power to challenge existing inequalities and oppressions can be augmented. Fortunately, many feminists, particularly black feminists, are aware of this possibility. That it is being named raises the likelihood of it being addressed, however cautiously (hooks, 1989; Collins, 1991). This approach is characteristic of the resiliency of feminism and indicates it does not hold predetermined solutions to the multiplicity of oppressions. Rather, any outcome has to be struggled for through the mobilisation of the necessary resources and people.

Feminist conceptual developments

Sensitivity to the use of language and receptivity to valuing difference have been conceptual developments which have penetrated the major schools of feminist thought. These are considered below.

Language

Language is a powerful conveyor of the taken-for-granted assumptions which reflect our individual and collective views of the world.

Seeking to refine our use of language so that it more accurately reflects power relations as they actually exist is an important element in feminist struggles (Spender, 1980). Thus, I am worried that the term feminist has been defined in ways which exclude rather than include women, without at the same time recognising our different experiences of gender oppression. I'd like to see the label reclaimed so that it is more inclusive – although that requires us to do much more work on identifying which elements of oppression are in reality common to all women and which are not, and on becoming capable of clarifying and celebrating our differences.

In addition, feminists, for example Gilligan (1982) and Tannen (1992), have revealed how differently men and women use language to communicate with each other and among themselves. The implicit power relations embodied in different styles and forms of communication will have to be taken on board if men and women are to reach the point of being able to talk *with* rather than 'to' or 'over' each other. Similar dynamics would also have to be investigated for their impact on communications among different groups of women.

Difference as a source of strength

Celebrating our differences is vital to showing respect for each other, valuing our uniqueness and creating equality between groups of women who currently are held to be unequal. In addressing this issue, feminists will have to tackle the problem of privileging, that is, the advantages which accrue to different groups of women because relations of domination benefit one at the expense of others. Our language and dichotomous thinking reflect this clearly. Each dichotomous pair has one aspect of it which is privileged, that is, cast as superior to the other, for example black over white, able-bodied over disabled, middle class over working class, heterosexual over homosexual, youth over old age (Collins, 1991). The list is endless. Such language portrays 'difference' as a 'deficit' which can only be overcome by becoming like the 'dominant' other. This solution is unacceptable in feminist practice because it reinforces relations of domination. But if feminists can transcend or dissolve binary oppositions by celebrating difference and creating egalitarian relations between different groups of women (Cixous, 1981), we will demonstrate through our actions that privileged groups can indeed cede power in non-violent ways. The omens provide a little optimism.

Feminists have responded to each other's criticisms in non-antago-
nistic ways (Eisenstein, 1994). Plurality is sought. Authoritarian ways
of working with each other are eschewed. Some material resources
have been transferred in feminist groups from women who are better
off to those who are not (Torkington, 1981; Curno *et al.*, 1981). But,
whichever way women respond, unity will have to be worked for. It
cannot be assumed and *will not happen of its own accord.*

Feminists should not be in the business of *assuming* either shared
experiences of oppressions or universal commitment to specific
demands made by other women. Sisterhood is created through the
actions of women. It is unlikely to materialise out of unbidden
historical forces, not only because history is created through human
action but also because women are implicated in the oppression of
others in their 'normal' interaction. Mothers socialising children to
heed relations of domination and women accepting prescribed roles
provide two illustrations of this. These examples should not be taken
at face value. Ordinary behaviour can both challenge and endorse
oppression, thereby shifting the terrain on which it is reproduced
and in which subsequent action, including resistance, takes place.
Relations of oppression can be infinitely renewed and challenged,
unless action is taken to break out of that dialectic.

The outcome of such action, is not predetermined. Much depends
on how those being challenged respond. As women, we live in
contingent realities which are not necessarily of our own choosing.
But, the other actors do not have it all their own way. People can
exercise their volition in unanticipated ways, thereby reversing power
relations. Unintended consequences can materialise (Giddens,
1982). Realising sisterhood, therefore, requires additional action
including research and development in both theory and practice. In
working out our commonalities as women, we have to validate the
differences that divide us more than we have done in the past. Even
though our objective may be the same, that is, the elimination of all
forms of oppression, these differences ensure that we do not all start
from the same baseline. If valued, differences can become sources of
strength rather than symbols of weakness.

The uses of feminism in social work

Feminism has gained a strong foothold in social work, primarily
because many issues which feminists address in their practice

concern welfare provisions which are the remit of social work. In addition, feminist practitioners have joined the academy to pass on their insights to students who were being badly prepared for work with women (Marchant and Wearing, 1986; Brook and Davis, 1985; Dominelli and McLeod, 1989; Burden and Gottlieb, 1987). Their activities have given rise to new forms of practice which address power relations between professional workers, 'clients' and the state as well as issues of gender. An example of feminist practice is depicted below:

CASE STUDY

Joe, a white working-class Englishman was living with Gloria, a black working-class woman in a run-down council estate in northern England. Although of Afro-Caribbean descent, Gloria was born in Brixton and saw herself as black British. Joe worked at a foundry, doing heavy work. He had very rigid views about his role in life and rarely got involved in doing either housework or looking after the children. But he always made sure that Gloria had money to pay the bills.

The couple had three children – Andrea aged five, Christopher aged three and Ben aged one. Joe and Gloria had been going out with each other off and on for several years before they began to live together when Gloria first became pregnant. Joe was a possessive man who jealously 'guarded' his partner and insisted that she stay away from other men. Although he had never hit her, he often shouted that she was a lousy housekeeper and would storm out of the house when he got angry about the things she did. At such times, he would go to the pub and not come back for hours or occasionally days. He always refused to tell Gloria where he had been and what he had been doing. As time went on, the relationship between the two of them deteriorated, but Gloria was worried about how she would manage to provide for the children if she left him. Moreover, she had lost most of her friends because she rarely had time to visit anyone. Looking after Joe and the kids took up all the energy she had.

One morning Gloria woke up feeling exhausted and weepy. She decided not to get up as she desperately needed to rest. She called Joe and suggested that he get the children their breakfast and then dress them. She was so tired, she could hardly move to get to the bathroom. Joe blew his top. Saying that it was her job to look after the children, he stormed out of the bedroom. He went downstairs to the phone and rang social services. He insisted that his wife had 'gone crazy'. She was in bed, pretending that she could not get up and attend to the children. He was worried about what she was up to. Could they send someone over straightaway.

A (white) feminist woman social worker arrived shortly afterwards to investigate. Up to that point, the children had yet to be fed and dressed. She asked Joe to tell her exactly what he thought the problem was. But he was incoherent. He kept insisting that Gloria should 'get up and get on with her jobs'. He did not take kindly to her suggestion that he should get the children dressed and fed. Meanwhile, the social worker said she would talk to Gloria while he dealt with the children. Then she went upstairs to the bedroom to see her.

Gloria was aghast that Joe had called in social services. She did not think they could help in her situation. She just wanted to be left alone to rest. The social worker replied that it seemed to her that resting was a reasonable thing to want. It could not be easy to care for three young children day in and day out. This was the key for Gloria to unleash her pent-up emotions. She then spoke of the pain of her isolation, her lack of support from Joe and the way she felt abused by the situation she found herself in. The social worker empathised with her and suggested that these feelings were not unusual. Other women going through experiences like hers felt similarly. Gloria looked somewhat relieved at this, but then sank back into her state of despondency.

The social worker then tried to get Gloria to talk about what she would like for herself if she were given the option. Gloria thought getting some help with the children and getting Joe to do more around the house and spend time with her would help. The social worker decided to explore Gloria's views about what she wanted from Joe to a greater extent. In the course of their conversation, it transpired that the children were being subjected to racist taunts by the (white) neighbours' older children. Joe constantly refused to take these seriously, saying that the neighbours didn't mean anything by them, it was their way of joking with their children. Gloria felt they were being abusive, but whenever she said so, she and Joe would have a dreadful row.

The social worker sympathised with Gloria's view about the taunts. Whether the neighbours meant it or not, their comments were hurtful and abusive. She could see how it would undermine the children's confidence and drain Gloria's energies when supporting the children. The social worker suggested that if Gloria would find it helpful, she could get a mother's help (sic), preferably another black woman, to assist her with the housework and the children a couple of days a week.

In the longer term, she felt it would be useful if Joe did some work on his attitudes towards women, his expectations about what it was appropriate for him to do around the house, and examine ways in which he could tackle racist abuse and seek help from the housing authorities in dealing with the neighbours. In fact, she thought it might be useful if a male social worker were assigned to work with Joe with the aim of getting him to become more involved in caring for the children's physical and emotional well-being. Such action would only be taken if both Gloria and Joe felt it would be appropriate for them. Meanwhile, she was prepared to support Gloria in taking up the issue of the racist taunts with the housing department if she wished to pursue it through that avenue.

From listening to Gloria, the social worker felt it was important to address the range of problems that she presented, thereby providing a holistic service to her. She also felt that there were a number of structural issues which needed to be tackled in the longer term. For the moment, however, she intended to focus on immediate needs. Moreover, Gloria's and Joe's differing accounts of the situation have revealed the complexity of the work that needs to be done if the family as currently constituted is to be assisted. Gloria's story indicates that Joe's stereotypical views of gender roles, lack of involvement with either childcare or housework and failure to take the racist abuse seriously were critical in precipitating the crisis. In the context in which Gloria does not live near an extended family or have close relationships with people around her for networking and help, her isolation needs to be addressed. For this, the social worker suggests that Gloria might like to join a women's group – a black women's group, a mother and toddler's group, playgroup or any other facility which sounds attractive to her. The social worker is also concerned about addressing the element of racism reflected in Joe's attitudes.

Critiques of feminism

The critique of feminist thought can be divided into two categories. First, *internal criticism* generated within feminism. This is a self-critique generally sympathetic to feminism's overall aim of ending the oppression of women in all its guises and introducing changes in social relationships which will support that objective. Second, *external criticism*. This is usually a hostile critique of feminism – what it stands for, its aims, objectives and methodology. The self-critique attempts to increase the relevance of feminism to a diverse group of women, improve its practice and generate positive developments in feminist theory. The latter has led to a backlash which has substantially undermined the limited gains that feminists have procured (Lyndon, 1992; Gairdner, 1992). Erosion of these has happened in the fields of equal rights, reproductive rights and welfare rights. In Britain, women's employment rights had begun to be reduced during Margaret Thatcher's premiership, for example through the abolition of the Wages Council which protected the working conditions and wage rates of low-paid working-class women and the loss of rights protecting pregnant women's jobs (Coyle, 1984). In the United States, Reagan's presidency was influential in cutting women's reproductive rights and blocking the passage of the Equal Rights Amendment (Sidel, 1986).

More opposition has come to light as men have gained confidence in attacking women's hard won rights. Men have organised a number of campaigns, sometimes helped by women who have felt threatened by feminist demands to reassert their privileged positions. For example, in Britain, the limited recognition of women's work in caring for children in the form of alimony following a divorce has been withdrawn as a result of the Matrimonial Proceedings Act of 1986 (Ruth, 1989). In the United States, fierce battles have been fought around women's reproductive rights with clinics providing abortion being attacked or firebombed and doctors providing these services being shot (Hanmer, 1993). That not all women subscribe to feminist insights is a matter of sadness for feminists. But feminists neither impose their views on other women nor insist that their version of events is *the truth*. Feminists are more concerned with responding to women's realities as women themselves see and define them. Feminists use women's questions about their insights as the basis for re-examining them in light of the information which other women provide (Frankfort, 1972; Hyde, 1989; Stanley, 1990).

In the academy, many men and women have refused to recognise the validity of feminist scholarship (Richardson and Robinson, 1993). Outright hostility has meant that feminist scholars have had to underplay their commitment to improving women's position. Feminists have often been passed up for promotion (if they got the jobs in the first place), even when they have been over-qualified for the jobs they have been seeking (Walby, 1990). As the backlash against feminist gains has gathered strength, the limited funding for ghettos in which feminists have been visible, for example women's studies, has been cut (Richardson and Robinson, 1993). Gender studies and men's studies have become more important in the academic lexicon. These have been developed at the expense of women's studies, with resources passing directly over from women to men (Richardson and Robinson, 1993).

The clawing back of hard-won feminist gains in both social policy and interpersonal relations has been possible because feminism has not succeeded in developing a constituency of adherents to its vision of the world which is capable of ensuring continuity over space and time. Antagonism to the feminist emancipatory project has always been around. For the moment, it has succeeded in amassing the 'allocative' and 'authoritative' resources necessary for taking control of some developments and lead them in anti-feminist directions.

Conclusions

The importance of systematically researching social work interventions cannot be overstated. Undertaking such work has been of limited interest to practitioners who feel they must be content to leave research to others while they get on with the job 'of doing': providing services and alleviating suffering (Davies, 1985; Bailey, 1982). Since social work can be used for good or ill, including the decimation of populations as happened in Nazi Germany (Lorenz, 1994), I would argue social workers should play a more active role in research – framing the research questions and methodology through which these are investigated, analysing and using the findings emanating from it – thereby leading it in emancipatory directions. Social work's own value base and commitment to individual self-realisation provide a basis which can orient practitioners towards liberationist paths. Furthermore, service users must be fully involved in the research process. Feminist research methodologies which place a greater emphasis on establishing a more participative relationship between the researcher and the subjects of the research (Roberts, 1981; Stanley and Wise, 1983) become germane in this context. Following this path calls upon social workers to commit themselves to research to a greater extent than they have been hitherto accustomed.

Notes

1 Client is a problematic term which assumes an expert helper and a dependent user. As this way of shaping the professional–client relationship is being questioned, I place quotes around it to denote its contested nature. I shall adhere to the 'client' convention throughout this book.

2 I use the term 'black' in this book in its political sense to encompass all people subjected to racism in predominantly white societies, regardless of their skin colour. The category is controversial. Some authors in Britain limit it largely to people of African and Afro-Caribbean descent.

   I do not subscribe to the view that black people are a homogeneous group. In using this term, I suggest only that racism in its personal, institutional, and cultural forms (see Dominelli (1988) for definitions of these terms) is a feature that black people have in common. However, their specific experience of it is varied and diverse.

   Black perspectives are rooted in black people's experience of racism and have been developed over centuries of exploitation to bring their world view into the social, including scholastic, arena. Anti-racist perspectives cover the activities of both black and white people challenging racism.

3 The Department of Health and Social Security was divided into two: the Department of Health and the Department of Social Security by Margaret Thatcher in the late 1980s to prepare the National Health Service for privatisation. This division also made it easier for government ministers to create 'moral panics' around the failure of unemployed people to get off Income Support and take up whatever job opportunities the market provided.

4 Following the 1991 Criminal Justice Act, probation officers no longer prepare Social Enquiry Reports on offenders, but Pre-Sentence Reports. These are allegedly more focused on offending behaviour but, in general terms, differ little from their predecessors.

5 bell hooks does not capitalise her name. I have observed her convention throughout this book.

2

Sociological Social Work

Arguments about the relevance of sociology to social work practitioners have been ongoing. These have focused on how far sociology could or should influence practice and the theories underpinning it. While its capacity to inform conceptual developments was cautiously welcomed, its potential to criticise and undermine existing practices and the privileged position of elites was feared. Back in the 1960s, Peter Leonard (1966) sought to introduce a sociological framework into the profession to dislodge its psychodynamic orientation. He argued that social work students have much to learn from sociological insights in examining a variety of questions about roles, status, power and organisational issues. These, he believed, would be immensely valuable in enabling students to acquire the intellectual skills needed to improve their practice and establish a sociologically based social work (Leonard, 1966). Heraud's (1970, 1979, 1981) attempts to develop a comprehensive sociological account of social work alongside other caring professions has met with limited success. Peter Day (1981, 1987) followed suit but has similarly failed to capture the imagination of either sociologists or social workers. Others, for example, Sibeon (1991) and Davies (1991), have attempted to develop a 'sociology of social work'. Martin Davies (1991) has tried to achieve this through an edited text. Although this book provides useful insights into practice, it creates neither the comprehensive intellectual backdrop necessary for promoting a 'sociology of social work', nor an analysis of practice which would make sociological thought attractive to busy practitioners. A contributor to Davies' book, Roger Sibeon, tackles some of the theoretical issues which need to be addressed in a sociology of social work and has written a book on the subject (Sibeon, 1991). This also fails to provide a comprehensive analysis of the 'sociology of social work' by neglecting the impact of social divisions in a profession dominated by gendered and racially stratified social relations.

Not one of these texts deals adequately with social divisions, their complexities in practice and the moral and ethical dilemmas associated with addressing them. A sociological analysis capable of accomplishing this task would have to explore separately each of the following and identify the interconnections between them: workplace relations binding employers and employees; professional relationships guiding 'client'–worker and worker–worker interactions; and expressions of institutional powers which include or exclude specific groups from organisational relationships which define, create and deliver services. It should also encompass an ethically and morally sound practice addressesing issues of oppression and social justice.

In this chapter, I explore the use of sociological constructs in social work and argue that practice can be enriched through sociological insights into society, which consider how it is organised and who benefits from the prevailing power structures and patterns of resource distribution. Understanding these requires social workers to unravel the 'politics of practice' and examine structural inequalities in social relations as a pre-requisite to improving practice. Moreover, I argue that social workers steeped in the knowledge of hardship, material poverty and emotional deprivation shaping the everyday lives of their clientele need to become political themselves in how they conceptualise their practice and activate their relationships with others outside the workplace. Their practice, therefore, should expose structured inequalities by drawing upon suitably anonymised information gleaned through systematic analyses of their practice; protest against the waste of human potential they encounter daily; and engage with 'clients' and colleagues in empowering ways. Sociological social work provides the analytical tools for developing such practice.

The role of social work in society

Social work's role in society is a contested and ambiguous one. This controversy makes it political in the sense of engaging in power relations at a number of levels, particularly in its own area of intervention – private life. The division of the world into a private sphere, which no outsider except a social worker under tightly defined conditions can penetrate, constitutes an element within the 'politics of practice' which sits unhappily with its professional ambition of neutrality in practice. Sociological social work is useful in transcending this division by identifying the public nature of private woes and gaining new insights into the boundaries between private and public matters (Gamarnikov *et al.*, 1983). Questioning its traditional limits enhances social work's commitment to social justice and social change. This stance has a fine pedigree. It has been endorsed, for example, by Clement Attlee (1920), a social worker who became prime minister, and C Wright Mills (1970), a renowned sociologist who spoke powerfully of the political nature of everyday life. But social workers' right to engage in such activities as part of routine practice has been challenged by some social work academics and practitioners. Having defined this approach outside the remit of social work practice, they demand its abolition (Pinker, 1979, 1993, 1994; Davies, 1981).

Davies (1981, 1985) claims that *the* task of the social worker is one of 'maintenance', not facilitating social change. He goes on to say that, despite wishing to see social work education retained within a university setting, social workers do not need sociology, but rather 'practice wisdoms' or practical know-how, knowledge of the law affecting social work, a knowledge of welfare rights and a working knowledge of the local community (Davies, 1985). I would argue knowledge of this practical nature is necessary but insufficient. Without sociological understanding, it can only lead to impoverished forms of practice. Social workers must understand how their profession fits into society's structures and is informed by its relationships with these. Moreover, good practice is underpinned by theoretical knowledge (Howe, 1987). Sociology is a key provider of theoretical underpinnings for practice. Yet, social workers appear to have a dread of abstract theory which seems tangential to practice. They claim they use theory rarely and do not recall many of those covered on their qualifying courses (Davies and Wright, 1989). Yet courses carry a commitment to testing students' ability to integrate theory and practice in both their written work and agency placements. Social workers are alleged to fear theory's potential both to mystify through its complexity and to undermine their performance as professional workers. Academics also assert that social workers neither focus on the theories underpinning their practice nor theorise about their work (Sibeon, 1991; Curnock and Hardiker, 1979). Large-scale systematic research backing such sweeping statements is missing. There are, however, small-scale studies which question these perceptions. For example, a limited study on the quality of practice teaching reveals that students welcomed their practice teachers' ability to integrate theory and practice. Moreover, they claimed that those who had been *both* accredited and awarded practice teaching awards were better at doing this than those who had not (Claytor *et al.*, 1994). The debate over the usefulness of sociological theory in social work practice is not only about the role of social work in society, but also the socialisation of social workers and their training for the profession.

There are two main sides to this debate: one focuses on 'maintenance'; the other on emancipation. Martin Davies (1985), a key architect of the 'maintenance approach', argues persuasively that social workers' principal task is a 'maintenance' function. This view carries the danger of automatically allying social workers with the status quo and their employers, regardless of the injustice their work may be exposing. This position is also reflected in discussions about the nature of social work and the training required for the profession. At times, this debate has been framed as the tension between care and control (Lee, 1982; Parry *et al.*, 1979). A maintenance function places more emphasis on the control than the care side of the equation. While I am not advocating that there is or should not be any degree of control in social work (such a position is neither tenable nor desirable), I would like to see a shift towards the care side, so that human needs are given primacy in reaching decisions about the kind of social work society should endorse. This is a matter of political deliberation and decision.

The counter to Davies' stance is most powerfully articulated by Paulo Freire (1972, 1973). He contends that social workers are responsible for empowering oppressed people by facilitating their understanding of social reality. This involves their demystifying social relations which disempower people by drawing on *concrete knowledge derived from their own experience* to unravel hidden power dynamics. Theory is thus drawn from the practice of life. Focusing on the liberating potential of an individual's life experience is attacked by authors such as Sibeon (1991) as 'woolly thinking'. The charge is misleading. Practitioners may not always be clear about their work. They can obfuscate what they do as much as academics. But in the current context, they have little time for systematically articulating the theoretical frameworks which shape their practice and should not be condemned for not doing so. However, critical theorists could assist them in getting their materials into print. After all, theorising about microlevel practice is a legitimate academic activity which places an obligation upon theorists to unpack the dynamics, relationships and theories encompassed by 'practical' knowledge rather than disparaging it. Moreover, unsubstantiated indictments against experiential knowledge reveal how mainstream sociological thought devalues people's capacity to draw on what they know to make sense of those aspects of social reality which they do not know (Adamson *et al.*, 1988).

British social work has taken Freirian approaches more seriously since the late 1970s. However, those allying themselves with the oppressed have been, and are, in the minority. Nonetheless, their academic opponents, opinion formers in the media and government ministers have exaggerated their influence and decried their concerns as 'political correctness' and stultified debate on the nature of social work in a participative and enabling society. I discuss this issue in greater detail later.

I would argue that all those with an interest in social work including social workers, social work academics, and users, should participate fully in defining the boundaries of social work activities – not just employers, the opinion formers who control the media, or have privileged access to it, and politicians. The issue is too important to be left primarily in their hands. I would add that we have to redefine citizenship rights to make the personal social services available to each individual by virtue of their presence in society. Rights involve obliga-tions. But these are matters of *reciprocity between the individual and the state* as the guarantor of individual freedoms.

The concept of 'rights' is a contested one. 'Rights' are not, as New Right theorists maintain, simply a question of how individuals provide for themselves. Insisting that individuals in extreme poverty fend for themselves, as Murray (1984) and Glazer (1988) do, is akin to passing a death sentence on people who cannot purchase the required services from a profit-oriented market. These include: working poor people whose jobs do not pay them enough for such purchases; unemployed people; women (mainly) who perform unpaid domestic work; and retired people lacking occupational pensions. These groups are excluded from enjoying benefits and rights, which are considered 'normal' in this society, by virtue of their structural position in it, irrespective of their individual will. The ability of marginalised people to safeguard their interests is limited by a lack of 'allocative' and 'authoritative' resources for mobilising resources and support for themselves. This is a sociological understanding that social workers, working with people excluded from decision-making processes, can employ in establishing the 'rights' of 'clients'. By using research to systematise their detailed knowledge of 'clients'' lives, social workers can highlight how these can be distorted and destroyed by structural realities over which individuals have no control.

Social workers have a professional value system which emphasises the 'right' of individuals to control their own lives and realise social justice (Kendall, 1978). They have an obligation to protect 'clients'' rights and argue for their extension (Mullaly, 1993). This is already being done to protect children from violence and safeguard the human rights of people with mental health problems. They can, therefore, legitimately espouse a socially aware form of social work. However, their potential for doing so is circumscribed. Bureau-professional social workers eschew the contamination of their professionalism by declaring that political positions are the remit of the active citizen. They have no time for the socially aware social worker. Their employers adopt the same view. Users interested in less bureaucratic and more responsive services do not (see Morris, 1991). Moreover, employers demand total allegiance from their workers. The argument that social workers should not criticise the state as their employer, denies employees, individually and collectively, the responsibility of acting within their consciences to challenge what they consider 'wrongdoing'. This stance leads to morally reprehensible 'cover-ups' in which malpractice cannot be publicly identified by workers who are in a good position to know about it and who are better placed than vulnerable 'clients' to expose it.

In Britain, safeguarding organisational interests has led to the authoritarian imposition of 'gagging clauses' in the contracts of individuals working for the welfare state (Baldock, 1982). Individuals who reject such strictures adopt a moral stance which challenges the unequal power relations their silence is designed to protect. Their taking a stand requires them to address the moral and ethical dilemmas encountered through social work tasks. Moreover, it reveals the interconnections between morality and action evident throughout social workers' interventions with their clientele.

Adopting a moral posture is different from moralising. The latter delivers a message of the 'superior' position of the moraliser while passing judgement about the 'inferior' worth of the other.

The sociological project

Sociology studies modern society and lays bare for systematic consideration the dynamics which underpin it (Comte, 1838). Having a sociological analysis of society does not mean sociology is on the side of the underdog. Sociology may describe society; there is no automatic commitment to changing it. Sociological analyses conducted according to a proclaimed neutrality permit existing oppressive power relations to continue unchallenged. However, social engineering and reformative measures have co-existed alongside schools of sociological thought espousing formal neutrality from their subjects, for example positivism and Parsonian functionalism. Despite this potential, few sociological findings have been controlled by oppressed people (Flaherty, 1995).

Oppressed groups are more likely to be objects of sociological research with information flows going from them to the ruling elite rather than the other way round (Nicolaus, 1966, 1973; Flaherty, 1995). This reality has caused some Marxists (see Nicolaus, 1966, 1973) and feminists (see Roberts, 1981; Stanley and Wise, 1983; Gamarnikov *et al.*, 1983) to question the research relationship and make accountability, to those traditionally treated as objects in the research process, a centrepiece of their approach. Yet, as is witnessed by the British government's reluctance to endorse the expansion of sociological studies, sociology's potential to expose power dynamics has made the ruling class reluctant to support it. Critical sociology in particular has been charged with being biased because the ruling elite has deemed its critique of society politically unacceptable (see Gould, 1977; Phillips, 1994).

These power plays are also evident in social work, where theories and practice drawing on critical sociology have been castigated for their political nature (Pinker, 1993, 1994), inability to deal with the 'realities of practice' (Harbart, 1985b), dogmatic and authoritarian imposition on others (Phillips, 1993), lack of substantiating research (Phillips, 1994), dearth of consumer involvement (Phillips, 1993, 1994), and radical careerism (Harbart, 1985a).

This litany of allegations misses the mark, but reveals much about the social positions of the authors singing it. These reflect the power and authority they wield: respected and influential professional social work academics, employers and journalists who seek to swing the debate over the nature of social work in their preferred direction. None writes as a 'client' of statutory provisions. On the contrary, they hold well-paid, established posts which provide the wherewithal for purchasing privately the goods and services they need. Their 'allocative' and 'authoritative' resources give them tremendous bargaining power – more so than their critics who do not have access to an equivalent panoply of 'allocative' and 'authoritative' resources. Moreover, their privileged access to the media means that they, rather than those they criticise, are better placed to mobilise public opinion in their favour.

These authors have consistently maintained that the 'politics of practice' (Galper, 1973; Halmos, 1978) have no place in social work. Employers seek practitioners who will not rock the boat by asking awkward questions and demanding organisational change favouring 'clients' (Baldock, 1982). Their position heralds a managerialist preoccupation with rationing resources and demands for service (Clarke *et al.*, 1994). Moreover, opinion formers who do not have to tackle the realities of working with people distressed by inequality in their day-to-day practice, are free to construct images that minimise the horrors it causes. Their reasoning espouses a value position which is no more or less valid than its opposite. Empirically, since the 1970s, more and more students, practitioners and academics have accepted the political nature of social work, even if it is simply to recognise its role in maintaining the status quo.

Notwithstanding their organisational advantages, these critics have failed to convince all professional social work academics, students or practitioners to uphold their views. Recognising how ideas take hold at particular points in time helps explain this outcome. An examination of their views reveals that the gender-blind and colour-blind forms of practice they advocate are deemed inadequate by the 'clients' and practitioners on whose behalf they purport to speak. Social movements among claimants, women and black people were formed precisely because *they* as *users* of its provisions had found the welfare state wanting. Moreover, their *experience* of welfare provisions has been backed by empirical research carried out by 'respectable' organisations including the

Council of Churches, the Home Office and the Lord Chancellor's Office.

Practice drawing on critical sociology is predicated on the experiences of oppressed people, and not an ivory tower view of what these are. Feminist practice, for example, has been developed by women *creating more appropriate services* by drawing on their experiences of 'professional' services they have *declared deficient*. Many of these arose in the voluntary sector and have moved from there into statutory and academic settings (Dominelli and McLeod, 1989).

Women's own biographies, subjected to analytical scrutiny, have served in model building. Through collective action sparked off by consciousness-raising groups, individual experiences have been generalised to develop woman-centred provisions. The attraction of consciousness-raising groups is that these provide women with the space to develop their own ideas about which services might meet their needs (Longress and McLeod, 1980). Consciousness-raising groups, therefore, act as 'reflexive monitoring' (Giddens, 1987, 1982) through which women's experiences, insights and understandings transcend time and space. Additionally, consciousness-raising groups are both 'allocative' and 'authoritative' resources which enable women who participate in them to collectively develop new forms of practice more in keeping with their egalitarian aspirations. Sibeon (1991) and Phillips (1993, 1994) miss the point when they define consciousness-raising activities in women's groups as authoritarian. The process of women enabling each other individually and collectively to discover for themselves what they want to do, and how, is central to feminist methodologies and liberating relationship building (Longres and McLeod, 1980).

Feminist social action also goes beyond the use of biography as a methodology for understanding society better and initiating social change. Feminist scholars have also placed social divisions *in the empirical domain*. Their research is demonstrable and can be replicated by others to expose the systemic oppression of women. Systematic patterns of oppression have therefore been uncovered and backed by people who hold neither feminist nor black perspectives (see ADSS, 1978; Brown, 1984; Taylor, 1981; Home Office, 1991). Similar research has been undertaken on other forms of oppression. But the important point for feminists is to take action on the basis of their experiential knowledge and/or systematic research (Collins, 1991).

Sociologists can claim that it is not for them to explore the implications of their theory in the field, although they will make information available to those who do so. Social workers do not have this option. They are in the business of 'initiating change' at the personal level as part and parcel of their work (Compton and Galaway, 1975). While they may have some choice about how they do it, social workers put their theoretical position(s) into practice, whether or not they wish to, regardless of whether or not they take action. This scope emanates from social work's remit of working with people to improve their life skills and ability to deal with their circumstances.

There is *no fixed answer* to the question of how to intervene. The dilemma of whether social workers help individuals and groups 'cope' with their situation by adapting, to negotiate more successfully their share of resources without challenging the system in which they live, or seek to change it, lies at the heart of social work. Considerable controversy surrounds the responses given by individual workers and society.

Any solution devised to the care or control dilemma is temporal, for its opponents will raise the question again in a new form. Currently, debate in Britain, Canada and the United States asks whether the social worker is accountable to the state or employer in resolving it. One argument put forth by employers is that they, as those who pay social workers' salaries, should define the job. This position emphasises the employers' greater power position, and places social workers in both a moral and political quandry. Should they worry about their 'meal ticket' or should they support 'clients', whose marginalisation precludes their having a voice elsewhere? This problem has to be answered by each social worker individually, although their organisations can take a more collective view.

The employers' resolution neglects one crucial element: the public trust vested in employers within the statutory sector. Those controlling state structures root this trust among undifferentiated taxpayers. In a liberal democratic state funded by all taxpayers through both direct and indirect taxes, the category of 'taxpayer' needs to be deconstructed. The tabloid media's and government's presentation of the taxpayer as a homogeneous conservative force is a myth. While some taxpayers might reflect this caricature, it does not fit all taxpayers. Besides conservative taxpayers, there are other kinds of taxpayers: liberals, radicals, oppressed and oppressing ones. Marginalised groups are among these, even though power holders act as if they were not.

In short, 'the taxpayer' consists of a complexity of groups, each of which hold different opinions regarding the nature of that trust and which definition of the purpose and role of social work can be accepted on their behalf. Hence, the category can be dissected along a number of axes, each of which has different interests from the others. Where does the employers' commitment to excluded people lie? Social workers are state employees paid out of public funds which include a contribution from marginalised groups who pay a disproportionate amount of their income in both direct and indirect taxes. Where is their accountability to these groups, who at least individually indicate their need for assistance when resorting to them? These questions are even more critical for politicians. Their claim to represent all their constituents should encompass marginalised groups.

Definitions of the 'taxpayer' should focus on the interconnections between people, not their separateness. For if marginalised groups did not exist, neither would social workers nor their employers. This contradiction does not justify people making safe careers out of serving marginalised 'clients' by making them dependent on either social workers or their organisations. But their vulnerability and contribution to social resources demands that all power holders become directly accountable to service users. Acknowledging this dimension of the 'politics of practice' calls for a sociological social work.

Sociological social work is what I call that form of social work practice which addresses directly 'the politics of practice'. It is founded on sociological understanding about the nature of society, human relationships and social interactions, social institutions and power relationships, and the distribution of resources and opportunities. It aims to enable individuals, groups and communities to take control over their lives within a framework which acknowledges the interconnected and interdependent nature of social life, and seeks to eradicate structured inequalities which privilege some at the expense of others. I now turn to exploring the sociological functions underpinning this type of social work.

Conceptual sociological frameworks

Sociology has concepts which are crucial in understanding how society works. These include status, power, roles, authority, legitimacy, institutions, organisations, responsibility, rights, relationships and division of labour.

Status

Status refers to the rights a person has within a group as a result of their social position in relation to others. It is closely associated with a person's role (Linton, 1936) and encompasses the notion of hierarchy with its attendant gradations of prestige and power. Weber (1968) divides this into two parts: 'status' and 'status groups'. The former is an individual's evaluation of the honour or prestige of another. The latter is the set of social relationships which follow from these evaluations. Weber maintains status groups are *independent* of class.

While useful, Weber's refinement of the concept fails to address the different ways in which social divisions such as 'race' and gender influence status and status groups because forms of power external to status classifications are ignored. These interact with forms of power derived from status and alter the experience of it. Thus, class impacts on status and status impacts on class in an ongoing dialectical relationship. Class and status are (re)produced through their interaction with each other. Similar dynamics apply with respect to other social divisions. A black woman's experience of being a district manager in a social services department is therefore different from a white woman's because the former encounters racism, the latter does not (Ahmad, 1992). Similarly, sexism makes white women's experience of management different from white men's (Eley, 1989; Hayles, 1989; Burgess, 1994). Sexism and racism affect black women's experience as managers. These 'isms' are reproduced through complex social interactions along both vertical and horizontal axes and explain what Lenski (1954) called 'status inconsistency' or 'crystallisation'.

Power

Power is the ability to act in accordance with one's wishes. For Weber (1968), power is a negative force imposed upon other individuals. It involves the notion of agency and covers rational choices and interventions which can be exercised over others. Parsons (1957) has argued that traditional views of power are 'zero-sum' ones. This means that power is considered finite; if it is possessed by one group, it is denied to another. This produces the dichotomous dyad: the powerful and the powerless. One group is included; the other excluded. Such power relies on the presence of others who accept the legitimacy of its being exercised over them. Weber (1968) termed this kind of power, 'authority'. Power is, therefore, a functional facility, which enables the powerful to get what they want. Marxists portray power as an economically determined structural phenomenon located within the ruling class for the purposes of domination (Poulantzas, 1978). Only class struggle can alter these power relations.

Feminists have argued that traditional concepts of power embody notions of 'power over' others (French, 1985). Power over others is about domination and is intricately linked with hierarchical relations. Power acting along gender lines privileges men (Firestone, 1971; Millett, 1970; Friedan, 1963). More recently, feminists have posited the idea of power as infinite – something that is constantly renewed and (re)negotiated during each social interaction. Power therefore, has many sources – economic, political, social, personal, institutional, and can be defined as 'the power to do' (French, 1985). Power *can* be positive as well as negative. No one is completely powerless (Collins, 1991). This conception of power means that women have the power to resist their oppression in a variety of ways. Women are not totally powerless and can act in pursuance of their own goals. These may or may not include liberation (see Jagger, 1983). Power is therefore a strategic and contingently achieved capacity (Giddens, 1987). Clegg (1989:211) describes three types of power: episodic, dispositional and facilitative which, he argues, people acting as agents use to stabilise their positions. Achieving stability may initiate a period of instability while a (re)new(ed) set of relationships are negotiated with others.

Roles

A *role* refers to that part of a social position which a person undertakes as part of an anticipated pattern of action. A role is defined by the obligations a person has within a group. Roles come with the position and are independent of an individual's personal attributes and expectations. Roles are the means whereby individual behaviours are socially shaped. Linton (1936) perceives roles as status entities associated with particular positions. These are reinforced by rather than changed through interaction with others. Mead (1936) on the other hand, depicts roles as tentative and creative because they arise as products of social interaction. This gives roles a dynamism which has provided symbolic interactionists with a springboard for analysis.

Sometimes, role refers to a social position with its attendant status (Neiman and Hughes, 1961). Role theory suggests that the same situation is perceived differently by the various actors involved in it because of their differing roles and status.

Merton (1957) extended role theory to include *role set*. A role set encompasses all the social positions with which any one social position is associated. It can also be used to refer to those with whom a particular role-holder interacts. Thus, the organisational flowchart of a social services department can represent the role set of a social worker. *Role conflict* arises when a person occupying more than one role finds incompatability between them. Role conflict represents a deviation from the norm but it does not have to be conflictual one. It may reinforce another role.

Goffman (1961) invented the concept of *role distance* to describe situations in which actors play a role while harbouring a motive that does not go with the role they are playing, that is, the person distances themselves from the role they are performing. Many black women, for example, use role distancing as a survival strategy when they pretend to accept their status as domestic servants, while knowing that they deserve more than this (see Collins, 1991). Role distance suggests that people will find ways of responding to situations as autonomous beings despite their subordinate status.

Feminists have argued that roles involve people in a set of interactions which are both determinate and indeterminate because people exert at least personal power in trying to shift the balance away from structural power and onto more personal forms. The capacity to exert personal leverage in social situations is a major ingredient in women's resistance to being defined as socially subordinate (Collins, 1991).

Authority

Authority has traditionally been considered a form of power, usually delegated power (Palmer, 1983). According to Weber (1968), authority involves power, consent, legitimacy or institutionalisation. There are, for him, three types of authority: legal-rational, traditional and charismatic. *Legal-rational authority* stems from organisations – something social workers would recognise. *Traditional authority*, which comes from cultural norms that people accept as given. *Charismatic authority* is derived from an individual's personal capacities to offer leadership. Barnes (1985) rejects this definition. For him, power is synonymous with discretion, that is, the individual's ability to make choices about whether or not to act. Authority lacks the dimension of discretion, so it is 'less than' power. Authority may have directive capabilities but these do not contain discretionary elements within them. Power uses discretion exercised through the agent's own judgement and decision-making capacities to direct routines. Barnes (1985) concludes that power-holders should never delegate their discretion because to do so leads to a loss of power. They should delegate only their authority. However, this situation becomes problematic for power-holders seeking stability and continuity. They must find ways of preventing authorities from becoming powers (Barnes, 1985) and devote energy to ensuring this does not happen.

Legitimacy

Weber (1968) defined *legitimacy* as 'a belief in the validity of an order'. It is a rational-legal form of authority characterising modern social organisations. In bureaucratic social work organisations, orders obeyed as legitimate, because they come from a particular office and follow appropriate procedures, typify this type of authority. Validity is defined by members of any given group. But legitimacy is also institutionalised power. Hence, legitimate procedures are deemed rational, fair and impartial. One problematic with the exercise of bureaucratic authority in Weberian terms is its failure to conceptualise actions which occur through non-action (Baert, 1989). In other words, legitimately *not taking* a decision is *making* a decision. Feminists have indicated the importance of non-action in both challenging the legitimacy of an order and endorsing it (Collins, 1991). For example, a black woman domestic worker complying with her employer's dictates, rejects the inferior place assigned to her, but only mentions this to confidantes. Her action of not openly rebelling gives her the space to be herself through non-action. That is, she does not directly challenge the employer's power to dictate the terms of her employment until she can do so safely (Collins, 1991). Acting through non-action becomes a coping strategy which relatively powerless individuals utilise in their interaction with relatively powerful others to survive (Dominelli, 1986a; Collins, 1991). An unintended consequence of such action, however, is that it perpetuates the system.

Responsibility

Responsibility means that individuals can be held morally account-able for their actions. Responsibilities of different kinds are associ-ated with different types of roles. They can be individual – as in a mother caring for her child, or collective – as in the pooling of risks through social security systems. Lately, the New Right has sought to reduce the significance of collective responsibilities and replace them with individualistic ones fulfilled through market provisions (Culpitt, 1992). Traditionally, social theorists assume that individ-uals have been rational in the way they exercise their responsibilities and conduct themselves. Feminist research into caring reveals a more complicated picture. Women often undertake caring roles which act against their personal interests. One person's rational choice is another's irrational burden. Yet, women have done this work willingly because life is more complex than theories based on binary opposition presuppose (see Ungerson, 1987; Finch and Groves, 1983; Graham, 1983).

Rights

In a welfare context, *rights* have come to mean entitlements. In liberal thought, rights previously referred to constitutional guaran-tees regarding individual action (Tong, 1989). Feminists have highlighted the gendered nature of welfare rights (see Pascall, 1986; Dominelli, 1991c; Dale and Foster, 1986). Rights in both their meanings are an important part of social work discourse. These are hotly contested and dependent on the value system and ideologies of those participating in the debate. However, rights cannot be realised without the necessary 'allocative' and 'authoritative' resources attending them.

Relationships

Relationships refer to the connections between individuals or the basis on which they interact with each other. Thus, relationships are sociopolitical entities providing a forum within which power relations are enacted. These may be intimate family relationships, or they may be impersonal contractual relationships negotiated individually or collectively between people, for example workers and their employers.

Relationships both form and occur within an organisational context. They may be inclusive or exclusive. In Marxist sociology, contractual relationships between employers and employees are exploitative (Marx, 1965) because they are embedded in exploitative relations of production which comprise the fundamental building blocks of society. They are also exclusionary, in so far as employees are excluded from participating in the key decision-making structures of the enterprise unless the employers permit it through agreements specifically authorising their involvement.

Feminists have added the notion of relatedness to intimate relationships (Chodorow, 1978). Relatedness, as the ability to associate with others, enhances the capacity for empathy – the ability to understand another person's position and experience, especially if it differs from one's own. It is inclusive without demanding a loss of self-identity or the absorption of one person's being by another. These attributes are essential to an ethic of caring (Collins, 1991) and of central importance in social work.

Institutions

Institutions represent ways of organising social relationships so that they are systematic and enduring. These can be regulatory and/or integrative. They represent a higher order of social practices than those depicted by roles, although institutions encompass these. Institutions may be based on social, economic, political, cultural, stratification or kinship considerations. Institutionalisation is the process whereby institutions achieve continuity or a sense of permanence. Functionalists see institutions as fulfilling the needs of individuals; phenomenologists view them as more responsive to human intervention. Institutions can be highly specialised and used to regulate conflict, thereby becoming vehicles which mediate the processes whereby individuals and groups are integrated into, and excluded from, the social fabric. Social work institutions are inclusive, insofar as they integrate individuals into the prevailing social order. They are exclusionary, insofar as they stigmatise people who deviate from normative standards or ration people's access to resources. Marxists argue that state institutions regulate class conflict in favour of capital. Thus, from the proletariat's point of view, they form exclusionary structures. This determinist view has been challenged by feminists and others. For example, Giddens (1987) suggests that although institutions ensure continuity in human relations over time and space, they enter constitutively into the actions of agents. At the same time, an agent's actions constitute and reconstitute the institutional conditions of others and vice-versa. Giddens's analysis is more akin to feminists' understandings of institutions as both structural and relational (Collins, 1991; Walby, 1990).

Organisations

Weber (1978) maintains that modern *organisations* are large bureaucratic centres of administrative power involved in social control. Organisations influence the behaviour of people and take a variety of forms. Their structures have usually been described as mechanistic – highly structured and bureaucratic; or organic – fluid and decentralised (Stalker, 1961). Giddens (1984, 1990) claims organisations are about the regularised control of social relations over time and space. In social work, this capacity slants the social work relationship towards control rather than care. The management of organisations and their personnel, that is, their regulation, has consumed much printers' ink recently as these are changed to adapt to international competitiveness, flexible allocation of resources, specialisation and managerial control (see Clark *et al.*, 1994).

Feminists have revealed the importance of social divisions, including gender, in the allocation of power and resources within organisations. Linked to their analysis is the significance of organisational cultures in excluding groups defined as outsiders. Organisational culture is created through shared values, beliefs and attitudes which shape customary or taken-for-granted behaviour. It is expressed through working relations which are accepted as legitimate. Sexual harassment provides one example of an organisational culture which excludes and controls women (Benn, 1983). Its legitimacy is currently being contested (Morrison, 1992).

Modern state social work occurs in large bureaucratic organisations. Since the late 1980s, British social services departments have been subjected to organisational change aimed at introducing quasi-markets and private business practices into a service-oriented enterprise (Challis and Davies, 1986; Price-Waterhouse, 1990; Orme and Glastonbury, 1993). This has led to the introduction of devolved budgets, decentralised decision-making, performance indicators and performance-related pay, as managers have sought to impose greater but more flexible control over professional employees. This has led to clashes between managerial cultures and professional ones.

Division of labour

The *division of labour* refers to the way work is organised. Marxists view the critical division as one between production in which wealth and exchange value are assembled, and reproduction in which use values are produced for consumption. In industrial societies, domestic work or unpaid labour done in the privacy of the home is carried out by women as an undervalued, largely invisible activity; waged work is paid work performed in the public domain, traditionally the prerogative of men. This particular form of the division of labour is a gendered or sexually segregated one indicative of modernity. In Western society, women across all classes have been increasingly drawn into waged work while doing both domestic and waged work; Bruegal, 1989; Walby, 1990). Feminists have argued that organising work in this way oppresses women and locks men into alienating jobs they dislike (Coyle, 1984, 1989; Collins, 1991). They have also argued that production and reproduction are parts of one process. In social work, the gendered division of labour is apparent – women at the caring edge; and men as managers (SSI, 1991b; Hallett, 1990). Black people seldom appear but, when they do, they are located in its lower echelons (Howe, 1986; NACRO, 1992). The division of labour in social work is both gendered and racially structured.

In summary, sociology provides a number of conceptual frameworks and tools for analysing and making sense of changes that take place in societies and organisations across space and time. Sociological concepts and insights about social relations and interaction are important to social work, regardless of whether it has set itself the task of controlling people who have been marginalised and excluded from the mainstream or that of facilitating their liberation. The following sections explore the relevance of sociological concepts to social work in greater depth and consider how they have been adapted to meet the needs of social work as an applied social science.

Social work as an object of sociological analysis

The suitability of social work as an object of sociological analysis has exercised the mind of many theoreticians (see Bosanquet, 1900; Heraud, 1979; Leonard, 1966; Younghusband, 1978; Sibeon, 1991). Those who believe that social work is an 'art' (see England, 1986) feel that its subject matter draws on complex, qualitative realities such as feelings, emotions, intuition and insight. These are transferred across settings when professional experts draw on 'practice wisdoms' (Phillips and Berman, 1995). Social work, therefore, cannot be reduced to scientific facts and is not easily amenable to scientifically orientated sociological enquiry, although it might be appropriate for some of its activities to be described in sociological terms (Elliott, 1990). Those expounding this view suspect that the uniqueness of social work and its methodologies can be obscured or damaged if it is subjected to the dry empirical paradigms of the natural sciences. These lines of thought have led social work academics endorsing social work as 'art' to devise booklists and exercises which draw on works of fiction, audio and visual art and poetry which can portray the human condition even more powerfully than texts bound by the rigours of scientific logic (see Morris, 1975).

Although held to be a social science, the scientific basis of social work is also disputed. Its link to sociology comes through this association. Those who believe that a 'sociology of social work' is possible, maintain social work is no less reducible to its component parts than any other complex human activity. These can be quantified and analysed objectively. Thus, social work, like psychology, is considered a 'science' and not an 'art' (Heraud, 1979; Sibeon, 1991). However, social work is persistently berated for failing to live up to the rigours of scientific paradigms through the sloppiness of practitioners and their trainers (see Sibeon, 1991).

Social work occurs within an institutional framework and engages in a series of interactions involving institutions, individuals and the state (Hanvey and Philpot, 1994). As such, its activities produce phenomenological material which can be subjected to methodological scrutiny and analysis. Because it relies on the exercise of judgement, intuition and understanding, and encourages 'clients' to be active in forming working relationships with practitioners, it requires many qualities normally associated with artists. Thus, I argue, that *social work is both an art and a science.* Its capacity to be both has been used by feminists to endorse holistic forms of practice which respond not only to the 'person-in-the-situation' but also to the person as a whole being with endless connections and inter-relationships with others (Simpkin, 1989). This analytical framework is potential dynamite in what has become a conservative state bureaucracy. Though never fully realised, its radical critique has initiated new forms of social work practice in opposition to psycho-dynamic approaches popular before the advent of radical social work (see Phillips and Berman, 1995).

Social workers are required to move through both fields if they are to work with the whole person in daily practice whether or not they explicitly subscribe to radical social work. The social worker–'client' relationship is strongly influenced by the social situation in which it is located. So, the organisational context within which professionals and 'clients' create a relationship is as important a feature of the work they do, as their own personalities, skills, knowledge and emotions (Compton and Galaway, 1975). Although a complex structuring of the social work relationship occurs within the care management framework, the resultant relationship is inordinately skewed by budgetary and managerial considerations. Consequently, it is distinctly different from that formed under previous organisational constraints.

In developing their relationship, both 'clients' and social workers are in the position of agents with the capacity to act constitutively, that is, to organise the interaction to their liking. Each affects the other's action(s) and the organisation in which the relationship develops. This does not mean that social workers as agents do not hold greater power than 'clients'. They do, by virtue of the greater 'allocative' and 'authoritative' resources attending their role as employees with particular responsibilities. But how this power is exercised at the level of the individual depends on the extent to which a social worker is prepared to use discretion as a vehicle for transcending organisational boundaries.

Sociological analyses can, therefore, unpack the impact of partic-ular organisational structures on social work relationships. Organisa-tional theory and conflict theory as extended and refined by feminist analyses is helpful in doing this. Using the concepts these make available, enables practitioners to make sense of the possibilities and constraints within which they work.

In a profession wanting an independent resource base, under-standing the limitations imposed on its professional boundaries by its social location is crucial to those who wish to explore its failure to achieve its full potential as an activity charged by society with securing the welfare of its citizens. Critical sociological theory has, for example, highlighted the contradictions between social work's control role and its caring one.

Social work as a state activity

The development of the welfare state since the Second World War in countries such as Britain, Canada and Sweden has meant that social work has been firmly located within the state apparatus (see Dominelli, 1991c; Armitage, 1975; Esping-Andersen, 1990). The roles of the voluntary and commercial sectors have been important, but not as *the* determiners of what transpires within the personal social services (Loney, 1987). However, this accommodation between social work and the state is breaking down under the impact of monetarist policies and the privatisation of the welfare state. In other nations, for example the United States, the state's role as the provider of services is less dominant than that of the commercial and voluntary sectors. However, *the state* plays a critical role in *funding* provisions, whether these be in the voluntary or commercial sectors in all of the countries mentioned (Dominelli, 1991c). Yet, in none of them is there a legally enshrined right of access to the personal social services based on need. Nor is there a legally enforceable commitment to providing social services to all those requiring them. Rather, public debate is shifting away from publicly funded institutional provisions (Levitas, 1986; Murray, 1990, 1994; Glazer, 1988; Esping-Andersen, 1990).

The British welfare state formed in the aftermath of war greatly expanded the personal social services (see Walton, 1975; Younghusband, 1978). However, these were neither accessed as a right nor comprehensively developed. The major thrust in their expansion occurred during the late 1960s and early 1970s when reorganisation of the local state and personal social services followed the publication of various reports, including the Maud Report on Local Government and the Seebohm Report on the Personal Social Services. The latter changed the face of social services in Britain dramatically until the 1990s.

Seebohm favoured the creation of generic rather than specialist provisions and their being housed under one department in an easily accessible locale in the community. Seebohm's vision drove the restructuring of social work, transforming activities located in small organisations, many under the remit of voluntary agencies, to the centre of large bureaucratic empires within the local state (Jaques, 1975). At the same time, social work moved away from being a profession managed by women to men deemed to have the organisational skills for handling the massive resources now under the auspices of organisationally complex departments (see Eley, 1989; Howe, 1986; Hallett, 1990; Coyle, 1984; Walton, 1975).

The location of social work as a small entity within a large social services department, has had profound implications for its organisation and structure (see Jaques, 1975, 1977). The magnitude of the problem was perceived to require the creation of a special unit to guide politicians and influence policy: the Social Sciences Research Unit at Brunel University (BSSRU). BSSRU produced a number of publications to facilitate the restructuring process. Under the leadership of Elliott Jaques (1977), these laid the plans for an administrative-bureaucratic form of social work. The resulting structures left social workers a minority in a vast social services bureaucracy while simultaneously strengthening their hand as an elite group of professionals. This was the arrangement and power base the Thatcher government set out to destroy with its privatisation programme and insistence on managerialist control (Clarke *et al.*, 1994).

A dependent profession

In Britain, the relationship between the state and social work is one of dependency. Social work as an activity has not possessed large-scale resources of its own to give either its practitioners or educators a powerful base independent of the state. Its origins as a woman-dominated industry located primarily within the voluntary sector have made it reliant on both the state and white upper-class men's patronage (Walton, 1975). The 'founding mothers' had to rely on their ability to extract resources from white upper- and middle-class men holding resources either individually or through the state to establish and maintain the profession. Social work remains a dependent profession. This dependency has subjected social work professionals, whether academics or practitioners, to a set of controls which have not arisen from either the professionals' concerns *qua* professionals qualified to carry out social work as a paid activity, or the demands of the 'client' groups which this particular enterprise is purported to serve.

Social work's remit for action, has been constantly mediated through its relationship with the state and white upper-class men as resource holders. Its fortunes have risen and fallen not so much on the basis of 'needs', as defined by either social workers or 'clients', but according to the resources the state has been prepared to release for such work (see Gough, 1979; Doyal and Gough, 1991). This has made social work vulnerable to political vicissitudes, a trend which has been exacerbated in recent times with the demise of the social democratic consensus over welfare provision and the ascendancy to political power of a New Right committed to privatising the welfare state, destroying the 'culture of welfare dependency' and getting claimants off the welfare rolls (Loney, 1986; Levitas, 1986; Culpitt, 1992; Clarke *et al.*, 1994). The acuteness of the dilemmas this poses are currently reflected in the underfunding of community care (George, 1995).

British social work's dependent status has intensified its social control function at the expense of service delivery to 'clients' (see Parry *et al.*, 1979; Langan and Lee, 1989; Oakley and Williams, 1994), for professional decisions are taken within an overall framework shaped by the political aims and objectives set by politicians. Recently, these have been led by the state's commitment to privatisation (Culpitt, 1992; Dominelli and Hoogvelt, 1994). Social work's dependency has intensified under this strategy and subjected social workers to tighter bureaucratic regimes and managerialist control at the expense of professional autonomy (Bailey and Lee, 1982; Clarke *et al.*, 1994).

Social work's location within the state apparatus makes it difficult for social workers to straddle the contradiction between care and control. Each part of this vast organisation is expected to comply with the overall policies and practices deemed appropriate by politicians, thereby leaving little room for professionals to assert their power as professionals, or for 'clients' to exercise their rights as citizens in shaping the political processes through which decisions about service provisions are formulated. The struggle to control the activities of an autonomous professional grouping such as social workers has been a constant feature of the personal social services post-Seebohm (Sibeon, 1991).

Social work struggles within state structures

The 'rediscovery of poverty' in the 1960s, the growth of critical sociological perspectives being applied directly to social work, including community work, and the rise of social movements, particularly the women's liberation movement, black civil rights movement and claimants' movements, started the questioning of the taken-for-granted assumptions about social work's mission and role in society. As a result of their agitation, the veneer of respectability and commitment to 'client self-determination' that lay as a core value of social work (see Butrym, 1976; Perlman, 1957; Hollis, 1964) was lifted to expose the hollow edifice on which this claim rested.

As the struggle over the purpose and meaning of social work raged among opposing sides, more sophisticated explanations of the dynamics inherent in the social work relationship emerged. This controversy exposed splits on the Left and defied traditional Left–Right fault lines. One side on the Left, led by Marxist-leaning intellectuals, took the view that social work was the handmaiden of the state, there to do its bidding on behalf of society unless professionals, in alliance with workers, struggled against it (see for example, Beaumont and Walker, 1981; Corrigan and Leonard, 1978).

Another 'Left' side, representing more liberationist, less structurally oriented intellectuals, attempted to establish less interventionist forms of theory and practice (see for example Mathiesen, 1974; Schur, 1973; Simpkin, 1979). They declared all forms of social work suspect for failing to improve the conditions of 'clients' (see Mathiesen, 1974). While accepting the contradictory nature of the state, their analyses have challenged the ways in which professionals wield power over marginalised groups to prevent their participating fully in the distribution of power and resources. Feminists and black activists sought less deterministic explanations and means for improving service delivery. Meanwhile, the traditional intellectual elite sought to re-establish more technicist forms of practice, more in keeping with the demands of employers and the state (see Pinker, 1979; Davies, 1981).

Profound questions about the political nature of social work, and its problematic relationship in supporting those who are oppressed escape those who oppress them, were being voiced, without a consensual resolution emerging. Marxist-oriented intellectuals working in radical initiatives like the Community Development

Projects (CDPs) raised concerns about the role social work played in controlling people (Bennington, 1976; CDP, 1977a, b). Using sociological perspectives associated with theories of political economy, they challenged psychodynamic perspectives for ignoring power relationships between professionals and 'clients' (see Loney, 1983; Bailey and Brake, 1975; Leonard, 1975a).

At the same time, the significance of power relations in welfare institutions was becoming a burning issue to people organising themselves in the new social movements. They, too, were adopting sociological constructs in making sense of the events unfolding before them, often in the same projects. For example, women and black people in the CDPs and American War on Poverty projects challenged the exclusivity of class analyses. A considerable amount of cross-fertilisation was also taking place between practitioners and intellectuals. Indeed, CDPs had been premised on the integration of theory and practice. Action research projects linked the activities of community workers in the field to those of researchers in universities (CDP, 1977a, b, 1978; Bennington, 1976; Dominelli, 1990).

Criticism of social work at this point drew heavily on Marxist social theory which had been articulated on the basis of class, to the exclusion of other social divisions. Feminists rejected Marxist critiques for subordinating women's interests to class and began to organise women in the community (Dominelli, 1990; Remfry, 1979). White Marxist and feminist analyses were questioned by black people who felt their experiences of class and/or gender had been fractured by 'race' and racism (Ohri *et al.*, 1982; Sivanandan, 1976; Carby, 1982; Bryant *et al.*, 1985). Black intellectuals set about developing different theoretical understandings to portray their realities and address the additional problematic of racism which their white allies were ignoring (Ahmed, 1978, 1982; Sivanandan, 1976, 1982; Gurnah, 1984, 1989; Ahmad, 1990, 1992).

These developments indicate that the whole terrain of social work is controversial. There are no easy delineations to be drawn among those believing they strive for the empowerment of 'clients'. Yet, their stance has placed them in oppositional mode *vis-à-vis* those controlling the state who demand that they remain within the boundaries expected of professionals. 'Their task was to provide people with information, not man (sic) the barricades', one Labour councillor told a troublesome Batley Community Development Project. It was closed down for supporting 'People Power' when workers joined tenants in direct action to protest against appalling housing conditions. This councillor was clear that professionals had a role, status, knowledge, personal contacts and other resources which had to be directed towards serving the needs of their employer, the state. From his point of view, the most 'professionals' were entitled to do on behalf of claimants was to provide them with 'information about their rights'. Supportive action in enforcing these rights was deemed 'unprofessional' (see Baldock, 1982).

In drawing this distinction between the role of a professional and a duty to 'clients', this councillor reflected a widely held view and one commensurate with his own social role as a power-holder seeking to shape public opinion in particular ways. That social work professionals involved in community action were seeking to redefine this role, is missing from this perspective. There is nothing given about this definition of professionalism. Nonetheless, the councillor's approach to the situation is symptomatic of the dichotomous way in which he saw the world. Workers were either professional or unprofessional. The two were in binary opposition.

Social workers supporting 'clients' through direct action are likely to find that they are castigated by power-holders on the Left for making demands of social services and privileging 'clients' who have won their attention, and by those on the Right for not sticking to their remit as 'neutral' professionals detached from political struggles. In short, both groups of power-holders demand organisational loyalty to the detriment of 'clients'' interests and professional autonomy.

Ties between sociological thought and the activities of social workers can be direct. Many young social sciences graduates in the 1960s and 70s left the academy full of their analyses of society to work with people and 'help them gain control of their lives'. The reality they uncovered was rather different. The CDP workers sent into communities to find pathology at both individual and community levels (Loney, 1983; Bennington, 1976; CDP, 1977a,b; Bridges, 1975) uncovered shocking truths among the grassroots. Their practice experience and the data they collected provided the materials with which they re-evaluated their position and began to develop new theoretical positions which moved away from personal pathologies on to structural inadequacies.

Marxism, feminism and black activism which dealt with the realities they found on the ground and keyed into the social movements then active – the labour movement, women's movement and black activist movement, provided the most appealing paradigms (see Remfry, 1979; Loney, 1983; Dominelli, 1982, 1990). Working with research colleagues located in nearby universities, community workers discovered that oppression was being systematically reproduced within such communities by multinational companies running down local economies (see CDP, 1977a, b; Bennington, 1976). Their findings opened up debates about the relationship between racism, imperialism and developments in declining industrial centres in Britain. These revealed the extremely conservative role of the state and of social work and community work as 'soft options' in controlling local populations (see Bridges, 1975; CDP, 1977a).

Initially struggling to find a ready-made analysis which made sense of this world, critical sociological texts by Karl Marx, Herbert Marcuse and R D Laing were scoured for prophetic insights to assist the development of analytical concepts and practice. The use of such literature was limited since theory cannot be applied in a mechanistic way in the field. Practitioners and researchers ploughed their energies into developing their own theoretical formulations and practice innovations. The task was eased by organising collective learning situations – study groups, seminars, conferences, and easily accessible publications in which to share and develop ideas. Refinements were made to theories and practice through what became identified as action research, to differentiate it from more positivistic approaches which neglected to do something about the realities they unmasked. In practice, critical sociology made social change part of its ethical value base (see Habermas, 1963, 1987). For women community workers like myself, this meant giving increasing emphasis to eradicating forms of oppression based on gender and 'race'.

This commitment to the oppressed, however vague and poorly thought out, put community activists on a collision course with their employers – the local state. As part of their reaction, local authorities sought to exert greater control over their workforce by introducing tight job descriptions which excluded professional employees from engaging in direct action on behalf of user groups (see CDP, 1977a; Bennington, 1976). They also closed down those projects which proved to be particularly problematic (Loney, 1983).

Although those elements of community development work emphasising grassroots organising were axed by local management committees (though not without a struggle), less controversial advice-giving work was allowed to continue, as indeed happened in Batley. On a national level, the rules for funding community action were changed to favour less radical forms of community work (CDP, 1977a; Armstrong, 1977; Dominelli, 1990, 1982). Consequently, most radical projects that applied for inner city funds found their applications refused (Armstrong, 1977). When the Thatcher government came into power, Lord Belstead announced that funding application's from 'political' projects would be rejected. Matters deteriorated further as the government's confidence in tackling such issues augmented and state funding for community work as community action virtually dried up (Dominelli, 1990; Loney, 1983). As these projects disappeared, so did the opportunities for critical thinkers to engage in paid practice as radical community workers or social workers. Some activists continued to undertake such work as part of their voluntary, unpaid work, while on the dole.

Nonetheless, over time, the spaces for undertaking such activities became smaller. Those who found employment in other parts of the welfare state, particularly in the health and educational sectors, discovered that legalistic measures for curtailing their autonomy – restrictions on their power to exercise professional discretion – became a major feature in their working lives (Baldock, 1982). Even the opportunity to put information into the public arena came under attack. The expectation that only non-political welfare rights advice be given was strictly enforced by the state as employer.

Consequently, the net around the disclosure of information deemed to be sensitive to those in power and overt critiques of suspected malpractices inside the interstices of the state has been tightened through so-called 'gagging' clauses. These aim to silence dissent and ensure that the initiative for what is or is not done remains in the hands of the state and the bureaucrats it can trust. By requiring that critiques of services proceed through the line management route, control of information flows is more likely to reflect the interests of the organisation or the employer than of 'clients'. It is also less likely to focus on structural inequalities and problems than on the individual, who will be defined as problematic, dysfunctional or incompetent for having exposed malpractice.

'Gagging' policies also threaten the posts of professionals whose remit society formally claims is to support its most vulnerable members. Without job security, or an organisational culture which facilitates the critical appraisal of policy and practice, poor practices are unlikely to be publicly exposed. For at the end of the day, social work professionals depend on being able to sell their labour power as the means of ensuring their livelihood. The loss of professional discretion, a source of professional power (see Barnes, 1985), also represents a closure for marginalised groups who expect professional expertise to be placed at their disposal (see Morris, 1991). People may also be caught in the 'gagging' net unintentionally. A good example of this recently is the lecturer in a college of further education who found that an anonymised, off-the-cuff comment on television about declining standards in the sector (not in his particular institution) resulted in his being charged with gross misconduct, which carries with it the threat of dismissal. Yet, being critical of the state, even if it pays an individual's salary must be a legitimate activity in a pluralistic democratic society.

Social workers' ethical code, value base, ideological commitment and training as professionals emphasise their role as helpers (see Lishman, 1991; Payne, 1991). Reality dents their expectations and leads them to disillusionment and demoralisation. For they have little room for manoeuvre in providing the services they professionally consider appropriate after consulting 'clients' (Clarke *et al.*, 1994).

Sociological analysis of organisations and power, for example Michels' (1962) and Weber's (1968, 1978), provide social workers with analytical tools for understanding these developments. Michels' (1962) work demonstrates how organisations exercise power in their interests. Weber's (1968, 1978) writings reveal how bureaucracies are in the business of self-preservation and aggrandisement. Social workers, enmeshed in conflictual relationships with their publicly funded employers, should not be surprised to find that their attempts to expose the inner workings of state bureaucracies are blocked by power-holders protecting their interests.

Social workers have to find ways of working with the minutiae of practice within a broader social framework as part of their distinctive remit. This means that social workers do not have the luxury of treating human suffering as an academic interest which does not require a response. Working within organisational constraints compromises social workers' scope for action and may jeopardise the quality of services to 'clients'. This is not arguing for social workers to be unaware of and not address organisational constraints. But *organisational constraints are only one among a number of factors that*

social workers have to balance in carrying out their work. Endorsing
social justice, facilitating marginalised 'clients'' ability to empower
themselves requires that, at minimum, equal weighting be given to
non-organisational issues. Otherwise, social workers are into a con
trip which frustrates 'clients' and may cause their own burn-out.
Social workers who choose to privilege their 'clients'' needs over
those of their organisations have to take into account the scrutiny of
their actions or their being opposed by others. Thus, they have to
consider contingent reality. No one agent or actor is in a position to
impose his or her will upon another (Giddens, 1987). Appearances,
or role-distancing by another name, suggest the contrary is the case.
This is demonstrated by the actions of the black domestic servant
described earlier (Collins, 1991) or 'clients' who 'play the game' to
get what they want.

Avoiding the constraints the state imposes on its workforce has
been a major incentive for social workers choosing to work in the
voluntary sector or as freelance practitioners. However, much of the
'space' these generate is illusory. The immediate, day-to-day
conditions of work may be under the control of the professional to a
greater extent than among their peers in a local authority office, but
the funds which the state provides determine the areas in which such
work can be undertaken. Under care management, the contracts
specifying how the job is to be done can severely limit a professional's
capacity to exercise discretionary powers (Challis and Davies, 1986;
Dominelli and Hoogvelt, 1994; Greer, 1994).

A 'scientific' social science that is appropriate for social workers
must deal with both organisational constraints and the aspirations
of oppressed peoples in ways that examine the multiplicity of roles
which people hold and the dialectical nature of the relationships
they form. In other words, an oppressed person is not simply an
oppressed person. They may be resisting oppression through a
variety of means. These may be active or inactive. In addition, while
being oppressed on one dimension, they may be oppressing others
on another. A white working-class man may be oppressive in his
relationships with women while being simultaneously oppressed on
the basis of class. In social interactions between a white working-
class man and a black middle-class woman, the man may be
oppressing the woman on both gender and 'race' dimensions while
being oppressed himself by the woman through class differentials.
This could happen if a wealthy black middle-class woman employs

a white working-class man as a gardener on low rates of pay. However, the nature of the oppression taking place in a particular encounter would depend on how the two people involved negotiate the 'allocative' and 'authoritative' resources they hold between them. Their personal bases of power would draw on those wider relationships endorsed by society and their own value systems (Mills, 1957). Both personal attributes and structural characteristics have to be addressed by a system of logic which considers reality in terms of its multiplicity (Collins, 1991).

Following through this analysis necessitates the reformulation of the 'scientific' base of applied social science to encompass both concerns. Critical sociologists have worked on it and different schools have found various solutions to the difficulties such a commitment entails. Anti-racist feminists, black and white, have responded by rejecting dichotomous thinking and adopting the principles listed below:

● examining the whole person
● recognising interdependency between people
● seeking the interconnections between different parts of social reality (Collins, 1991).

These principles undermine and replace those characterising the dichotomous thinking which underpin positivistic approaches to science and sociology. Holistic approaches enable individuals to maintain the connections between their personal and public lives. Working with the whole person also makes it easier for social workers to make sense of 'clients'' lives as *they* define them instead of imposing arbitrary professional definitions. It also facilitates their ability to work with 'clients' in non-oppressive ways.

The variety of possible approaches in a given practice context may mean that work promoting a 'client's' ability to make decisions is poorly theorised and explained by practitioners (see Davies, 1981). Their interventions are popularly classified as 'do-gooding' or the outpourings of a 'bleeding heart'. Social workers have been slow to question such caricatures although they reflect badly and inadequately upon their work. Instead of justifying the scientific and humanistic bases of their interventions, social workers often present these as intuitive materials which they find difficult to either articulate or have validated by their employers.

Social workers' efforts in squaring 'client' needs with the limited resources which society makes available is misconstrued as the worker's ineffectual response to a complex reality or the witless expression of the worker's ideological leanings (see Harbart, 1985a, b). Their attempt to respond to the needs of oppressed groups is ruled out of court in the name of a neutral (natural) science-based professionalism founded on a technicist appreciation of practice. To gain a deeper understanding of the dynamics being elaborated, a more thorough examination of what a social worker *actually does* and *an extension of the scientific paradigm in new directions* is required. From a critical sociological perspective this includes redefining 'scientific paradigms' to encompass the complexity of people's realities as they live them rather than fitting people into pre-determined categories. It also requires a rethinking of profession-alism to be more in keeping with 'client' aspirations and the work these require of social workers.

Giddens's (1984) 'structuration theory' provides useful insights in developing a sociology of the helping professions. Structuration theory posits people as agents who write their own history in interac-tion with others. It has much in common with anti-racist feminist theory. People are knowing subjects with a capacity for acting in and reacting to the situations in which they are located. Their ability to mobilise 'allocative' and 'authoritative' resources in structuring their reality allows social work 'clients' to be neither 'passive victims' nor 'change agents' with a predetermined status and patterns of behaviour. Envisaging 'clients' in this light, enables social workers to draw on the knowledge and skills of social work as both science and art. And, working along these lines leads to social services which respond to human need (see Doyal and Gough, 1991).

Sociological social work: a model for empowering practice

Sociological social work, as I have defined it, is a form of social work which is rooted in exploring how structural inequalities impact on individuals' lives and seeks to limit the damage these cause in the lives of individuals or 'client' groups. It also incorporates a dialec-tical view of human behaviour which recognises that structures are created by and through the actions of people. Thus, structures both influence individual activity and are influenced by it. There is a constant dynamic between people and structures which enables both people and structures to be socially (re)created by human action over time. This fluidity of movement makes social action both the same and constantly different. Social work based on this insight into social action seeks to understand the relationship between the individual and society, and holds both responsible for the situation in which individuals live. Sociological social work also acknowledges the importance of various forms of power in social work relationships and the political nature of social work at both micro and macrolevels. By engaging with the multiplicity of life and acknowledging the individual's power to influence their own situation, sociological social work provides practitioners with a model for empowering practice.

Sociological social work has (re)emerged in British social work, through radical social work initially and, subsequently, social work developed by feminists and black activists. It draws on knowledge provided by critical sociology. Key theorists whose concepts may promote its further development include:

- Foucault's (1980) concept of power
- Goffman's (1961) analysis of closed institutions
- Gilligan's (1982) insights into gendered psychosocial development
- Marx's (1965) understandings of class exploitation
- Hall's (1989) analysis of black cultural identities
- hooks's (1984, 1989, 1982) analyses of gendered and racialised politics
- Morris's (1991) analysis of gender and disability
- Phillipson's (1982) work on old age
- Weeks's (1981) insights into homophobia
- Davis's (1982, 1989) analyses of 'race', gender and class exploitation
- Sklair's (1991) work on the global economy.

This list indicates that social work theoreticians need to draw on a systematised eclecticism to develop a theoretical base addressing the complexities of practice. Moreover, the connection between theory and practice is one in which one grows out of the other, influences the other, and is in turn influenced by this new combination. In this way, knowledge is constantly being amended and growing.

A major difficulty social workers encounter with sociological theories is that those developed by academics without a practice base fail to address the realities of practice. To carry credence with practitioners, both the theory and practice component in social work have to be addressed. That is, the practice relevance of theories must be made explicit. This connection has been poorly made to date.

The practice relevance of many theories has had to be developed by practitioners through the details of their daily practice, for example Marxist social work in Britain (Sibeon, 1991; Harbart, 1985a, b). However, there is no expectation that social workers undertake developmental work on theories as part of their job. Such work has proceeded in an ad hoc unsystematic way which minimises both the significance and use of theory (see Curnock and Hardiker, 1979; Davies, 1981; Davies and Wright, 1989). Sociological social work is one way of bridging the practice–theory gap.

Finally, sociological social work has an explicit value base which is concerned with issues of social justice and a commitment to 'clients' acquiring the resources, skills and knowledge needed to control and make decisions about their lives. This approach becomes an oppositional one in a society that is not devoted to unmasking relations of domination and subordination. Yet, social work must have the freedom to act in this capacity if the lives of marginalised 'client' groups are to be socially validated rather than stigmatised and their demands heard by powerful groups who benefit from their exclusion from social power and resources. That the relationship between social workers seeking social justice and the state does not have to be an antagonistic one is evidenced by the Greater London Council's successful implementation of anti-sexist and anti-racist strategies prior to its abolition (Livingstone, 1987). This example also demonstrates that gains cannot be guaranteed by any particular segment of the state. They will last only as long as powerful actors can sustain enduring alliances which give stability to their position (see Whitlock, 1987; Dominelli and McLeod, 1989; Giddens, 1987). In other words, they are retained as long as social reformers succeed in organising 'allocative' and 'authoritiative' resources to work on their behalf.

Conclusions

The role and nature of social work is hotly disputed by employers, practitioners, academics, politicians and users. The 'politics of practice' are often submerged in an alleged neutral professionalism which disguises social workers' subservience to their paymasters. The rejection of critical theory has played an important part in maintaining this state of affairs. However, this need not be the case. Sociological social work draws on critical sociological theories and concepts to expose injustice and inequality and provide an analysis which can guide action aimed at rectifying them. Making sociological social work a routine part of daily practice has to be worked for at both macro and microlevels. The task is not as daunting as it sounds because, as we will discover shortly, pre-figurative guidelines for assisting the process already exist.

3

A Sociology of Social Work and Feminist Sociological Social Work

Social work is a male-dominated profession with women workers managing front-line encounters with 'clients', the majority of whom are women. Any sociology of social work must engage with the gendered realities of social work if it is to make sense of them. Gendered relations permeate its working relations, organisational structures, decision-making procedures, service provision and service delivery. Yet, women's needs, whether workers or 'clients', are poorly served (Dominelli, 1984; Marchant and Wearing, 1986). Paradoxically, male dominated and patriarchally structured as it is, social work fails to respond adequately to *men's* needs if they are seeking liberation from the controlling confines of traditional social work responses to them. It is as if 'women's work' is out of bounds to men 'clients' or suitable only for 'dealing with' women 'clients' who must be made to conform to stereotypical female behaviour.

Feminist sociology is well-suited to rise to the challenge thrown up by the imperative to seek a 'new' sociology of social work. This is because feminism has challenged mainstream sociology's epistemological and ontological base (see Smith, 1979; Eichler, 1980, 1988; Adamson *et al.*, 1988; Stanley and Wise, 1983; Gamarnikov *et al.*, 1983) and sought to include women who had been excluded from its explicit concerns. Other reasons are integral to feminist thought itself. These include:

- relating to the whole person
- the integration of theory and practice
- linking the personal and social dimensions of life
- understanding the processes of achieving change as part of its epistemological base

- its capacity for self-evaluation and self-critique
- its commitment to non-exploitative, egalitarian social relations
- its relevance to all people, regardless of gender.

I use the term 'feminist sociology' to encompass the sociological insights into women's condition provided by both black and white feminists. Hence, an anti-racist feminist sociological social work constitutes the essence of this chapter. Combining the understandings acquired from both black and white feminist thought requires a theoretically sophisticated model of social work which is easy to use in practice. It draws on the foundations of what I termed sociological social work. The development of this model, its extension and reproduction occurs as part of daily practice in the field and academy. Feminists, individually and collectively, will have to demonstrate its relevance to the lives of both social workers and 'clients' as each sees them, regardless of their status in the social hierarchy or the forms of oppressions which impact upon them.

Implementing the model in practice will not be easy, given the hostile environments in which feminists, black and white, currently work. However, feminists' constant efforts to transcend opposition will maintain the continuity of this effort over time and preclude closure of the debate on this subject. The stability necessary for these activities to unfold comes by practising in ways which are consistent with feminist principles. Existing feminist interventions in social work and health care settings give substance to the model. These prefigure alternative ways of working alongside 'clients', delineate approaches in which practice priorities are shaped and defined by those involved in the interaction, and engage in a process whereby theory is informed by practice and vice-a-versa. This approach to practice challenges the view of the professional as controlling expert. It does *not* mean that the professional is not an expert in a knowledgeable sense. They must have cognitive and technical knowledge and skills. This includes knowing what the job is, understanding what works, why and how, having a vision of what might be, and planning how it might be realised. In short, what is required is a critical competent practitioner who challenges orthodoxies and works in egalitarian directions (Dominelli *et al.*, 1995). This chapter considers the conceptual framework which helps to contextualise and develop a professional fitting this description.

Feminist conceptual frameworks and analyses of social work

Feminists' challenges to sociology have brought new insights which are crucial in creating feminist sociological social work. I will explore some of its most crucial concepts before examining case study materials which indicate how feminist social work uses sociology to enhance practice with 'clients'.

Language

Feminists have identified the importance of understanding the power relations which are inherent within words and have subjected language to systematic analyses (see Spender, 1980; Tannen, 1992; Gilligan, 1982). These analyses reveal the taken-for-granted assumptions embedded in visual, written, verbal and non-verbal forms of communication and reflect the way the world is organised around the social ranking of various groups. Particularly important in this regard is understanding those who are included and excluded by any given term (Spender, 1980).

For example, feminists have highlighted how policy-makers say 'the family' when referring to women doing caring activities and men being heads of households. Having made the point, feminists favour gender neutral language and more accurate descriptions of specific situations in dealing with these hidden power dynamics. Thus, the term 'lone mother' is preferred to 'single parent' if describing a woman supporting children on her own (see Abramovitz, 1991) because both the gender and role are made explicit. Similarly, the gendered nature of poverty is obscured by euphemistic terminology like 'the elderly'. Thus, poor elders and white older women is preferable to 'the poor elderly black' (Hughes and Mtezuka, 1989; Scott, 1984; Sidel, 1986). Moreover, the works of Tannen (1992) and Gilligan (1982) have revealed how communication processes become sites which reproduce relations of domination. These show that women's patterns of communication emphasise relationship building and connection while men's articulate separation and control.

Citizenship

Feminist critiques of citizenship as a status signifying access to the public domain have highlighted the extent to which women have been excluded from many entitlements (Eisenstein, 1994). The British welfare state was predicated on the notion of universal citizenship (Marshall, 1950). However, women's access to its provisions has been denied unless mediated through their position of assumed dependency on male partners: fathers in their youth; husbands in adulthood (see Pascall, 1986; Dale and Foster, 1986). Structuring welfare benefits around women's dependency has enforced white women's reliance on their menfolk for economic support. The situation has been rather different for black women. Black men are discriminated against as workers. Neither black men nor black women can rely on accessing welfare arrangements open to white people (Gordon and Newnham, 1985). Moreover, because black women are primary earners in many black families, they experience the barriers imposed by both sexism and racism. Their exclusion from welfare provisions has compelled them to develop alternatives which draw on the support networks they have created.

The welfare state has been a major employer of women, who now form the bulk of the workforce in the public sector (Walby, 1990; Coyle, 1984). Both black and white women work in the welfare state. However, the labour hierarchy is gendered and racially strati-fied, with black women on the bottom rungs (Bruegal, 1989). Women have sought these openings as an avenue for achieving financial independence – free from direct control by individual men with whom they are intimately connected. The welfare state has undermined patriarchal relations by granting women their own (limited) monetary resources and contact with other women while simultaneously reinforcing them by ghettoising 'women's work', tying their access to benefits to men acting in the role of 'protectors'. These 'freedoms' have made this gendered labour hierarchy of low-paid, part-time and insecure jobs a lesser issue than demanding employment options consistent with their caring responsibilities (Coyle, 1984, 1989). Walby (1990) has designated these develop-ments a shift in patricarchal relations. Private patriarchy dependent on individual men within the family has given way to public patriarchy under the aegis of the state.

Moreover, citizenship has been associated with the public arena, where men, particularly white men, are the dominant players. Black women, black men and white women have had limited access to the opportunities holding this status provides. Decisions about who has access to citizenship rights had been taken largely by wealthy white men who had excluded all others, until those so denied agitated for inclusion. Notwithstanding the eventual granting of the franchise to adult men and women nationals, citizenship rights remain circum-scribed. Young people are excluded by being made financially dependent on their parents for lengthy periods. For example, 16-to 18-year-olds can no longer claim state benefits (Becker, 1991). Others are also left out. Black men and women currently living and working in Britain, who do 'not meet the "residence test" by having a close connection' with this country, defined by government legisla-tion as having a parent or grandparent born here, are excluded from citizenship rights by their immigration status (Gordon, 1992). Even those holding citizenship status may be excluded from enjoying some of its benefits by conditions of eligibility which pre-empt the realisation of their formal rights. For example, a black British woman caring for a dependent child overseas is denied child benefit because the law says the child must *reside* in Britain rather than be financed by a parent who works and is domiciled here (see Gordon and Newnham, 1985). Young women with children are also threatened with the withdrawal of their eligibility to state support as govern-ment ministers hold them responsible for exacerbating housing shortages and driving fathers away from their families. Citizenship is, as feminists have pointed out, conditional. Its conditionality may at times extend to disenfranchising citizens themselves.

Power

Feminists have challenged monodimensional understandings of power by revealing its multidimensional forms and questioning its conceptualisation as a finite entity. Masculinist definitions of power as hierarchically exclusive *power over others* (Brittan, 1989) have been replaced with the idea that power, infinitely (re)created through social interaction, can be shared among all those involved in social exchanges (Tong, 1989; Collins, 1991). White men's power to define both white women and black people as 'other' has enabled them to collar positions which allow them to organise social relations on their terms. Categorising people as 'other' typifies their exclusion from social processes and is deeply implicated in patriarchal hierarchies (De Beauvoir, 1974). Women and black people have resisted this characterisation of social reality and proposed more creative and less intimidating ways for handling power. In social work, their resistance has led to the development of new forms of practice based on feminist and black perspectives.

Social stratification

A person's position in the social strata is an important means of identity and provides the individual with roles and status. Within the social stratification of waged employment, social work is part of the secondary labour market in which women are principally located in its low-status echelons. Sociologists have traditionally assigned women's places in the social stratification system through the occupation of their husband if married or their father's if not rather than their own. Feminists have challenged this assignation and insisted that research examine women's own specific situations to develop more relevant classifications. The importance of the issue became evident when studies highlighted that women had been denied equal access to resources within the family (see Pahl, 1985), thereby undermining the assumption that women are adequately provided for in the privacy of their homes. Moreover, Pahl revealed that when resources within the family are short, women usually go without so that children and men can get the lion's share of whatever is going. Within black families, the woman as the main provider shares whatever she has with her husband and children by going without so that the others can have their entitlements (hooks, 1982, 1989; Stacks, 1975). The scarcity of resources also deters women from leaving violent or abusive relationships (Dobash and Dobash, 1980, 1991).

The problem of how to deal with women as main breadwinners and holders of social position and status in their own right has yet to be resolved by mainstream sociology. However, this reflects a reality which black and white working-class women have known for some time (Collins, 1991). Today, the dual income family has become the norm. Indeed, a husband landing a well-paid job which enables the whole family to survive and the wife to quit work is so rare its achievement becomes a tremondous source of pride for working-class men and women, for it symbolises upward mobility – a highly desirable good. High-status posts for women at the same level as men in the social hierarchy are, however, viewed in a poorer light (Eley, 1989). Even in the educational sphere with its long-standing equal opportunities policy, women holding the same rank as men and having similar or higher qualifications, earn less than men similarly ranked. In social work, white women managers are not considered as powerful as white men managers (Eley, 1989; Coyle, 1984; Hayles, 1989; Burgess, 1994). Black women managers have the additional obstacle of racism to contend with, particularly if they question management functions enforcing oppression (Durrant, 1989; Ahmad, 1992; Burgess, 1994).

Social divisions

Social divisions reflect the fractured nature of current reality and represent the numerous dimensions upon which differences exist between us. Class was initially given pride of place by Marxist theorists. However, feminists were among those who questioned the all encompassing nature of class as a category (Coulson *et al.*, 1975; Smith, 1979; Dalla Costa and James, 1972; Benston, 1969). Arguing that women's experience of class was mediated through their gender, feminists were able to challenge the terms of its universal applicability. Like other social divisions, class could be fractured by an individual's personal attributes including gender, age, 'race', sexual orientation, and disability (Davis, 1982). Deconstructing class highlights how relations of domination and subordination are reproduced through it and exposes society's failure to value the unpaid work women do in the home, an outcome consistent with women's place as second-class citizens.

The early gurus of white feminist thought advocated an automatic sisterhood by presupposing that all women experienced a similar form of gender oppression (see Morgan, 1970). Black feminists quickly rejected this position for failing to describe the realities they confronted daily. By asserting their own perspectives and definitions, black women have unleashed new developments in feminist theory (hooks, 1984; Lorde, 1984; Collins, 1991). These emphasise valuing 'difference' by rejecting the view of 'difference' as a 'deficit' depicting inferiority and accepting the urgency of eradicating all forms of oppression as part of the liberation process. The common goal of ending oppressive relations can become a unifying force for bringing together the diverse fragments women represent.

Status

Feminists have exposed status as a gendered phenomenon with differences in the way women and men experience it (see Tong, 1989). Status is fractured by social divisions, including class and 'race', so that the rights and obligations of citizenship do not fall equally upon those holding a lower status. The relations of domination (re)produced through status become another source of exclusion. Feminists have devoted time to developing alternative organisational forms which reject hierarchical relations. For example, the development of collectives – entrepreneurial and voluntary – reflect aspirations that hierarchies be flattened and decision-making shared among members to reduce status differentials (Dominelli and McLeod, 1989). While the ambition to enact egalitarian relationships has been imperfectly realised in practice (Barker, 1986), the attempts to effect them have been genuine. These efforts have provided prefigurative forms of organising which enable women to exercise the right to determine what occurs within organisations in the here and now (Dominelli, 1992a). Thus, women enact roles as agents by developing resources which meet their needs as they define them. For example, women developed 'Well Women Clinics' with flattened labour hierarchies to enable professionals and unpaid volunteers to work along more egalitarian lines with health service users (Foster, 1989).

Role

Feminists have shown that traditional social roles, arranged as binary opposites, give one set of role-holders a dominant position over others. The dominant member in a role dyad is more valued than the subordinate one. For example, the manager's role supersedes that of the front-line worker. Most roles holding superior status have been defined so as to favour white men. Resisting relations of domination and subordination in any given organisation requires careful, systematic analyses which demystify the underlying power dynamics and focus on the gendered and racialised nature of such stratification. Feminists have (re)defined roles as fluid entities which people (re)create through social interaction rather than being things-in-themselves (Abbott and Wallace, 1990). Thus, a woman in a secondary role in the labour hierarchy as a secretary accepts her boss's authority over her in defining the parameters of the job, but she draws the line at sexual harassment.

Division of labour

Feminist scholars have worked hard to unpack the implications of a gender segregated division of labour in the waged workplace and the domestic hearth (Coyle, 1984; Walby, 1990). Consequently, the public arena of waged work has been exposed as segregated along gender and 'race' lines. The secondary labour market, as the site of low pay and poor working conditions, has been accessed predominantly by white women and black people. In social work, childcare work has the highest status while residential care the lowest. Black men and women are more likely to be concentrated in the latter sector. The worth of work in the secondary sector to society, like that of the domestic economy, is low. Indeed, domestic labour is not considered work at all, and does not entitle women to welfare rights on the basis of having done it, usually for years (Pascall, 1986). The tasks women perform at home remain invisible except when they have not been done.

This gendered division of labour accounts for the low standing of residential work and its replication of divisions of labour found in the home, for example 'house-mothers' and 'house-fathers'. Fortunately these terms are being replaced. Nonetheless, white men exercise their option for social mobility by leaving the residential sector for childcare as quickly as possible; black people are stuck there (Howe, 1986). In organising the division of labour in gendered terms, feminists argue, society maintains the public and the private as two separate entities in which individuals lead fragmented and intensely private personal lives (Gamarnikov *et al.*, 1983). This division also endorses the subordination of women and children who inhabit the private, less important social sphere (Zaretsky, 1976). But the incorporation of skills developed in the private arena into the public one has changed the nature of patriarchy by shifting it away from private family life and onto the welfare state (Walby, 1990). New Right ideologues claim this represents the 'cuckolding' of the patriarchal master in the home by the 'compassionate state' (Gilder, 1981). This worries them as it represents the loss of male power. This analysis and its accompanying concerns fuel their determination to destroy both the welfare state and feminism (Murray, 1984, 1990, 1994; Glazer, 1988).

Working relations

What happens in the workplace is an important focus for feminist analyses. Feminist scholars have identified how working relations stratified according to gender, 'race' and class, shape workplace experiences for black and white women and black men. Gendered and racially stratified working relations mean men and women occupy unequal positions in the workplace. Women, particularly black women, hold the least desirable jobs, have little formal power and seldom rise to the top ranks (Bruegal, 1989). In social work, black women have yet to be appointed to the ranks of either director of social services or chief probation officer. Only 12 per cent of these positions have gone to white women, although they form the bulk of the workforce (SSI, 1991b; NACRO, 1992). A handful of black men have made it to the director's chair for short periods, but none has been promoted to chief probation officer (Alfred, 1992).

The segregated division of labour in social work has direct implications for the ways in which working relations are structured, conducted and elaborated. The taken-for-granted assumptions, about what should be done and who should do it, reveal that black women, black men and white women are considered second-class workers. White women managers, for example, are expected to serve the 'tea' in mixed meetings. *All* eyes turn to her when it arrives. Even the woman bringing the tray may set it next to her without thinking. Such interactions indicate the pervasiveness of sexism and how well it has been internalised by both men and women. In the case of a black woman manager, the chances are that, the moment she walks into a building where she is unknown, she will be taken to be a 'client', or even the cleaner. Her experience of gender will be refracted through a deeply ingrained racism which shapes her experiences and makes them substantially different from those of the white woman manager formally holding a position of equal status. The 'commonsense givens' of working relations in social work have to be probed to clarify their meanings rather than being automatically acted upon.

The range of issues feminists have included in examining working relations has been wide, covering initiatives from unequal pay to sexual harassment. In this, feminists have both analysed the situation, (re)defined the problem to be addressed and taken action to improve matters. Action then provides the framework for further reflection and action. In the case of sexuality, for example, feminists have shown that sexual harassment features regularly in women's working lives. Eliminating it is crucial to establishing safe and congenial working relations between men and women (see Benn and Sedgley, 1984; Morrison, 1992).

Sexual harassment is differently structured for black and white women. Sexual harassment of white women depicts the abuse of gendered power which assumes women are objects of men's desire. Black women's experience of it includes racist stereotypes of the readily available sexually active black woman. If the alleged harasser is a black man, racist stereotypes of the oversexed and violent black man come into play (see Moynihan, 1965). Racialised stereotypes increase the vulnerability of black women and black men in the workplace (Collins, 1991). These are exacerbated if the 'victim' is a white woman (Collins, 1991). The readiness with which, even in 1994, white Americans believed the white woman who alleged a black man had hijacked her car and two toddlers when she had drowned them in a lake herself is an indication of the strength and persistence of these stereotypes. Racialised stereotypes also ensure that allegations of sexual harassment are more likely to be believed without proof if a black man is the accused because white people use these to shape contingent reality. Although drawing on different notions of sexuality – aggressiveness in Afro-Caribbean women and passivity in Asian women – racialised stereotypes about black women's sexuality enable white people to disbelieve or trivialise the sexual harassment if the victim/survivor is a black woman. The United States Senate hearings into the Hill–Clarence case demonstrated the 'race-ing and engendering' of sexual harassment (Morrison, 1992).

Feminists have made safety, particularly for women, a critical concern in workplace relations. In social work, where front-line practitioners often become the target of frustrated 'client' anger, the issue may be one of life and death (Marchant, 1994). Years of sustained campaigning over the issue have compelled managers to take safety issues more seriously. Violence against social workers has been increasing in recent years; a trend reflecting the rise in more generalised violence (Marchant, 1994; Mayhew and Hough, 1990). Evidence also suggests that male violence against women has increased as women have challenged traditional gender roles and intensified men's fears about their own status and roles (Bailey and Lee, 1982).

Women's gains at work, whether these involve safety, equal pay or better working conditions, are under threat (Walby, 1990) because our working reality is a contingent one. The struggles over these issues are constantly being re-enacted since women have yet to secure the organisational and institutional forms which will maintain these gains across space and time. Even on the employment front, for example, public expenditure cuts have decimated the size of the labour force in full-time work. Women, as the largest group of employees in the welfare state, have experienced the greatest impact in the unemployment stakes and lowered wages that followed. Moreover, as privatisation and competitive tendering force many of the jobs previously located in the higher paid public sector into the private sector, women with already low rates of pay and poor working conditions see these fall even further.

Professionalism

Social work has been struggling for recognition as a full profession since its inception. Back in 1915, the verdict given by white men in the USA when the Flexner Report was published was, that at best, it was a semi-profession (Flexner, 1915); a position Toren (1972) claims it retains. Part of Flexner's rationale in reaching this conclusion was that a profession must have a discrete body of knowledge controlled by (professional) experts who specify the training, which provides access to its area of expertise, and who determine admission to its ranks. Moreover, there must be an authoritative professional association – a closed shop of professional peers, capable of exercising control over individual practitioner's performance, professional competence and development, and passing judgement in questions of malpractice.

The exclusion of social work as a profession staffed by women who seek different forms of professionalism (and suspect on these grounds alone) has rarely been voiced in public. But, the medical profession stands as an example of how work, initially devalued for being undertaken by women, becomes redefined as a high-status exclusive arena for men to practice (Ehrenreich and English, 1979). However, this achievement requires the transformation of medical practice into 'scientific medicine'.

Social work, as a profession concerned with caring, has had a more direct connection with, and is more readily labelled, 'women's work'.

As such, it is more easily devalued than medicine and of less interest to men (see Hugman, 1991a,b). Nonetheless, the social work profession remains under male control, despite the preponderance of women at the front line. Men control the managerial echelons where decisions about policy and resources which affect practice are taken.

However, professional boundaries are mutable. Soviet medicine became redefined as women's domain when Stalin's industrialisation programme lessened its importance (Sidel and Sidel, 1977; Dominelli, 1991c). Meanwhile, the caring side of medicine and nursing remain dominated by poorly paid women worldwide (Sidel and Sidel, 1977; Dominelli, 1991c). The racialised stratification of medicine is also evident. In Britain, black doctors are located largely in the lower status specialisms (Littlewood and Lipsedge, 1982). Black women predominate in the lower ranks of nursing (Doyal *et al.*, 1981). The American situation portrays a similar segregation (Sidel and Sidel, 1977; Navarro, 1979,).

Women in social work have struggled (unsuccessfully) to redefine professionalism in different terms (Callahan, 1994). By seeking to empower users and women workers, women have attempted to create a profession for themselves while serving others. The full implications of this insight require further investigation. At this point, it suffices to say that women have sought to redefine the division of labour in ways more to their liking, mobilising resources for this project, even if the gendered division of labour has been reproduced in a new form.

In the last two decades, feminists have been challenging hierarchical notions of professionalism. Their activities have sought to redefine the purpose of a profession, improve the quality of services provided, and increase 'clients'' involvement in decision-making (see Ruzek, 1978, 1986; Foster, 1989; Dominelli and McLeod, 1989). Consequently, power sharing between 'clients' and practitioners is the norm in feminist work (see Hatton and Nugent, 1993; Dominelli and McLeod, 1989). In British social work, the arguments for rejecting traditional definitions of professionalism have focused on keeping the profession open to a wide variety of people by not limiting training to the university setting or requiring practitioners to be licensed.

While discrimination based on the exclusion of women from university campuses has ended, women remain less likely than men to take higher degrees. Differential access also exists because institutions of higher education organise courses in ways that disadvantage women who are raising families. Moreover, women who earn less than men have greater difficulty amassing the financial resources necessary for being out of the labour market for a lengthy period. A looser profession which is not exclusively based in universities is more likely to meet the needs of working-class and black women, argue its adherents. There is merit in this position, but it remains problematic. In the current configuration of the labour market, it ghettoises women in social work and facilitates the retention of lower paid and less qualified workers, thereby paving the way for the deprofessionalisation of social work (Dominelli, 1996).

Men have been a minority on social work courses (Walton, 1975; SSI, 1991b; Hallett, 1990), although they formed a larger proportion of the student body when social work's prospects were brighter at the height of the Seebohm reorganisation. However, once in the profession, white men flourish in a way white women, black women and black men do not, rapidly ascending the managerial ladder to run the profession (Howe, 1986; Hallet, 1990; SSI, 1991b; NACRO, 1992; Burgess, 1994).

Redefining professionalism also has major implications for the socialisation of new recruits into the profession and their training. In Britain, debates indicate a split between those favouring academic qualifications and those endorsing in-service training through National Vocational Qualifications (NVQs). The latter argue NVQs provide formal recognition of the devalued work in social care done by women. Feminists are ambivalent about the degree to which they support such initiatives because these also provide employers with the opportunity to obtain social workers on the cheap and lower the status of the profession even further (Dominelli, 1996; Issitt, 1994). Currently, the majority of those supporting NVQs over more expensive DipSW training are employers, the government and CCETSW.

Social organisations

Feminists have identified the importance of examining unequal social relations in organisational structures. These embody values justifying the subordination of women and ideologies endorsing their implementation in practice. Social organisations provide the means for perpetuating and maintaining relations of dominance, irrespective of the 'will' of an individual, and ensuring their continuity over time (Giddens, 1984).

Relations of domination are not confined to gender. They include 'race', class, disability, age and sexual orientation. Women, represented among these other social divisions, may be at the receiving end of a number of dominances which interact with each other to 'keep them in their (subordinate) place' (Collins, 1991). Multiple social divisions account for the absence of a definitive experience of women's oppression which is shared by all women. Instead, there are a number of different experiences of oppression which have in common the fact that women are socially dominated by men. Moreover, women's experience of social status is different from men's at similar points in the system. Because their experiences are gendered, the impact of racial oppression on black working-class women will be different from that of black working-class men. Racism also makes black working-class women's experience of gender oppression substantially different from white working-class women's (hooks, 1984; Davis, 1982, 1989).

Feminists have also begun to argue that establishing a hierarchy of oppressions, as Marxists have prioritised class (see Anderson, 1976; Offe, 1984) or black nationalists the supremacy of racial struggles (Perry, 1989), is invidious and unhelpful (Collins, 1991; Dominelli and McLeod, 1989). Individuals who have to deal with more than one form of oppression in their lives should not be forced to choose between them. Their need is to tackle all forms of oppression at the same time. However, the forms of practice which will enable this principle to be fully realised have been poorly developed and thought out. Hence, the experience of most women enduring multiple oppressions is that of being put in the position of having to prioritise which 'ism' they will address first. For example, black lesbian women having to choose anti-racist struggles over anti-sexist and lesbian ones (hooks, 1984; Lorde, 1984; Collins, 1991).

Organisational culture

Feminists have uncovered the importance of organisational culture in keeping relations of domination going. Organisational culture sustains these through the taken-for-granted assumptions which oil daily interactions and routines. It has proven extremely difficult to shift, and is a major factor in the failure of formal equal opportunities, anti-sexist and anti-racist policies (Collins, 1991). Transforming organisational cultures is essential if people are to move their attitudes and belief systems in egalitarian directions (Dominelli, 1995; Broadbent *et al.*, 1993). In social work, this includes redefining the organisational culture's view of sexism as unproblem- atic because the profession consists primarily of women and racism a non-issue unless black people are present. It also has to address the significance of society's broader norms and values in structuring inequality in the workplace and professional relationships at both macro and microlevels of interaction.

Social institutions

Social institutions have been critical in maintaining the long-term viability of relations of domination. These include both macrolevel and microlevel institutions ranging from the global economy to the family. In between these two extremes are the nation-state, local and central government, religious orders, educational systems and the media. These institutions are guided by particular definitions of masculinity and femininity which affirm the supremacy of the former over the latter and are deeply implicated in the social control of individuals – men or women, black or white. Those running social institutions act as if there were a fixed definition of acceptable social relations which they are in the business of upholding. This definition is normative and provides the yardstick by which all activities are evaluated. The guiding assumptions on which this measure is currently predicated establish the hegemonic position of white middle-class men. However, these are being challenged by women and black people.

Black feminists have also conceptualised social institutions in ways which clarify their differential impact on black and white people (Lorde, 1984; hooks, 1989; Collins, 1991). Moreover, feminists have shown that institutions are situationally located and that social relations among and between people are enacted through and in them.

The welfare state

Feminists' attitudes towards the central and local state are ambiva- lent. For British women, the welfare state nationally and locally has been a major site of waged employment. Although most of the jobs have been low paid and hold little status, they have provided women with access to an income independent of men and greater freedom in choosing how to live. Tying into feminist demands for women's economic self-sufficiency, this has been welcomed as a precondition to liberation. Yet, it has ghettoised women in the secondary labour market and intensified their exploitation in the workplace (Beechey, 1980). Moreover, many of the tasks assumed by the welfare state have been those women have traditionally undertaken at home (Segal, 1983). The modest amount of power and status which has accrued to women as the result of fulfilling these domestic roles has disappeared. Finally, welfare state employers exploit women's labour by paying scant attention to women's training needs (Coyle 1984, 1989). Indeed, because these jobs mirror those done for their loved ones, employers expect women to walk into them with ready-made skills requiring little if any training. Black women have been hard hit by these dynamics. Not only have they been crucial in providing the labour power which initially set up the welfare state, particularly its health services (Mama, 1989; Bridges, 1975), but their poorly paid labour has kept it going during periods of austerity (Mama, 1989).

'The family'

'The family' is another contradictory institution for women. Women's oppression at the interpersonal level and our socialisation into relations of subordination take place within its fold (Eichler, 1983). Substantial numbers of women and children have experienced brutal treatment at the hands of their male 'protectors' through physical, emotional and sexual abuse (Rush, 1980; Gordon, 1985; Mama, 1989). But, families have also acted as sites of resistance against the daily onslaught on the personal integrity of oppressed peoples (see Staples 1988; Thomas Bernard, 1994). The organisation of white working-class families to resist class oppression during labour struggles, for example white working-class women's activism during the Miner's Strike of 1984, illustrates this (Rowbotham, 1986). Black working-class women demonstrate similar skills and strengths when organising families and communities during their workplace struggles, for example Asian women's strike at Grunwick's in the mid 1970s (Rogaly, 1977). Moreover, women's *raison d'être* is validated through familial relationships. These become sources of power for women in their own right.

In addition, black families have enabled black people to resist racial oppression and taught black children survival skills for successfully negotiating around obstacles to their progress, enacted through racist social relations (Comer and Poussaint, 1975). However, traditional sociologists like Mount (1982) have defined 'the family' as the white middle-class heterosexual nuclear family. This definition has been used as the yardstick to label other family forms deviant and pathological (Eichler, 1983; Brooke and Davis, 1985; Dominelli, 1993). Feminists' work has countered this by celebrating diversity in 'family' forms and encouraging women to choose their lifestyles.

Networks

Networks and campaigns have been major vehicles through which feminists have sought to promote social change (Dominelli and McLeod, 1989). Hierarchical organisational structures and elitist forms of leadership have been eschewed as instruments that distort feminists' attempts at establishing egalitarian relationships among all women (Frankfort, 1972). Avoiding the formation of hierarchies in relationships with each other has been a major preoccupation of feminists. Consequently, working in small groups, particularly consciousness-raising groups, networks and campaigns, has been their favoured means of mass mobilisation. These organisational forms are advantageous in producing innovative practice and challenging women to think of new ways of relating to each other. This is problematic. Organising dispersed and disparate organisations is difficult. Communication can suffer from time lags between calls for action and a response, as each group receives basic information, considers it and decides how to respond. Nonetheless, the effectiveness of feminist forms of organising on a large scale has been demonstrated by the women's shelter movement (Dobash and Dobash, 1991), the Greenham Women's Peace Movement (Cook and Kirk, 1983; Dominelli, 1986b) and various campaigns for women's reproductive rights (Greenwood and Young, 1976).

Gains that feminists have introduced through their own efforts are constantly being contested by traditionalist and fundamentalist groups. These attacks signify the intensely politicised nature of sexual politics and women's rights. Moreover, they indicate the feminist movement's failure to mobilise the organisational means securing widespread institutional support for their activities across space and time. Nonetheless, feminist campaigns and networks have demonstrated how effectively women use self-help initiatives to stretch limited resources in pursuit of their goals.

Empowering structures and relationships

Feminists have focused on the empowering – of oneself and of each other. Arguing that individual experience is a valid basis for commenting on social realities, feminists have encouraged each woman to speak out and name her own pain (Friedan, 1963) and resist calls aiming to silence other women's voices (Frankfort, 1972). Work in feminist groups has attempted to live up to this ideal. Sharing knowledges, skills and powers with each other has been an important plank in its realisation. Women have made many sacrifices for feminism. These have ranged from being ridiculed and ostracised to losing their lives, as happened in Germany when Hitler had thousands of feminists liquidated as part of his campaign to recruit women to the Nazi cause and silence opposition to his evil ways (Lorenz, 1994; Adamson *et al.*, 1988), or in the USA when countless black women faced death through brutality and enslavement for trying to hang on to those parts of themselves they deemed important, for example, passing their culture on to their children and maintaining their dignity and their personal integrity (Collins, 1991).

Black feminists have taken the commitment to empowerment further to promote 'racial uplift', the empowerment of all black people, regardless of their gender (Collins, 1991; Winant, 1994). White feminists, with one or two exceptions (Dominelli and McLeod, 1989; Eisenstein, 1979; Segal, 1987) have been slower to argue feminism's relevance to white men. These initiatives are now taking off as feminists work with men to address ways of ending men's domestic and sexual violence against women and children (see Fagg, 1993; Dominelli, 1991a). Feminism is rooted in women's experience of being oppressed as women, with women as its starting point. However, the realisation of its goal – ending oppression – requires the liberation of men from patriarchal masculinity. Feminist principles and ways of working can apply to and be applied by men pursuing this task (Segal, 1987).

Social change

Feminism espouses a commitment to social change. This feature differentiates feminism from other woman-centred approaches (Dominelli and McLeod, 1989; Adamson *et al.*, 1988). Although feminists began by demanding that women be included in men's world, their demands have gone beyond this. Feminists now want a new world order based on a vision of a different society. One that is non-exploitative, sensitive to environmental issues, cognisant of the interdependence of all our lives, committed to a peaceful resolution of differences between people and aimed at righting past wrongs. Bringing this about will be no mean feat, but women are working towards it in countless ways (Segal, 1987). These include resistance through everyday activities, working on identity politics and transforming broader political activities including the electoral process (Dominelli and McLeod, 1989; Collins, 1991; hooks, 1990, 1989).

Feminist sociological social work

Feminist insights have already influenced developments in social work. The women's movement has provided the framework for the development of a form of social work which bears its name – feminist social work (Dominelli, 1992a; Burden and Gottlieb, 1987). Although feminists have had a significant impact on social work theory and practice (see Dominelli, 1991b, 1992a), it is not as strong as might be anticipated, given its commitment to more appropriate services for 'clients'. The mobilisation of support for its tenets has been slow and incremental (Dominelli, 1991b, 1992a). Some feminist messages have been adopted by practitioners more readily than others, for example the development of equal opportunities policies and work with male sex offenders. One of the reasons for this lukewarm response has been the lack of support for feminism at the highest echelons of government (Dominelli and McLeod, 1989); another is its failure to speak directly to the majority of the population by mobilising opinion-formers on its own behalf. Feminist messages and actions have been filtered for public consumption by a hostile media (see hooks, 1992). The relentless attack on feminists' views, orchestrated by opinion-formers in the media with spurious and unproven allegations, has become an important barrier to promoting feminist theory and practice (Dunant, 1994).

In social work, the government and media have been crucial in endorsing a backlash against feminist claims and aspirations, including their seeking academic respectability (Dunant, 1994). 'Moral panics' have been created around 'single parent women' and 'politically correct' ideologies (Phillips, 1993; Appleyard, 1993; Pinker, 1993). However, we should not be too pessimistic about a backlash. It indicates contested terrain. As such, both feminists and those spearheading the backlash will engage in activities which seek to advance their position. In the process of doing so neither will remain unaffected by what the others say and do. At the end of the day, the compromises reached will reflect their relative abilities to mobilise others. The outcome of this particular struggle to (re)establish another hegemonic professional regime in social work will not be determined solely by those commanding greater 'allocative' or 'authoritative' resources, but on their ability to deal with the counter position, and speak to people's reality as *they* experience it. In the section below, I examine the use of feminist theories and practice in social work, identifying in the process, how feminist social work leads to better practice because it takes as its starting point people's realities as they experience them.

CASE STUDY

Mary was a (white working-class) mother of three children, Dorothy aged five, Daniel aged four and Angela aged two. As she had not maintained steady relationships with men, each child had a different father. All of the fathers were (white) working-class men. The last man Mary had lived with for over two years had been sent to prison on assault and theft charges. With him gone, Mary went on Income Support and found it hard to cope with the bills. The most difficult for her to pay regularly were the gas bill and rent. She was becoming extremely depressed with her situation, but didn't know what to do. The doctor who was prescribing medication for her condition referred her to social services for assistance. A male social worker came to call, decided that the children were not at risk of being abused, and sent her for debt counselling so that she could learn to manage her money better. With that, he felt the case could be closed.

This course of action might look good on his performance ratings, but his intervention has not met Mary's needs. To begin with, Mary is not being considered as her own person. She is being related to on the basis of stereotypical roles – a man's partner, a mother, a housekeeper. The case notes reveal a number of sexist assumptions which reflect badly on Mary's abilities as a woman. These cover her relationships with men, mothering capacities and skills in managing her life. The social work problem has been defined around the safety of the children, although Mary also needs assistance. Crucial debilitating presumptions guiding the social worker's interventions are:

- Mary's failure to maintain long-term relationships with men
- medicalising her financial problems
- casting doubts on her mothering abilities
- defining her problems as financial mismanagement
- ignoring Mary as a woman with needs of her own.

If handled by a feminist social worker or a male social worker working through a feminist perspective, this intervention would have been substantially different. It might not necessarily challenge the status quo outside Mary's immediate environment, for feminist ethics preclude abusing a vulnerable individual by using their specific suffering for the broader goal of changing society. However, the insights and information collected from one case can be incorporated in this wider strategic objective. In other words, structural inequalities would *not* be challenged by placing a specific individual under the spotlight unless they personally wished to be a 'test case'.

Feminists assessing Mary's situation would have begun with a recognition of Mary's social position as a woman and examined both her own specific needs and those of her children. Included in this consideration would be a question about whether there are social divisions other than gender which might have a bearing on her position. Mary would have been contextualised as a whole person living in a particular social milieu with the advantages and disadvantages accruing to her because of it. This woman and her children are white working class, but the social worker writing these case notes does not think it important to consider this fact. Hence, I have placed them in brackets.

In terms of microlevel practice, Mary would not have been labelled a failure for not maintaining her relationships with men.

Nor would a feminist social worker jump to the conclusion that the problem was Mary's inability to manage her financial resources. However, she would explore her financial situation with her to ensure that Mary was receiving all her welfare entitlements (or refer her to the appropriate advice centre if unable to do it directly). She would also explore other ways of increasing her finances, for example a loan from the Social Fund, a grant from a charity. The social worker would have created space for Mary to marshal as many resources as possible to help her make decisions about and take control of her life. In the longer term, if Mary felt that she would like to enter the job market, this might also include examining Mary's employability, training needs and childcare requirements.

A feminist social worker would have asked Mary to participate actively in the assessment of her situation and the decisions made about the assistance she requires. During the exploration of her needs, Mary would be encouraged to define what she wants from social services instead of having a number of (inappropriate) assumptions made about these. She would not be pathologised for the position she is in, but her physical, emotional and financial needs would all be explored. So, for example, Mary would be asked to express a preference regarding the gender of her social worker, in recognition of the fact that some women prefer to talk to women about certain aspects of their lives. A relationship of trust would be built up between them by the social worker treating Mary with respect and dignity as a matter of right rather than condescendingly because there are class differences between them.

Mary might talk of her isolation, in which case the social worker would respond to that, perhaps by telling Mary about resources and groups which would enable her to develop a variety of friendships and networks. Mary might identify the need to get support with the exhausting task of caring for three children day in and day out without a break. Here, the social worker would inform Mary about childcare and home help resources she could tap into, particularly if social services did not have any which it could offer her directly.

Working from a feminist perspective does not mean that resource shortages are ignored. These concerns are shared fully with the 'client' and other ways of addressing the situation considered. Rather than merely accepting material scarcity as an unalterable constraint, the social worker would focus on 'enabling hope', that is, seeking other practical solutions to the problems they have identified.

Together, they would look for alternatives to surmount these difficulties. Joining an informal childminding network with other mothers might be one way of responding to her childcare needs. Another possibility that could be pursued would be to see whether organisations working with the partners (wives) of prisoners could assist her. These would offer Mary support from groups of women able to appreciate her particular experience. Mary's isolation would be specifically addressed, although becoming involved in childcare networks and support groups would also go some way towards reducing it.

The intervention might end up affirming Mary's role as childcarer and society's division of labour. But it would have initiated small-scale changes in Mary's everyday life through her involvement in a more enabling form of social work practice which gives *her* control over her life. Though small-scale, the changes Mary might make are not insignificant. By seeking non-family based resources to support her in caring for the children, Mary's consciousness of her situation would have been altered. She would see other possibilities to doing everything herself and feeling bad or unsuccessful when she asks others for help. Feeling validated despite needing assistance would give Mary confidence in doing new things. She would begin to feel empowered.

The needs of the children would have to be taken on board in their own right. A feminist social worker would try to do this without satisfying the needs of the mother at the expense of the children's or vice-versa. This might require the social worker to bring in other workers. Both Mary and the children would have their specific needs considered and further discussions focusing on these would have to ensue. The children's views and experiences would be included as far as possible, whatever their tender years. The children would probably benefit from having a mother who felt more in control of her life and a feminist social worker's overall aim would be to find ways of helping the woman achieve this in terms which take account of her (re)definition(s) of the problem(s) to be addressed.

The social worker would also discuss Mary's depression and seek ways of enabling her to connect with other women who have undergone similar experiences. It would not be assumed that Mary's depression was unrelated to the situation in which she lived. But equally, the medical option would not be ruled out without careful consideration.

In summary, Mary would be fully engaged in the process of empowering herself. She would not personally bear the burden for initiating societal change. This approach contrasts with the actual intervention Mary received. For at the end of that process, she was disempowered. Her individual plight had been used to reinforce the status quo in a way that was likely to exacerbate her depression rather than reduce it. This is an important point, for depression is often women's response to feeling powerless and out of control (Rowe, 1983). A feminist helping relationship is empowering because different types of power are shared on a number of different levels. However, power sharing does not mean ceding formal authority – the social worker remains a social worker accountable to employers, society and the 'client' for the work that is done. Moreover, that work is always open to public scrutiny and feminist social workers, like other practitioners, have to be able to defend their actions publicly.

CASE STUDY

Marcia, a black social worker had been with Hometown Social Services since she had qualified seven years ago. She had risen through the different levels and become a principal social worker. Then, the Team Manager was taken ill and Marcia became Acting Team Head in her place. During her tenure as Acting Manager, everyone had praised her work. After she had held this position for fifteen months, a permanent vacancy for a team leader's post came up. Marcia applied and was interviewed. She was the only black woman among the five applicants shortlisted. The remaining four candidates were white men. None of them had had previous experience as team managers. One of these men secured the position. When Marcia queried her performance at the interview, her white male supervisor who had been on the Interviewing Panel told her she needed to get more experience before seeking a promotion.

This example demonstrates how organisations use women's talents for their own purposes and fail to recognise their quality and merit when it comes to advancing their status and position within the organisation. Given the information presented above, it is difficult to ascertain whether Marcia's full contribution to the organisation had been devalued because she was a woman or because she was black or both. This would have to be determined through an investigation of the case. However, feminist research has revealed that men supervising bright women find it difficult to acknowledge the merit of their work by suggesting promotion to them (Coyle, 1984) and consistently devalue its worth (Eley, 1989). Black women managers' contributions have also been devalued (Ahmad, 1992; Durrant, 1989). Women managers can also fail to appreciate high quality work performed by other women if they themselves feel under pressure to conform. The undervaluing of women's managerial skills is evident in this example, despite the interviewing panel's judgement to the contrary. Marcia had been doing the job of Team Manager effectively. It might even be argued that had the position come up in her own team, she should have been promoted as a matter of course on the basis of having demonstrated that she could do the job.

Working with men

The relevance of feminist perspectives in working with men (Bowl, 1985; Tolson, 1977; Seidler, 1992; Dominelli, 1991, 1989) has become more and more evident. For example, probation services have made extensive use of its insights in working with violent men (Fagg, 1993). Men have also set up men's groups which explore the relevance of feminism for their relationships with other men and between men and women. These range from the generalist *Achilles Heel Collective* (see Seidler, 1992) and *Working with Men*, to self-help groups aimed at addressing specific problems such as MOVE's work with men who assault women (Fagg, 1993). Their work has highlighted the importance of rethinking masculinity both theoretically (Thomas Bernard, 1994; Hearn, 1987; Brittan, 1989) and in practice settings (Cordery and Whitehead, 1992; Dominelli, 1991a, 1992b).

CASE STUDY

A white male probation officer, worried about the number of unemployed young men roaming the streets and ending up on his caseload, thought about getting a voluntary agency to establish a young men's group. This would enable them to focus on their masculinity and give them something to do. His work with young offenders suggested that many of them were having identity crises but had few legitimate outlets in which to explore these. The young male subculture focused on bravado and holding your own. Toughness, not sensitivity, marked their struggle for survival. Feelings were considered a weakness and therefore not admitted.

A group for young men was set up in a youth centre under the auspices of a voluntary agency. It received referrals from probation and social services. It also invited young men in the community, aged 14 – 15, to join. It attracted ten members. The activities of the group were to be agreed between the group facilitator (a white man) and the group members. The facilitator had hoped that at least some of these would examine masculinity and the expectations the young men had for the future. Imagine the facilitator's consternation when the group decided to paint a mural!

As the probation officer had agreed to support him in the work, he discussed his worries with him. The probation officer assured him that he need not worry. He could use whatever opportunities arose from the conversations the young men had while painting the mural. To the facilitator's delight, there was no dearth of materials produced. The group members shared their hopes and fears for the future, concerns about relationships with others – parents, male friends, girlfriends – offending behaviour and employment prospects. The facilitator skillfully used their banter to get them to examine their feelings about themselves and others and their roles in life. Their enforced bravado, sense of despair, willingness to support each other in difficult moments and humour, all came out.

This case study reveals how men workers can support rather than compete with each other. It also highlights men's emotional side. Given the chance, men can reflect upon and get in touch with themselves and their emotions.

Conclusions

Feminist sociological social work focuses on gender dynamics in all situations and tries to identify their significance in specific ones. Moreover, feminist insights can be applied in working with men. Feminists have been crucial in raising the problematic nature of masculinity for both men and women and revealed how men are limited in expressing the full range of their emotions and organisa-tional skills because certain characteristics have been defined as 'feminine' and out of bounds to them (Bowl, 1985; Tolson, 1977; Festau, 1975). Housework, childcare and forming close relationships with others are just a few areas in which men's experience is limited. Feminists (Segal, 1987; Walby, 1990) have argued that men's lives could be enriched if they participated equally alongside women in such activities. Moreover, feminists have highlighted the importance of men examining masculinity – the norms it espouses regarding their relationships with each other and less socially powerful groups. Prime among these have been violence against women and the sexual abuse of children. Feminists have addressed these issues by working directly with men (see Dominelli, 1982), encouraging men to work with other men as they do in MOVE, Working With Men, and the Achilles Heel Collective (see Seidler, 1992) or men and women co-working (Thompson, 1993).

It is becoming increasingly clear to feminists that anti-sexist work is the concern of both men and women (Davis, 1982; hooks, 1984). The world has to be changed for both men and women if the oppression of women is to be eliminated. Anti-racist feminist social work has an important role to play in producing a better world for all – through microlevel practice by responding to individual needs in ways that promote self-empowerment, and macrolevel intervention by undertaking research and social action aimed at challenging inegalitarianism in all its forms. A sociology of social work from an anti-racist feminist perspective provides us with the conceptual tools and analyses necessary for realising this task and evaluating our efforts.

4

The Institutional Parameters of Social Work

Institutions provide one social means whereby people seek to ensure continuity over time and space (Giddens, 1987). As Goffman, (1961) has demonstrated, institutions are powerful organisational forms which impact on the lives of individuals because those in control seek to secure their position by structuring relationships and using resources to prioritise managerial and administrative objectives over those of 'clients'. Institutions become instruments through which agents exert organisational power and influence those requiring services. The nature of the relationship between the two parties to the transaction usually disempowers those receiving the services because agents exercising institutional control use the greater 'authoritative' and 'allocative' resources they have at their command to pursue their interests.

In social work, institutional power enables social workers to exercise control over 'clients'. When the interests of those running the organisation conflict with those of users, the 'allocative' and 'authoritative' resources the institution endows on social workers give them the edge over their 'clients'. Thus, in negotiations about needs, 'clients'' definitions may be subordinated to organisational ones, as in residential homes where staffing levels limit the independence of residents (Goffman, 1961; Henwood, 1986).

Institutional power exists insofar as its reproduction is negotiated with other actors including 'clients'. However, its constraining influence is effective only to the extent that users are unable to replace existing relationships with another set because institutional power is never absolute. It is dependent on the capabilities of others to (re)create and transform the institution's existing parameters, whether these be areas of jurisdiction, policies, practices or resources.

Thus, institutions are constantly changing as those in formal control of them attempt to (re)define contingent reality from their perspective and respond to others' reactions to their actions.

The fluidity of institutions involved in social work is substantial. Individual agents, whether 'clients' or employees, are constantly negotiating and renegotiating organisational relationships and introducing interpersonal change via their interactions and the choices they make when taking action. Legislative, political, economic, cultural and other changes also continually affect its institutional base. Social work institutions are therefore characterised by uncertainty as much as certainty.

Key questions which a sociology of social work seeks to answer about institutions are:

- Who controls social work institutions?
- Who owns institutional resources?
- Who defines institutional ways of working?

This chapter examines these questions largely in terms of developments in British social work.

Social work: a state dependent profession

Social work in Britain is primarily a state activity. Its funding comes from the central state, although specific expenditures are determined locally through the representational structures of the local authority. A social services committee oversees budget expenditures and policy at departmental level. Social workers and their managers must operate within limits set by local councillors, although there are organisational mechanisms through which they can influence their decisions. For social workers, this includes using collective bargaining procedures endorsed by their unions.

Councillors' sphere of action is controlled by central government funding – usually to a predetermined formula which has been constantly altered to reflect conservative political priorities since 1979. These operate in favour of reducing state activities and are being driven through financial instruments which restrict the monies allocated for welfare purposes. Block grants, capped budgets, standard assessments and administrative control form the cornerstones of the government's strategy for containing public sector expenditure and establishing the framework for 'contract government' (Greer, 1994).

'Contract government' has created the infrastructure for moving state activities into the private sector. Through it, the central state restricts local authorities to purchasing rather than providing welfare services in community care, by compelling them to either put services out to tender or make contractual arrangements for their provision. Community care supplies an active example of how 'contract government' is privatising the welfare state (see Orme and Glastonbury, 1993; Le Grand and Robinson, 1984). Councils have challenged budgetary allocations made by the central state but their efforts have had limited success (see Le Grand and Robinson, 1984). This outcome is not surprising given the Tories' commitment to curtailing local government spending using financial mechanisms rather than conducting an ideological confrontation over political priorities. The influx of monetarist principles into local government has also impacted on social work professionals. Financial disincentives have seriously diminished operational possibilities by curbing the discretional powers social workers and their managers exercise. Moreover, in subjecting professional decisions to economic exigencies, social work has become depoliticised and technocratised (Dominelli, 1996).

Practitioners' ability to influence the definition of social work's remit is limited. Service users have even less potential to redefine it except insofar as they exercise their right to vote and select politicians who act on their behalf. Social work professionals can at least access formal decision-making structures to express their views through their trade unions, professional organisations and line managers. In addition, the day-to-day implementation of policies, the expenditure of budgets determined at the political level, and the provision of services to individuals lies in their hands. There is little input from 'clients' at these points. Service users' influence is more indirect – through their relationship with individual social workers, or when they organise protests against closures of facilities. Even then, their resistance is restricted by a dearth of collective forms of organisations sustainable through time and space. Under the provisions of the Citizen's Charter, users can exercise negative influence by utilising established complaints procedures. I call this 'negative influence' because it is reactive rather than proactive. The 'client' can only complain *after* receiving a service they deem poor. This makes the subject of the complaint the individual social worker and does not enable the 'client' to question the overall policy or the provision of services which fail to respond to user-defined needs.

The question of who owns social work's resources is also problematic. The theoretical owner is the taxpayer through the state. In practice, a local authority 'owns' the facilities of the social services department under its jurisdiction. Contrary to popular opinion, this institutionalised ownership does not ensure service stability. Much depends on the priorities and vicissitudes of the political process. Whenever resources are scarce, economic and political exigencies can force the sale of welfare facilities to balance the books. The 1980s are replete with examples of these. Homes for older people, children's homes, nursery provisions, youth services and education welfare services have been treated as assets ready for stripping and transferral to the private sector rather than as provisions that the state holds in trust for vulnerable groups. Even sustained opposition to closure has not guaranteed the survival of any given facility in the public sector (Culpitt, 1992).

The definition of what constitutes social work and how it is done is strongly influenced by the political process. This may produce policies and practices inimical to the interests of users. In the 1980s, government ministers intervened directly in shaping practices which in other professions were determined by professionals and their professional bodies. Ministerial interventions have been particularly forceful in relation to lone mothers and young offenders. The plight of the two is often linked. Government ministers claim that the absence of fathers in single parent families is responsible for young male delinquency and blame mothers for not providing an environment conducive to the two parent heterosexual couple (see Gairdner, 1992; Richardson, 1992). The political agenda of these developments reflects the demonising of single parent women and young people as particular categories of poor people. Such treatment aims to cast them in the role of 'undeserving' users who can be excluded from public provision by denying them sympathy and support from either 'deserving' users or enfranchised citizens.

The term 'underclass' used to refer to the 'undeserving' poor encapsulates the less than human status into which these people are being forced (Morris, 1994). In the case of 'lone mothers' and young offenders, more punitive policies seek to return them to the fold of 'normal' society by compelling them to enter waged work to support their families instead of relying on Income Support. Yet, their predicament is marked by inadequately remunerated childcare provisions (Showstack-Sassoon, 1987; Becker, 1991; Dominelli, 1993).

Young offenders are to be sent to secure training units which aim to instil socially sanctioned values into their conduct without any acknowledgement of the role society has played in putting young people on a collision course with it. Young people who feel they have no place in social life will carve out their own response to the struggle for existence. In this context, that their response may be anti-social is irrelevant (see Newburn and Hagell, 1994). Many young people, particularly young men, are being switched off from society. This is evident in crime statistics which reveal one in three men under the age of thirty have been convicted of a non-motoring offences (otherwise, the figures would be substantially higher) (Graef, 1992). Moreover, custodial facilities for young offenders are to be placed under the auspices of the private sector rather than the publicly run Prison Service (Sone, 1995; Evans, 1994; Tissier, 1994; Rickford, 1995a), thus providing another point for the privatisation of state facilities. The British state's treatment of young people has been condemned internationally for neglecting the rights of children. The country's response to children's needs – including the alleviation of poverty among them, has been so appalling that, in early 1995, the United Nations declared Britain had broken international law on children's rights (Rickford, 1995a).

Similar disparaging views about woman-headed families and young offenders are being expressed in the United States where institutional arrangements for social work are different, although the British ones are becoming more like them as the mixed economy of welfare and the market environment take hold (see Murray, 1984, 1990, 1994). In the United States, those demonising the poor also play the 'race' card to promote the myth that poor black people are genetically pathological (see Murray, 1994). Drawing on a biologically driven pathology enables policy-makers and taxpayers to absolve themselves of the responsibility for making unstigmatised public provisions readily available to poor people.

In Britain, the seamless web of local authority responsibility for creating and delivering services to 'clients' is being broken down through the introduction of the purchaser–provider split initiated under community care legislation. This has made the privatisation of the personal social services easier. The government has used

economic instruments such as cash limits, specific funding arrangements and legislative fiat to change the organisational culture of
welfare organisations and make it more accommodating to private
entrepreneurs (Culpitt, 1992; Dominelli and Hoogvelt, 1994).

It is still too early to reach more than tentative conclusions on the
changes taking place, but the old professional definition of social
work is being sorely tested. Specialist interventions in the statutory
sector, for example child protection, have become increasingly
determined by bureaucratic procedures rather than professional
relationships, although legislation in the Children Act 1989 espouses
a concern to let users, especially parents, control their own lives
(Frost, 1992). Nonetheless, the case management approach to social
work has reduced the space for professionals to explore the needs of
the 'person-in-the-situation'. This trend is most evident in
community care where social workers have become engrossed in
chasing other professionals and service providers to deliver 'packages
of care' which focus on a discrete aspect of a 'client's' life rather than
addressing their circumstances in a holistic way.

Moreover, this approach turns ethical dilemmas into technical
problems as the social worker has to decide between competing
needs and resource availability, without having had a say in the
allocation of resources. Their lack of influence in the overall
decision-making process has marginalised social workers' professional concerns and judgements. For example, a social worker may
have assessed two older 'clients' with Alzheimer's Disease as both
being in need. But, the resources available in the devolved budget
allow for meeting the needs of only one. Consequently, social
workers are placed in the position of having to find ways of *excluding*
one person from eligibility, even though legislation says *both* are
entitled to provisions. Under current arrangements, even the
possibility of fudging the issue by exceeding the budget which
existed previously is no longer theoretically possible. The emphasis
on making costs visible has put the spotlight on the failure of
resources to meet needs as an unintended consequence of pricing
policy. However, its impact in shaking the conscience of policy-
makers is muted in a climate driven by economic forces.

The social worker avoids confronting the moral and ethical
dilemmas non-provision poses not by challenging the policy, but by
refining the bureaucratic criteria to further differentiate between the
needs of two users. For in a context in which the room for profes-

sional discretion has been minimised, economic priorities take precedence. The social worker's responses in the above situation can be: placing one 'client' on a waiting list which can be very long; waiting for an older person currently receiving services to die, thereby freeing up resources previously allocated; or finding other creative ways of breaking the vicious circle. Responding to these situations in innovative ways which challenge the initial political decision about the overall budgetary allocation is virtually impossible for social workers employed to work within a given budget. Challenging financial constraints in social work requires organisational work to be done in mobilising 'allocative' and 'authoritative' resources to bring an alternative scenario to fruition. A key dimension in realising this endeavour is time – a resource that social workers are desperately short of, given the high demands of administering and servicing cases in the quasi-market (Orme and Glastonbury, 1983).

A small study I have undertaken has revealed that 35 per cent of social workers' time is spent on meeting administrative demands imposed by the new managerialist direction in the profession. Service provision plays a poor cousin to the administrative side's voracious capacity to devour resources in the name of holding social workers responsible for their use of resources and accountable to management's guidelines in service delivery. These demand social workers provide discrete services and record their activities in tightly defined and rigidly monitored ways. New technological developments in computing have made managerialist surveillance of social workers' activities much more intensive and invasive (Dominelli *et al.*, 1995).

The introduction of technologically based forms of surveillance has given management an instantly accessible monitoring system. However, these systems require probation officers and social workers to spend more time simultaneously processing 'clients' and preparing the materials through which their work will be monitored. By engaging in their own monitoring process, social workers become implicated in their own social control. Reproducing these forms of practice leaves little scope for entrepreneurial social workers to use professional discretion in developing new services which respond to users' definitions of the services they require. The fragmented world being created through the purchaser–provider split brings a new form of organisational power to the fore as the managerialist techno-bureaucrat replaces the bureau-professional. Similar processes are evident in probation where the Home Office has been systematically keeping tabs on probation officers' activities for some time. Probation services are introducing new computer technology under an initiative called CRAMS. By measuring workers outputs, CRAMS will make an even more thorough evaluation of worker productivity possible.

Another way of influencing developments in social work is by controlling the training of qualifying practitioners. Social work training in Britain is governed by government policy, largely articulated through a quango, the Central Council for Education and Training in Social Work (CCESTW). Recently, this body has come under sustained attack by academics who have resented its bureaucratic interference in their professional remit (see Pinker, 1986, 1993, 1994). Academics' own organisations, The Joint Universities Council – Social Work Education Committee (JUC-SWEC), the Association of University Professors in Social Work, the Standing Conference for Heads of Social Work Courses, the Standing Conference of Probation Tutors, have failed to substantially influence developments in training. Yet an intensive power struggle to determine the shape of the profession erupted between academics and CCETSW in the mid 1980s prior to the introduction of the Diploma in Social Work (DipSW) (Sibeon, 1991) and the 1990s over revisions to the DipSW curriculum.

Practitioners have been unable to exert much power in defending their interests. The British Association of Social Workers (BASW) is experiencing a decline in membership (Rickford, 1995b) for failing to raise the standing of social work and claim the allegiance of a broad potential membership. The trade union UNISON, the product of a merger of the National Association of Local Government Officers (NALGO), National Union of Public Employees (NUPE) and Confederation of Health Service Employees (COHSE) which formerly represented social workers, has had little impact on improving either working conditions for social workers or services for 'clients', despite having supported several strikes to these ends (Joyce *et al.*, 1987). Only the National Association of Probation Officers (NAPO) which claims 80 per cent membership levels among probation officers has had limited success in defending the profession's social work base. But even this has been subjected to a sustained attack which threatens to turn probation into a uniformed service led by former army personnel trained in-house (Sone, 1995). Meanwhile, cuts already imposed on other parts of the welfare state are being inflicted on the criminal justice system at a fast pace. The extent to which NAPO, the Association of Chief Officers of Probation (ACOP), Association of Black Probation Officers (ABPO), National Association of Asian Probation Staff (NAAPS) and the Central Probation Council (CPC) can withstand this onslaught is unclear (Ward and Spencer, 1994). The government has been attacking it with increasing vigour since the introduction of the Statement of National Objectives and Priorities (SNOP) and the privatisation of some provisions in the criminal justice system during the mid 1980s (Rickford, 1995b).

Meanwhile, CCETSW has succeeded in restructuring social work education and training to enhance the influence of employers in curriculum design and implementation. This has occurred by requiring that universities and employers form consortia which are responsible for delivering DipSW training. Such arrangements have proven costly and bureaucratic (Duckworth, 1994). Lacking provisions for student representation, these consortia have reduced the scope for students to influence curriculum development. During the mid 1970s, CQSW courses like the one at Warwick University genuinely involved students in negotiating course content with their tutors (Warwick Course Handbook, 1976).

DipSW consortia do not allow 'clients' to sit on their decision-making structures either. Indeed, the whole thrust of consortia arrangements has been to take power in determining course content away from the universities in favour of employers. This favours the model previously set by the Certificate in Social Services (CSS). CSS focused on training practitioners with the discrete skills required by employers rather than 'bogging' them down in theories and critical thinking as did CQSW (see Harbart, 1985a, b). Whether the employers' group can sustain unanimity over a vocationally oriented training under their control remains to be ascertained. Private sector employers' interests are not necessarily the same as those of directors of social services departments. Nor are the constraints under which they operate identical. Private owners have already formed their own organisation as proprietors. The unanimity employers have maintained over the demise of CQSW may break under the strain of accommodating different interests.

The DipSW has encouraged the formation of Employment Based Routes (EBR) in which students register to train with a college while remaining at work. This development presumed an innovation – that of having students working on employers' premises, as if the placements which traditionally constitute 50 per cent of a college-based course are not directly supervised in the workplace by practitioners employed by service providers. The problem with DipSW's EBR provisions is that 'students' remain employees, undertake placements within their own workplace, with limited guarantees that line managers will, in practice, not become directly involved in their supervision and assessment. Consequently, a student's ability to stand back from the pressures of day-to-day responses to the job or be critical of practice may be seriously compromised. In the context of severe underfunding in the social services (George, 1995), employers have found EBRs which safeguard the students' interests through the provision of independent supervisors and mentors too expensive to implement. Some social services departments are now rethinking their strategy and coming to the view that sending students to university is the cheaper option (Duckworth, 1994).

Additionally, the introduction of National Vocational Qualifications (NVQs) for social services workers has meant that jobs once undertaken by qualified social workers are now being done by people, mainly women, with lower level NVQ qualifications. This will produce further organisational shifts which will reduce the power of social work professionals in the workplace and may re-orient or displace existing training alliances, depending on employers' emphasis on staff development for NVQ holders. Meanwhile, NVQs have drawn monies previously allocated to DipSW training. Devolved budgets and compulsory competitive tendering hive off training departments in social services departments and demand these demonstrate viability and the ability to extract value for money from the training resources they dispense. Under these conditions, new values and commitments can dramatically shift trainers' allegiances away from DipSW consortia.

NVQs have been endorsed by CCETSW which has been closely involved in developing the competences for such qualifications. Nonetheless, CCETSW maintains that DipSW is *the* recognised qualification for social workers. Its endorsement of both NVQ and DipSW provisions without adequate resourcing for either, coupled with the absence of a clear ladder of progression between the two qualifications, gives the impression it is backing both sides in the training debate.

Meanwhile, CCETSW is busily enforcing a competency-based approach to social work which favours the employers' and government's interests over those of the professionals and users (see Dominelli, 1995; Jones, 1994a). CCETSW's method in pursuing this strategy has been to involve professional interests in hurried consultation processes which have been heavily criticised for failing to engage with the real issues, relying on outdated and discredited sociological theories and undermining social work's value base. These consultations have been labelled a 'sham' by black external assessors which CCETSW had itself selected (Black Assessors, 1994). The resolution to the hotly contested terrain of social work education and training is not a foregone conclusion.

The trend towards giving employers more say in developing social work training is likely to become more entrenched if the government succeeds in pushing all social work training to in-house NVQs popular with employers. Having little space for critical thinking and reflection, these emphasise 'competences' – the skills for doing the job on a day-to-day basis. In-house provisions are likely to mean that employers will develop programmes to meet their specific needs. The extent to which a nationally recognised award will then exist becomes debatable. Employers insisting on value for money are unlikely to subsidise training provisions for competitors.

Employers are already questioning the degree to which DipSW is necessary for their workers. The development of case managers, as the organisers of packages of community care, has diminished social work's focus on relational and interpersonal skills. This weakens the case for DipSW as *the* award for social workers, as does the de-professionalising of social work as a consequence of in-service training and developments in the competency-based approach to practice (Dominelli, 1995). Employers are saying that scarce training resources would be better used in providing less expensive training through NVQs to cover more unqualified workers (Issitt, 1994). Consequently, many agencies have reduced the number of students sent on DipSW training courses.

Students' abilities to fund themselves through two-year courses are limited by the commitments many have to families and mortgages. Training in-house on a salary becomes a preferable option to surviving on meagre student grants, making NVQ-based training a more likely scenario than continuing with DipSW as *the* qualification for social workers. Consortia arrangements, and the focus on 'outcomes' without an equal concern about inputs and process, may result in haphazard teaching. Students in one agency may cover a curriculum very different from those working in another. In these circumstances, establishing equivalence in qualifications (even if they carry the same name) is difficult.

These trends may jeopardise the recognition of British awards in the international arena. Already, the CQSW and DipSW have hit snags in being recognised in Europe by not meeting the three-year minimum period for qualifying professional training prescribed by the First Directive of the European Union. Thus, the list of those who stand to gain by the current developments in British social work education is short. Users, students, practitioners and academics are likely to be the biggest losers. Whatever outcome emerges will be contested in due course. In a profession *lacking a consensus* about its purpose and role in society, the dynamics driving developments are unstable. This instability represents dissent. Consequently, the results of a contingently produced reality can only be temporary – lasting until someone mobilises sufficiently strong 'allocative' and 'authoritative' resources for mounting an effective challenge.

Gender relations produce another set of dynamics which have undervalued the professional work carried out with 'clients'. Employers, the government and the public generally, consider social work a women's profession concerned primarily with caring. Moreover, they assume that caring is something women do 'naturally' with a 'commonsense' skills base. Virginia Bottomley, as Secretary of State for Health, declared, 'any streetwise granny' can do social work. Such sentiments expose the low priority accorded to high quality training at university level for social workers. They also exacerbate its vulnerability to political vicissitudes which endorse an anti-intellectualism and deprive groups such as women and black people access to higher education for developing their skills by locking them into a lowly qualified educational ghetto.

Gendered and racially stratified management relations

Social work's workforce is made up primarily of women – about 80 per cent. However, only 9 per cent of chief probation officers (NACRO, 1992) and 12 per cent of directors are women (SSI, 1991b; Hallett, 1990). The demographic make-up of the labour force in social services departments and the probation service reflects the phenomenon of the 'glass ceiling' – a term describing women's failure to penetrate managerial ranks in substantial numbers. There are various reasons for this. Systematised prejudice against women as 'management material' is one of them (Coyle, 1984). Women are not credited with having the ruthlessness required of modern-day managers (Hayles, 1989). There is no mentoring system through which women are encouraged to go for promotion when they are ready. The informal networks which exist favour men (Coyle, 1984). Women are also not keen to enter managerial ranks. Those that do it have confirmed other women's suspicions when they relate how unattractive management has been for them (Hayles, 1989).

The labour force picture is also more complex. Although men are the main occupants of the higher echelons of the social work labour hierarchy, their career patterns at the lower levels of the social services department do not mirror women's. Men's rapid rise through practitioners' ranks and early entry into management is the opposite of women's career path (Howe, 1986). Unlike women who remain at the lower, women-dominated levels, men do not get locked into women's ghettos. So, men who enter residential work, soon leave for childcare posts and from there move into management (Howe, 1986). Women are less likely to transfer out of the sector or even seek higher level qualifications to enter a managerialist environment that they consider non-'client' centred.

Black people fare considerably worse than women as a group. Few enter the social work profession. If they do, it is mainly in residential work. They tend to remain stuck in that sector, rising at most to Head of Home (Home Office, 1986). The operation of a 'colour line' is evident in that there are no black women at director level, and only a handful of black men have reached such heights. The picture is equally bleak in probation. Only three per cent of the workforce is black. No black person has made it beyond the grade of assistant chief probation officer (NACRO, 1992; Burgess, 1994). Black people in the higher managerial echelons of social services have left these posts after being in them a comparatively short period of time. Josie Durrant, the first black woman to reach a senior tier of management, in explaining her departure from the post of assistant director, emphasised the lack of job satisfaction which stemmed from having a highly regimented, bureaucratically oriented job concerned with managing cuts rather than facilitating people's needs and favouring a management style appropriate to that task (Durrant, 1989). Eley (1989) and Coyle (1989) have found similar concerns expressed by white women, many of whom refuse to entertain a managerial career.

They are put off by the definition of management as remote, competitive and uncaring, preferring to remain practitioners where contact with 'clients' makes up for some of the more bureaucratic and less satisfying elements of the job (Durrant, 1989; Coyle, 1989). Sadly, with the increasing managerialism driving developments in both social services and probation, these trends are likely to intensify (Burgess, 1994).

Women's actual experiences of a management structure headed mainly by men have been resource focused and lacking in inspiration (Coyle, 1989). Men's managerial approaches have been described by Parsons (1957, 1968) as 'instrumental'. Reflecting male ways of behaving, they keep 'clients' and workers at a distance and do not offer good role models for women to emulate. Moreover, workers have seen women who have broken through the 'glass ceiling' expend endless energy fighting battles not of their making and failing to implement the changes they think necessary for improving working relations and service delivery to 'clients'.

Research undertaken on this subject by feminists reveals that the experience of women managers is often one of frustration and isolation (Durrant, 1989). Male colleagues do not facilitate women's entry into their ranks. Their conduct and attitudes freeze a woman manager into the position of 'outsider' (Hayles, 1989). Men do not have the informal exchanges of information with their women colleagues that they do, without thinking, with men. Sites in which such exchanges take place are often barred to women, either because they are inappropriate, for example men's toilets, or because women feel uncomfortable in surroundings geared primarily to making space for men, for example pubs and recreational sports facilities (French, 1985).

Organisations respond differently to men and women. Consequently, feminists have made changing the organisational culture a critical goal. Whether or not women are the majority of the workforce, the dominant culture supports white men's needs and definitions of roles and function. Indeed, my discussions with women managers have prompted me to develop what I call the 'seepage theory of authority' to begin theorising what is taking place (Dominelli, 1993).

The seepage theory of authority

Feminist research has exposed weaknesses in Weberian formulations of organisational structure. The roles, status and authority which Weber claims are inherent in any managerial position seems to be present mainly for white men. When a woman is appointed to a top position, the roles, status and authority seep away. She comes to the post to find an empty structure which she has to fill by dint of her personality, skills and charisma. Only when she has done this and 'proven' herself, does she begin to be taken seriously as a manager with a major contribution to make to the organisation's work. However, her feeling of always having to be on guard and having to prove herself never abates. Everyone is watching to see her fall flat on her face and demonstrate that 'she is not up to the job'. Her activities are under constant scrutiny. If she makes a mistake, however trivial, her critics will exaggerate and amplify it. Things which would be ignored in a man manager, precipitate major crises. Hence, she is under constant pressure to perform better than her male colleagues. Her experience of management is significantly different from theirs.

Being taken as the one to serve the tea is the least of her worries. The personal slights against her are very subtle and involve both men and women in their perpetration. For example, a woman manager is expected to be self-sufficient. A male manager is deemed to need more 'caring' from his secretary. Things that secretaries will do for male managers, are not done for women managers. This might include practices which should be declared out of bounds for all managers, for example doing men's personal shopping during the lunch hour, but it also includes simple things which if they are provided, should be made available for both men and women, such as preparing the manager's papers for meetings. A man manager can take many things his secretary does to oil the wheels for him for granted. She will do them unbidden because it is what is traditionally expected of her and is not questioned. It is taken as part and parcel of the organisational culture. A woman manager will have to issue specific instructions if she expects anything to be done for her. If she does so, she is labelled demanding and officious.

Differing expectations about men and women make the relationship between the man manager and his secretary qualitatively different from that of the woman manager and her secretary, even if the same secretary is involved (as is often the case). Indeed, in such situations, the woman manager may be saddled with the ways of the previous male manager. She will often be told 'This is how X wanted this done', if she attempts to change office routines. This comment signifies irritation with change, but it also betrays the assumption that 'men's ways' of doing things are superior. These dynamics indicate how sexist social relations are reproduced through social interaction. Moreover, if she intends to introduce a more participative style of management, inclusive of the administrative grades, she is likely to encounter resistance, even if the new methods aim to improve office efficiency. Involving others in decision-making may even be defined as a sign of weakness, further feeding the view that she is 'not up to the job'. Whatever her shortcomings, she may count on these being amplified. Because she *is* an exception, her activities will be noted, remembered and exaggerated to confirm people's prejudice that women should not rise above their allotted place in the lower ranks.

Even her supporters have different expectations of the woman manager. She may be seen as a major change agent who will put the world to rights, or at least end many discriminatory practices which have developed in the office over the years. If she fails to fulfil this 'saviour' role, those who warmed to her coming will feel betrayed and move away. She will also find that whether she wants to or not, she will be identified as the person with the 'woman's brief'. Any issue to do with gender will be shoved her way, and she will be expected to provide the 'expertise' in working through the dilemmas which arise whether she wants to deal with them or not. This puts her in a contradictory position for, while her contribution is devalued because she is a woman, she is expected to be an expert on matters that relate to women. Similar pressures do not exist for white men managers. They have greater scope as individuals for choosing which areas of work they will specialise in.

Black managers encounter similar difficulties in relation to 'race' issues. Whether male or female, they will be expected to provide the expertise for dealing with racism and addressing the needs of black 'clients' whether they wish to or not (Rooney, 1987; Ahmad, 1992). They will also be constantly watched to see whether or not they are 'up to the job', and have any trivial matter which is mishandled, blown out of all proportions (Small, J, 1994). The human capacity to make mistakes and learn from them is denied to black managers regardless of gender, as it is to white women. Black women managers are expected to be superhuman while simultaneously having their work devalued as both sexism and racism operate against them (Collins, 1991; hooks, 1989; Ahmad, 1992). Moreover, they will be asked to nurture everyone but themselves as individuals with their own sets of needs and demands which cry out to be met (Ahmad, 1992).

Men and social work management

White men entered social work management in substantial numbers when large bureaucratic empires were created following the Seebohm Report (Walton, 1975). Many of these men did not hold social work qualifications and had little understanding of social work tasks. This incursion was justified on the grounds that they held qualifications relevant to management (Walton, 1975). These included MBAs and management experience in large organisations. This recruitment policy did not ask whether managing a service sector and professional staff required different skills from those necessary to run a factory mass-producing commodities. Appointing these men marked a departure from previous working practices in which social work practitioners rose to managerial positions. Concern about the lack of career structures for practitioners subsequently prompted social workers to take this up as an issue arising from the reorganisation of the personal social services. Success on this score has eluded them to date.

Even if one accepts the Marxist argument that labour power becomes a commodity in the exchange process, the labour of social work professionals is qualitatively different from that of other skilled workers and draws on different elements of expertise and traditions. Despite this, the new breed of male managers who lacked social work knowledge made decisions which had a direct impact on work done by front-line workers who were mainly women (Walton, 1975). Moreover, this policy failed to recognise the important managerial skills held by women who had managed smaller social work agencies prior to reorganisation. As they tended to be practitioners who had worked their way up the ranks, they were familiar with the tasks practitioners faced on a daily basis (Coyle, 1984). What they lacked, because their employers had not provided the requisite training, were the managerial skills for handling massive resources within a large bureaucratic framework. The absence of adequate managerial training geared to enhancing women practitioners' skills in this area becomes even more critical in the purchaser–provider world of community care which demands sophisticated financial and budgetary knowledge. Appropriate training may enable more women to acquire skills relevant for managerial roles.

The entry of men managers without social work qualifications into the profession also coincided with the promotion of corporate management techniques in local authority decision-making (Ginsburg, 1979). Corporate management intensified the instrumental approach of social services managers and called for measures leading to greater financial and professional accountability. Social workers were asked to justify how they spent their time. Workload management and other techniques for controlling the labour force were borrowed from the sociology of work and private enterprises. These developments were intensified under 'contract government' when social work management was shaken up during the late 1980s, profoundly disrupting social workers' professional culture in their wake. The declining popularity of time-consuming and ineffectual psychodynamic and therapeutic approaches to social work led to the espousal of more tightly controlled and less involved forms of intervention. Rejecting a focus on the whole person, these sought to address narrowly defined needs in a limited time frame. Task-centred social work (TCSW) and contract social work became the methods management favoured. Social workers critical of therapeutic approaches' neglect of underlying problems, such as poverty and the disempowerment of 'clients', were also receptive to these (see Doel and Marsh, 1992).

Empowerment

Some academics and practitioners lauded TCSW for empowering 'clients' by securing their consent to a contract specifying activities to be undertaken by themselves and their workers (Doel and Marsh, 1992). This clarity of expectations is to be welcomed, but it can hardly be classed as empowerment. Contracts do not reduce the greater power of workers to shape these by accepting or rejecting suggestions made by the 'client'. Nor does TCSW acknowledge the impact of structural inequalities and forms of power outside the individual 'client's' capacity to directly influence through contractual negotiation, for example power stemming from organisational sources, resource constraints and legislative fiat.

Empowerment, according to Stuart Rees (1991) addresses structural inequalities. Barbara Solomon (1976) suggests empowerment involves a redefinition of the 'problem' to be tackled by the oppressed for they have been pathologised and problematised by social work processes which enforce their powerlessness. Thus, empowerment demands more than the 'client's' signature at the bottom of a contract which is driven by agency requirements.

Empowerment means that 'clients' are in a position to define their 'needs' and affect how social work agencies consider them. However, the question of who determines 'needs' is hotly contested. Professionals have differing opinions of what constitutes need; the government offers another version; 'clients' have their own; taxpayers provide additional perspectives. Agreement on what constitutes an acceptable 'need', which can be met through public provisions rather than being procured by the individual concerned independently through the private market, is not easy to achieve (Le Grand and Robinson, 1984). Although Doyal and Gough (1991) argue that 'human needs' are driven by economic exigencies, a situation encompassing divergent priorities among those involved in reaching a verdict makes the subject more complex than this. The problem is not only what is deemed affordable, but the ideological spin given by politicians and opinion formers in the media. Despite these tensions, social workers daily engage in responding to 'needs', whether these are identified by practitioners, a referring agency, a 'client', their agency, legislative fiat or government policy. Opportunities for professionals to empower 'clients' are severely circumscribed if TCSW is the main vehicle for achieving this.

Social work within the larger societal context

Social workers are charged with meeting the welfare needs of the population. The government gives the misleading impression that it provides the lion's share of services to those who need 'care' (Higgins, 1989). Most of society's caring work occurs within 'the family', primarily through the labour that women do 'for love' (Graham, 1983). For example, Higgins (1989) has worked out that in one area of care alone – elder care – the state makes provisions for only five per cent of the eligible population. The Family Policy Studies Centre has calculated that women provide £3.7 billion worth of home care for the over-75s free annually, compared to £928 million of actual government expenditure (FPSC, 1984). These figures reflect the position before community care was introduced. They are likely to have increased since then.

Women's hidden subsidy to the welfare state is considerable without their low-paid waged work being taken into account.

Until feminists identified the important role that domestic care has played in the provision of welfare resources, it had been taken for granted. To some extent, little has changed. Women who are not in the waged labour market do not get welfare credits for the unpaid caring work they do. After years of unwaged caring for children, elders or dependent adults, women still lack social security provisions covering their old age (Pascall, 1986). Similar problems arise when women leave marital relationships. The time spent servicing their husband's needs while he forged ahead with his career is not fully compensated when resources are divided after the dissolution of their union. Women now have better access to their partner's financial resources, including pension plans in some countries, for example Canada. However, women experience a drop of 75 per cent in their income when a marriage ends; men can expect a 45 per cent rise in theirs (Ruth, 1989).

The domestic economy of welfare is the invisible linchpin of welfare provisions in advanced capitalist societies. The state promotes policies drawing on women's taken-for-granted unpaid caring labour. Doing so without acknowledgement enables it to stretch welfare resources and ration eligibility to publicly funded services. That women shoulder such burdens as a 'labour of love' (Graham, 1983) indicates the range of pressures and interests guiding women's actions. Women's 'willing' participation in this process enables others to mobilise their labour, by making women's work serve others' purposes. Women personally lose out in such transactions through forgone opportunities (Ungerson, 1987). Their willingness to serve others may indicate their lack of sufficient power to strike a more equal bargain. This inequality perpetuates caring as an exploited form of labour.

The domestic model of welfare encapsulated in 'the family' model of service provision provides the prototype for public services. Thus, residential homes replicate 'family' relationships in institutional form. In them, women do the caring work which carries less status while men perform the more valued managerial tasks (Howe, 1986). Public institutions both mirror and reinforce a gendered division of labour which leaves women in a subordinate position.

The majority of black and white working-class people are not recipients of welfare services. Of that small, but significant proportion which is, many require personal social services for limited periods, usually during crises until they amass their own resources (Morris, 1994). While the image of large numbers of 'welfare scroungers' or 'welfare dependent' individuals is not borne out empirically (Morris, 1994), the myth of the 'dependency culture' is an important ideological artefact. It enables ministers who wish to reduce the state's role in providing these services to move with greater ease. And, it allows members of the public who lack alternative information to scapegoat 'scroungers' for the social ills present in industrial societies. Defining these as self-created woes destroys feelings of human solidarity with victim-survivors and makes it easier for individuals who do not require public welfare services to continue their lives uninterrupted by their concerns.

The personal social services have been developed to cater for the needs of a small minority of people 'in need' by those *not* 'in need'. Those *not* 'in need' have further divided those in need into 'deserving' and 'undeserving' categories. Moreover, those who might be 'in need' according to specified criteria can be excluded from receiving benefits on character grounds, as has happened historically to unmarried mothers (Sidel, 1986). Meanwhile, claimants considered salvageable by those in charge are enjoined to change their lifestyles to remain on the 'deserving' list. These coercive dynamics intensify the political and ideological sides of social work and mock its pretensions to neutrality and non-judgmentalness. Decisions about the worth of individuals and their eligibility for assistance are judgements. Not condemning people for being in this predicament is something else. Nonetheless, social workers attempt to distance themselves from the decisions they take by hiding behind bureaucratic procedures.

The 'founding mothers' of social work were clear they could only provide services for specific needy groups (Walton, 1975; Mowatt and Loch, 1961). The remainder of the population was expected to fend for itself. Except for a brief period after the Second World War when socialists put universal welfare provisions on the agenda, this has traditionally been the case. The thrust of Reaganism in the United States and Thatcherism in Britain are but modern variants of this old theme. Meeting the needs of the most needy is targeting 'the deserving' by any other name.

The increasing importance government ministers give family-based welfare provisions is part of an ideological shift seeking to withdraw the state from the welfare arena. Public services played an important role in war-ravaged Britain, for the state intervened when individuals could not pay to look after themselves and their families throughout their lives at a socially acceptable standard, that is, cover their own reproduction. Politicians then accepted that having state intervention on this front was one way of getting the economy going. This policy became the basis for the Keynsian welfare state which provided the consensus around which postwar social democracy flourished. The 'social compact' this represented was sundered by Thatcherism. In today's more competitive international context, the capitalist nation state is less interested in assisting the reproduction of well-paid workers in the old industrial heartlands. For manufacturing is in decline and a flexible, casualised labour force is the order of the day (Hutton, 1995). The attack on workers' hard won welfare rights – whether backed by state or private provisions through the workplace – indicates this change in emphasis. A disempowered labour movement, as the product of a carefully strate-gised policy of shifting the balance of power in workplace relations towards managers (Clarke *et al.*, 1994) makes it more difficult for workers to successfully mount counter-offensives. Employers have acquired further room for manoeuvre by relocating manufacturing enterprises in Third World countries lacking public welfare provisions or Eastern Europe where these are being rapidly disman-tled. These developments signify an indifference to the needs of working-class people who are at the sharp end of industrial decline. These companies' moves also perpetrate new forms of racism. The old racist idea that some people are less human than others remains central to the emerging world trade patterns. The new racism legiti-mates the inhumane treatment and exploitation of Third World and Eastern European peoples to the greatest degree that multinational corporations can get away with. And, it enables employers to ignore the protection of the environment and workers' health in the new sweatshops of the world, despite the lessons evident from experiences in the West (See Carson, 1963; Sklair, 1991).

The limited development of publicly funded welfare follows such policies. Implementing personal social services provisions on a universal basis is unnecessary if families and women pick up the tab. For in the absence of other arrangements, people will mobilise resources through kinship and friendship networks to ensure their survival (Stack, 1975). Spreading the costs of reproducing themselves across as wide a pool of others as they can access characterises many of the survival strategies people living in appalling social conditions develop. The creation of subcultures of support among homeless individuals also illustrates this (Jacobs and Popple, 1994).

The United States, as a major industrial power has avoided the development of a substantial public welfare state by relying on family and friendship cultures of assistance (see Stack, 1975) as well as market-based provisions. It has also furnished other countries with the model for dismantling publicly funded institutionalised provisions in favour of a residual welfare state as part of its economic and ideological strategies. The ideological drive has been realised through its influence in international financial institutions such as the World Bank and the International Monetary Fund (IMF). These organisations have insisted that economic restructuring which reduces the borrowing state's input into welfare facilities be a condition of obtaining loans (Kaseke, 1994; Sklair, 1991). The British welfare state was one of the first western democracies to experience these constraints. Back in 1976, the IMF insisted that Labour pull back from its electoral commitment to welfare subsidies aimed at removing the stigma from public provisions provided by the health, education, housing and social services departments.

The IMF's policies have traditionally subordinated social policy to economic exigencies (Kaseke, 1994). Yet, in Britain, the electorate of the time had voted for a radical extension of Labour's welfare programme. Electoral politics have proved a poor vehicle for promoting welfare rights. During the Thatcher era, this political contradiction was resolved through Thatcher's support for withdrawing the state from the welfare arena. Consequently, the subordination of social policies to economic ones has been intensified during her reign and John Major's. The struggle to overturn this equation has not succeeded to date, although small concessions have occasionally materialised, for example the freezing of child welfare benefits instead of their abolition in the late 1980s.

The debate around having social policies determined by human needs rather than economic exigencies has yet to capture the public's imagination. Culpitt (1992) argues that as an unintended consequence of market discourse in a market-driven climate, talks about citizenship rights based on moral or altruistic motivations will be rejected because these are identified with weakness. Only those who are successful in market terms capture people's attention. Viewed in this light, we should not be surprised that social workers have been subjected to such an onslaught in the press. They are condemned for acting to protect children from sexual abuse, as happened in Cleveland where they were labelled a 'nasty, authoritarian bunch' with little respect for parents' rights (see Brewer and Lait, 1980; Bell, 1987); and damned if they do not prevent children from being killed by challenging parental declarations about the well-being of their children. In Culpitt's (1992) terms, these social workers have failed because they have not given up their altruistic values to focus instead on unacceptable flaws in human nature. This would mean eschewing 'client' self-determination and getting 'tough'. The altruism which has guided the British welfare state in the past (Titmuss, 1970) is far removed from today's market-oriented doctrines.

Social workers have not divulged their detailed knowledge of the havoc market discipline wreaks in individual and family lives excluded from purchasing its goods and services. Traditional professional ideologies confirm those not wishing to do so by legitimating the belief that such action is political and beyond the remit of neutral professionals. Social workers who challenge such views lack the financial and organisational resources to promote alternative ideologies. Telling traditional colleagues that in not acting they are behaving politically is unlikely to deter them from pursuing their stance. They will interpret the comment as either a meaningless statement or their colleagues peddling their ideology again. Traditional professionalism, with its attendant division of the world into binary dyads, cocoons them against receiving other messages.

Yet, information that social workers collect on a case-by-case basis can be crucial in opening new areas of debate about citizenship rights. It can also be used to pose awkward questions about the direction of public policy. To what extent can societies that are losing their industrial base – a resource that is unlikely to return – ignore the suffering and hardship of people who, having been excluded from the economic oxygen of the marketplace, cannot participate in society's political decision-making processes and social life? Until these people become socially included, social workers must raise public consciousness about their plight and work with them to free up their talents and energies to create a better life for themselves and their children. Otherwise, the numbers of excluded people will continue to rise and legitimate the unacceptable face of civil society. Sociological social work from an anti-racist feminist perspective yields important intellectual tools for assisting practitioners in this process. It equips them with the theoretical concepts for challenging and transcending 'practice wisdoms' which are constrained by the institutional parameters within which social work is currently located.

Conclusions

The institutional parameters of social work provide the means whereby the stability of social work practice can be maintained over time. These include organisational, legislative and professional constraints. Constraints do not have to operate in conservative fashion by controlling 'client' aspirations and demands. Feminist social work has provided an alternative paradigm which has demonstrated that institutions can promote rather than hinder 'client' well-being.

5

Care and Control Dynamics in Caring Relationships

Throughout social work's history, practitioners and policy-makers have failed to agree the balance to be struck between its controlling dimension and its caring one. In recent years, (social) control has become a dirty word in the minds of practitioners. The literature identifies the negative effects of social control on social workers and 'clients' (Corrigan and Leonard, 1978 Parry *et al.*, 1979). This skews 'client' needs by squeezing them to fit the resources available. Rationing via eligibility criteria becomes one way of achieving this. For some practitioners, this constitutes an immoral form of practice proscribed by their professional ethics.

Social control has also been employed to blame 'clients' for their predicament. Pathologising those at the receiving end of unequal social relations holds them responsible for their situation and obviates investigations about the role social structures play in creating inequality. Moreover, people who internalise such pathology are unable to challenge social injustice and inequality. By internalising society's social dicta, individuals make them their own. These become normative, and guide individual behaviour to be consistent with them. This reduces the likelihood of 'clients' questioning their position or seeking new solutions to their problems. The actions of those rejecting socially accepted norms undermine this dynamic. People's behaviour indicates that they both internalise and reject social norms. That is, individuals are constantly choosing which norms they will adhere to. Their choices will take a number of different factors into account. These include not only the dominant norms, but the constraints they face and other options open to them.

Control is seen as the unpleasant side of social work. Practitioners suggest that enforcing social control or 'exercising their authority' brings unpalatable elements into their relationship with 'clients' (Langan and Lee, 1989; Bolger *et al.*, 1981; Davies, 1991). It is something that is not talked about or else is shied away from. However, there are situations in which control over others is desirable, for example protecting children from sexual abuse. Securing the evidence, charging an offender and bringing him before the courts may be unpleasant, but it is undeniably the 'right' thing to do.

The decision to be made is not always so obvious. Social control can operate at very esoteric levels, like reinforcing sexism by endorsing women's roles as carers when they ask for assistance in altering these and perpetuating racism by not enquiring about the lack of interpreters in the office to communicate with non-English speaking residents (Oakley and Williams, 1994).

Caring is associated with the idealistic dimension of social work: its commitment to providing people with the help and support they need. Reality has not been clear cut on this issue. 'Clients' have difficulty asserting their needs and seeing them being fulfilled (Oakley and Williams, 1994; Doyal and Gough, 1991). They have had to argue convincingly to get their definition of needs given priority over or even equal worth with that pronounced by policy-makers and practitioners. The state has not accepted responsibility for meeting people's needs for formal care, preferring to respond mainly to those for whom family care is unavailable (Warner, 1994; Higgins, 1989). This tendency has been accentuated in recent years as privatisation of the welfare state accelerates.

Caring driven by a control function aimed at delegitimating 'client' demands or excluding certain groups from eligibility produces residual services which are stigmatised, and stigmatising for recipients. Questioning the appropriateness of this response requires an open debate about the kind of social services people are entitled to as a right in an advanced democratic capitalist society which endorses social inclusion and integration. Having the decision made by default via politicians, who can afford to purchase services or count on women partners or relatives providing them for free, is unacceptable.

There is little relish for such debate. The neo-liberal economic regimes ushered in by Thatcher in Britain and Reagan in the United States have skewed the public debate in one direction – keeping the state out of people's private lives. This division is artificial. As C Wright Mills (1970) indicated, it is easy to talk about the sanctity of the private sphere if one is speaking from a position of comfortable privilege. But as feminist scholars have shown, much happens in private lives that is a matter of public concern. Physical violence and sexual abuse are only two areas which demonstrate that private woes cannot be kept within the confines of 'the family' (Gamarnikov *et al.*, 1983; Showstack-Sassoon, 1987).

Another instance which evokes this issue is challenging the double burden women carry. Women do not have freedom from caring functions – housework, looking after children and caring for dependent relatives (Oakley, 1974, 1980; Walby, 1990). Research has shown that while women are expected to work in the office and the home, similar expectations are not held for men (Oakley, 1974; Showstack-Sasson, 1987; Walby, 1990). The question is, 'Who cares for the countless women caught in this situation?' Private woes such as these must become public concerns. Redefining the boundaries between the private and the public is a feminist project. Feminists have brought such issues into the open by asking 'who cares for the carers?' (CNA, 1992; Oakley and Williams, 1994).

Feminist research and action has challenged the traditional portrayal of caring work in sociological texts as in Parson's work (Parson, 1957). These have concealed the specific experiences of women carers and denied the reality of the difficult choices they make between caring for others and self-fulfilment, whether through marriage, having children or acquiring a career (Bonny, 1984; Ungerson, 1987, CNA, 1992). Women have felt obliged to undertake caring responsibilities whether they personally wish to or not. Ignoring women's realities is a form of social control. It deligitimates these experiences and discourages the questioning of assumed responsibilities rooted in a sexist division of labour. Feminists have, therefore, exposed caring as socially valuable work (Walby, 1990) and highlighted its political nature (Ungerson, 1987).

Feminist sociological social work examines these complex matters from the perspective of those disadvantaged by traditional definitions of privacy and identifies the position of those privileged by them. Its aim is to reduce the inequalities between the two groups through social action which brings matters into the public arena. Power differentials which enable certain definitions of privacy to prevail are brought into the open and challenged. This redefines the issue to promote the interests of the disadvantaged person, for example the victim-survivor in sexual abuse, and demand that action be taken to safeguard their well-being and repair the damage (see Driver and Droisen, 1989).

Similar dilemmas about the balance between care and control, the public and the private, and who draws the line between them occur in other helping professions such as medicine and education. Early feminist initiatives seeking to redraw professional boundaries focused on health issues and the unresponsive methods doctors used when working with women patients. They demanded that doctors listen to women, reorient their styles to empower women and respond to their needs in caring ways (Ruzek, 1978, 1986; Frankfort, 1972). When doctors refused to respond to the message, women created the women's health movement and developed alternative health care services which did not require expensive technological interventions (Foster, 1989). These efforts revealed that many of those being used were not only unnecessary, but positively harmful to women (Ehrenreich and English, 1979; Frankfort, 1972; Ruzek, 1978, 1986).

Social workers have colluded with assumptions that hold women responsible for caring work by exerting pressure on daughters (in-law) to provide support that social services are either unable or unwilling to offer (see Hughes and Mtezuka, 1989). At times, social workers have acted in sexist ways even when a son (in-law) has been more readily available than the daughter (in-law) either by personal preference or domicile.

Besides locking women into caring functions unnecessarily, such actions deny men the opportunity to become carers and develop the nurturing sides of their personalities. That some men are willing to do this is witnessed by the small, but significant proportion of spouses who care for sick wives and young men who care for sick parents (Nissel and Bonnerjea, 1982; Ungerson, 1987). The assumption that *one* gender, usually the woman, is exclusively responsible for *all* of society's caring is not borne out by recent research investigating different kinds of carers. Nor is this assumption desirable from an egalitarian feminist perspective. Both men and women have nurturing potential (Walby, 1990). Enforcing the sexist premise that men cannot do such work is a subtle form of social control which denies both men and women the right to decide how and when to express their caring capacities. Thus, feminists have broadened the debate on caring to argue that it is the responsibility of both men and women. Moreover, feminists have maintained that people should have choices about whether they receive home-based care (care in the community) or institutional care (see Finch, 1984; Bonny, 1984; Finch and Groves, 1983).

Feminists have criticised community care for exploiting the unpaid work of women and other family members (Finch and Groves, 1983). Instead of being a fully resourced option which keeps people in contact with friends and relatives in their home base, it has become a cheap option promoted by a state intent on cutting caring provisions (Dobson, 1994). Although the concept has been around for some time (Titmuss, 1968), it became enforced government policy when cuts in the welfare state and privatised services flourished (see Wistow *et al.*, 1994).

Janet Finch (1984) has argued that institutional care can be attractive rather than of poor quality. Young people in foster care support her view. Through the National Association of Young People in Care (NAYPIC), they have insisted that residential care is preferable to other forms of care at various points in their lives. Marginalised people dependent on public services should not be denied the right to a choice about their placement if they are to receive responsive individual care. This right is currently enjoyed by privileged people who can purchase the services they desire. People who argue they do not want to contribute towards welfare provisions required by poor people ignore the fact that many of the facilities they 'purchase' are subsidised through the state, that is, 'the taxpayer' – which includes marginalised people who are not using them. This subsidy is usually hidden as tax breaks or infrastructure provisions, for example access roads. They rationalise their position by disregarding the interconnectedness between payers and users; and the changing roles that the 'same' individual can occupy as they progress through their lifecycle. Services that endorse principles of social justice require high quality universal provisions to be available to all at the point of need. They are paid for collectively through a truly progressive income tax. Sadly, these principles have yet to be accepted in the sphere of the personal social services. But developing such provisions is a prerequisite to the elimination of structural inequalities in life chances.

Decisions taken by social workers can alter the balance between community and residential care provisions. Warwickshire Social Services Department was among the first to abolish residential care for children as inappropriate and costly (Baldwin *et al.*, 1993). It was not long before social workers discovered that a small number of children needed residential care. These had go out of county because local provisions were lacking.

This option created additional problems. Children ended up in facilities far removed from home, making it difficult for family and friends to visit. This jeopardised their relationships with close others, a loss which intensifies children's feelings of isolation and disloca- tion. Moreover, children, particularly older ones, who positively opted for residential care were refused their choice. Social workers felt frustrated by being denied access to necessary facilities. Cost rather than need or professional assessment became the principle guiding policy-makers (Oakley and Williams, 1994; Culpitt, 1992).

These developments indicate how day-to-day routines with 'clients' are determined outside the social work relationship by people not responsible for doing the work. Users' powerlessness in influencing service provision is paralleled by practitioners inability to shape services in ways they feel professionally appropriate. Social workers' loss of professional autonomy in decision-making in the publicly funded welfare state becomes a major source of inefficiency and frustration (see Carter *et al.*, 1992). A lot of time can be fruitlessly consumed chasing limited placements. Poor information flows about occupancy rates in residential provisions in other parts of the country exacerbate this problem.

I am not arguing that bureaucratic decision-makers be replaced by professional decision-makers. Rather, I envisage all parties with an interest in social work having an equal say in the kinds of provisions that are created. These include: politicians, employers, academics, practitioners, informal carers and users. Ensuring that these parties have an equal say may require that each be treated differently. For example, users will need access to information and other resources to thoroughly develop their case on par with politicians and employers who can take such resourcing for granted. Greater accountability to those who are at the receiving end of service provision is an important democratic criterion which needs to be incorporated into the decision- making structures operating within social services departments.

Reinforcing oppression through social work intervention

Social workers can enforce oppressive social relations when amassing resources for their 'clients'. Their response to older 'clients' can illustrate how such processes work in practice.

Jane was an 83-year-old Afro-Caribbean woman with severe mobility problems caused by arthritis and angina. She had a bright, alert mind and wished to remain in her own home for the remainder of her life. But, she needed assistance with her shopping, cooking and some aspects of her personal hygiene.

Jane had three children. Her eldest, a son named Bill, lived about four miles away from her. He was a manager in a branch of a well-known food chain. Her second child was a son called Alan. He lived about 100 miles away and taught at a grammar school. Her youngest child, Lisa, lived thirty miles away. She ran her own designer studio and had two children. Neither Bill nor Alan had children although they were both married.

One icy winter day, Jane slipped when collecting her daily pint. She broke her arm and fractured her leg. She spent some time in hospital but, when it was time for her to go home, there was no one available to support her.

The white woman social worker who took up the referral saw Jane in hospital and took her details. She was extremely busy, with a workload heavily weighted down with child abuse referrals. Having asked Jane about her children's availability, she decided that Lisa, as the self-employed person with the highest degree of flexibility should help support her mother. Social services were prepared to offer Jane three meals a week through the Meals-on-Wheels Service.

This case exposes the taken-for-granted assumptions about women's place in society, particularly regarding their caring role. If one used objective criteria such as employment status and distance from her mother's house, Lisa would not have been the obvious choice. Rather, the social worker's decision conveys assumptions about whose job she deems less important. A counter argument is that, as a self-employed professional, Lisa has less flexibility than her brothers. Working for large firms, they might get time off without incurring a financial penalty. In any case, flexibility should be determined through discussion and agreement with the people concerned, not arrived at on the basis of stereotypes in the social worker's mind. It may well be that all three of Jane's children would like to support their mother and might have suggested alternative solutions had they been asked.

That a woman social worker reaches these conclusions indicates how far women have internalised expectations about their own roles as society's nurturers and carers. The social worker's own conditions of employment left much to be desired. It is clear that the department placed little emphasis on working with older people. Social workers who juggle the conflicting priorities this engenders collude with institutionalised forms of oppression. From a feminist perspective, the question of why the social worker was so overworked would be examined in the light of how gender issues interacted with inadequate resourcing. The lack of appropriate facilities for the care of older women would also be considered in gendered terms. Institutional sexism was taking a variety of forms in this particular locale. Both the social worker's and 'client's' suffering would have to be addressed for the ensuing practice to be substantially improved.

Moreover, the social worker did not identify the relevance of other social divisions. One of these is age. The social worker did not initiate a facilitative discussion with Jane. Rather, she went to see her with fixed ideas based on what social services could offer and proceeded to work within that framework. The infantilising of older people – that is, denying them the right to make their own choices by treating them as dependent children – is a recurrent theme in social work practice (Leonard, 1984; Scrutton, 1990). Also, she colluded with institutional ageism which allows providers to avoid taking responsibility for making appropriate facilities available to older people. 'Race' is another social division which is ignored. The social worker did not explore how an Afro-Caribbean woman might want to use her relationship with her children and others within her broader community networks to get support.

The case study below examines oppression in family work.

CASE STUDY

Sal is a 32-year-old black woman with two children, Andrea aged five and Alice aged three. She is also pregnant. Sal is in the process of seeking a divorce from her partner, a white man called Pete. Pete is an engineer in a car factory. Sal has been having a relationship with a black woman named Elsie for the past eighteen months and they want to set up house together, keeping the children with them.

Pete opposes her having custody of the children and is determined to challenge her in court. He is not interested in the child Sal is carrying because he does not believe it is his. However, he is convinced that she should not be allowed to keep that child either, as she is an 'unfit' mother.

The white male probation officer writing the Court Report has great difficulty amassing the information he requires. Conflicting demands are made by both partners. Sal is adamant she is capable of caring for the children and offering them a good home. She will not work to look after them as she has done with Pete. Her new partner, Elsie, will be earning their livelihood as an accountant with a major firm. Elsie's relationship with the children is a good one and so is Sal's.

Pete gets on well with the children. He has helped Sal care for them in the past, including for days on end while she attended summer school.

The probation officer thinks both Sal and Pete are good parents. But he needs to choose between the two. He decides to back Pete's application for a residential order enabling Andrea and Alice to live with him. Both parents will keep their parental rights. As far as the unborn child is concerned, given the question about its paternity, he feels it may be better for the Court to consider its fate once the child is born. However, he feels that if Pete can make arrangements for the baby to be cared for, it could become subject of an order in his favour. He feels that that the three siblings should be kept together.

This case represents another bungled intervention. The white probation officer is responding to both Sal and Pete on the basis of stereotypes rather than looking at the situation in creative ways which do not pit father and mother against each other and divide the children's feelings for both parents. His failure to apply the criterion of the best interests of the child to each of the children means he has failed to consider the nature of the relationship *young* children need with their parents. This is particularly evident in the case of the unborn child where he is prepared to take it away from its mother, soon after birth. Yet, the mother may be breastfeeding! Neither has he adequately evaluated Pete's ability to provide long-term care for the children. Looking after them for a brief period while the mother is away on a training course is less strenuous than constant, long-term care. The operative word in this context is 'helped'. He helped Sal look after them rather than taking full responsibility for their daily care. The probation officer also does not ask whether Pete will continue his job and who will care for the children while he works. Will the care of a substitute carer be as good as that currently being provided by the mother? This question has not been addressed.

The poor weighting he gives to Sal's mothering abilities are more an indication of his homophobia than a thorough assessment of what she has to offer the children. The degree to which racism enters his thoughts is more difficult to ascertain, but it is highly likely that the fact that both women are black means he doesn't quite accept their ability to provide a comfortable middle-class home for the children. In any case, he has shown no interest in meeting Elsie to examine her views on her prospective role. It is almost as if she doesn't exist.

The example below focuses on women with disabilities.

CASE STUDY

Cressie was a 21-year-old white woman with severe spinal injuries from a car accident. She was bound to a wheelchair and her face badly scarred. There was little that could be done about her spinal injuries, but she was on the waiting list for plastic surgery regarding her scars.

When her long-awaited appointment arrived, Cressie was asked to report to the hospital the night before. While she was in bed, a white male orderly slipped into her room and sexually assaulted her. Cressie was mortified. She did not know if she had simply had a bad dream. Nothing made sense and she became very fearful of being in the room alone. She felt unable to discuss her predicament with anyone and went ahead with her treatment on the prescribed day. That night the orderly returned again. This time, he had sexual intercourse with her. Cressie felt the pain between her legs, but still wasn't sure that it wasn't all a bad dream. How could anyone do this to her?

A few months later, Cressie discovered she was pregnant. She felt ashamed and on her own. The nurses and doctors who provided the antenatal care included both white and black doctors. They made it clear that they could not believe that she could be sexually active. Moreover, they did their best to convince her that she should terminate her pregnancy.

Cressie agonised over the decision which was thrust upon her. In the end, she decided that, although she now knew she had been raped, she would go ahead and have the child. The disbelief in the eyes of the doctors and nurses hurt her dreadfully. No one offered her social work support and no one took an interest in what would happen to her or the baby. She felt as if she were being punished for thinking that she of all people could be a mother.

This case reveals the lack of sexual and reproductive rights endured by women with disabilities (Morris, 1991). Cressie was silenced by her oppression as a disabled woman who was deprived of the control of her body, abused by others and denied the assistance she required. Moreover, a criminal offence had been committed, but this remained unacknowledged. As the assault had not been reported, the offender would be free to strike again. Other vulnerable women might be engendered by him.

Enabling relationships

Each of the last three case studies reveals the failure of the helping professionals to accord the 'client(s)' involved dignity, respect and an appropriate service. As a result, poor practice ensued and the practitioners were unable to address issues around social divisions and structural inequalities. Moreover, they were unable to respond to the 'clientws'' specific needs. Hence, they perpetrated oppression at the personal, institutional and cultural levels. Meanwhile, the 'client' in each particular case failed to receive either an appropriate service or see justice done in their particular cases.

Professionals can become involved in empowering 'clients' through careful interventions which take users' perspectives as their starting point. Empowerment is not a 'good' which can be 'given' to 'clients'. Indeed, Oliver (1990) suggests that the most social workers can do is stop disempowering people through their practice. Empowerment is something people do for themselves. While I accept the note of caution in Oliver's advice, he provides an incomplete view of empowerment. Empowerment is a process. As process, it is enacted through relationships with others. In the 'client' – worker relationship, this includes both practitioner and user. Social workers and other helping professionals can play an enabling role in the empowerment of others even if, traditionally, they have not done so. This is done by encouraging rather than discouraging individuals' belief in themselves and their capacity to act on their own behalf. In other words, empowerment is an enabling relationship each person negotiates in and through interaction with others. Its empowering potential is released when professionals treat users with respect and dignity, increase their self-confidence and enable them to exercise power in controlling their own affairs.

Full empowerment cannot occur if gender, 'race', age, sexual orientation, disability and other social divisions are not addressed directly. Stereotypical responses full of condescension have to be avoided. These represent control which, disguised as caring, reinforces control and disables people. Empowering caring tips the balance of power towards 'clients' and releases new opportunities for action. To achieve this, social workers have to establish open and honest communication with 'clients' and obtain information about their particular experiences of oppression from them. Treating a 'client' as part of a category, for example a black disabled woman, is inadequate. Categorisation provides useful background information for contextualising what this woman might say. But, at the end of the day, the woman is a unique individual in her own right. Understanding *her* biography must become an important part of the data collection process in which social workers engage. For social workers in the business of responding to the individual in their social context – or as Younghusband (1978) put it, 'the person-in-the-situation', such an approach is essential for enacting sensitive and relevant practice. Every person is entitled to the best service that society can provide through the agents it entrusts to deliver services on its behalf.

Policies endorsing equality of treatment and outcomes are lacking in the case studies presented above. The answer to this problem is not the development of a formal policy which everyone ignores, as happened in each of them. The close scrutiny of everyday practices and routines is an important complement to appropriate policies. To scrutinise practice effectively, people's work needs to be monitored. A key purpose of such monitoring is to improve standards. The ensuing findings should guide staff development and training thereby linking it to the realisation of this goal. The process whereby the quality of an individual's practice is improved should also reflect a sensitive approach to the task of changing people's cognitive and behavioural patterns.

The opportunity for people to learn freely and openly how to move their practice in anti-oppressive directions is the backbone of this approach. Only when the educational process has been exhausted and practitioners continue their poor performance, should disciplinary means be adopted. Even then, it is vital to ensure that the procedures used in following through on this are fair and just. Even people accused of oppressing others have the right to be treated with dignity and respect. Otherwise, those handling the allegations will be diminished in their humanity through their mistreatment of others. Implementing this aspiration can be difficult. Investigating claims of poor practice requires careful work in which support systems are needed for those making the allegation, those facing the charges and those undertaking the investigation. Such work is slow, time-consuming and expensive. Oppressing people is costly too. But different people pay the price. Resources misused in oppressing others could be better utilised. Working to empower people is to work for the eradication of oppression and a valid use of public resources. Its final pay-off is that all people can develop their talents to maximum potential.

Conclusions

Social workers are constantly juggling the interests of society, employers and 'clients'. Since many of these are in contradiction with each other, social workers need to be fully informed of research findings, theoretical developments and practice initiatives which can lead to better practice. Discovering ways through the resultant maze which are compatible with the overriding concern to empower 'clients' requires practitioners to be critical, reflective and competent.

This requires a balance to be struck between the caring side of social work and its controlling one. In striking this balance, 'clients' need to be fully involved in decisions about their lives. Otherwise their interests will be sacrificed on the alter of professional and bureaucratic priorities.

6

Professionalism and Training

Professional ideology, values and ethics are critical in the reproduction of particular kinds of professionals. These give an indication of what the profession stands for, identify the principles guiding practitioners' work, enforce standards and generate forms of social control that are internal to the profession.

Traditional professions such as law and medicine have developed powerful associations, for example the British Medical Association and the American Medical Association to:

- define the profession – its boundaries and remit
- control access to it
- uphold its standards
- authorise those who can practise within it
- eject those deemed unsuitable for it
- promote new developments.

Control over the professions' activities and entry into its ranks enables doctors and lawyers to police themselves, direct their training and socialisation processes, and keep a tight reign on professional developments (Heraud, 1979). In subscribing to the association's edicts, members are assured professional standing and the high power, status and remuneration which accompany it (Hugman, 1991b).

Power, status and authority in professional bodies have been organised along elitist and hierarchical lines (Hugman, 1991b; Hatton and Nugent, 1993). Thus, powerful professional associations act like closed shops which determine how one's livelihood is organised and services delivered. Moreover, their control over practising members ensures a uniformity of standards and introduces a certain predictability in what a professional will or can do. The power of such organisations is immense. In some instances, their power has been so extensive that governments attempting to radically alter their direction have had little option but to abolish them. This happened in Russia when the Bolsheviks wishing to shake up the medics abrogated the Pirogov Society (Field, 1989; Sidel and Sidel, 1977), and in China under Mao when the Chinese Communist Party closed down the Chinese Medical Association (Lampton, 1977; Sidel and Sidel, 1982). In other cases, powerful professional groupings have prevented governments from introducing new policies, as the American Medical Association did when it prevented Franklin Delano Roosevelt from initiating a public health care scheme (Lampton, 1977).

Social work in Britain has not reached such heights of power for a number of reasons. To begin with, social workers have not generally aspired to organise themselves as mimics of the medical profession, even though they desire full professional status. The reasons for adopting this path are explored below. In the course of this exploration, I draw comparisons with developments in other countries.

Elitism versus democratism in a profession

Who controls the social work profession?

British social workers have been struggling to acquire fully fledged professional standing for their occupation for over a century (Walton, 1975). However, they have been torn between a desire to subscribe to the controlling requirements imposed on traditional professions and their wish to allow open access to theirs. This latter approach reflects an attempt to redefine professionalism on a more democratic footing. The 'founding mothers' of social work sought to secure a sound 'scientific' base for the profession – an aspiration requiring high quality university-based specific training which would exclude those not so trained from practising it; and retain an open recruitment base which enabled anyone wishing to enter its ranks to do so (Walton, 1975). Their commitment to both being open and straddling a scientific paradigm has created a contradiction which lies at the centre of social work. Some critics have characterised this as the profession's 'woolly thinking' and failure to adhere to professional standards (see Sibeon, 1991). I prefer to recast their vision as an attempt to provide an alternative professional paradigm to the prevailing masculist oriented ones. Rather than excluding people to enhance their own professional expertise and power as men did, these women wanted to involve those they worked with in their professional activities. Valuing 'client' self-determination can be interpreted in this light.

Social work, a caring profession rooted in work which women have traditionally undertaken at home on the basis of close relationships with those they care for, has a workforce composed primarily of women. Callahan (1994) has argued that social work became a profession developed by women because men were not interested, so heavily was it identified with 'women's work'. Its weakness in the eyes of men became a strength in those of women. By providing women, particularly white middle-class Victorian women, with the opportunity to develop a profession in their own image, women could follow aspirations differing from those endorsed by medicine which had been collared by men who deliberately barred women from being trained to join them (see Oakley and Williams, 1994; Ehrenreich and English, 1979). This strategy had the distinct advantage of enabling women to create the parameters of their profession without having to compete directly with or exclude men.

Unfortunately, women in Victorian England, having limited access to resources in their own right, had to rely on male patronage and support to secure their ideas (Walton, 1975). Getting men to back their plans meant that women could not simply get on with the job of creating a profession to their liking. They had to convince men to put money into their deliberations. Doing so required compromises about what was an acceptable professional activity and what was not. That is, it necessitated a negotiation of contingent realities. Neither existing paradigms nor the role models offered by the longer established professions could be completely ignored. Consequently, the fruition of the dream that was realised by women who wanted to use their talents in the service of others in a formal, systematic and recognised way, was not precisely what they had started out with (Walton, 1975; Callahan, 1994).

Furthermore, the state became involved in this project as the holder of massive resources the 'founding mothers' wanted to access. To realise their ambitions, the fledgling profession needed to establish its credentials. This required: a clear vision of its purpose; an identifiable clientele; knowledge of its 'client' group; an articulated theory; a methodology of intervention; a statement of its training requirements; and legitimation from the broader society.

Sadly, the act of specifying these requirements turned them into contested issues. The search for financial backing intensified the controversies that interventions in peoples' lives usually generates. At this point, the different views about the domain of knowledge and practice which social work could legitimately call its own, proved problematic. Although people agreed that helping others was an important aim of social work, they disagreed about who might receive assistance and how. Much depended on the protagonists' analyses of society and their prescriptions for curing its maladies (Walton, 1975; Parry *et al.*, 1979). The key groups struggling to acquire the power to define the remit of the profession fell into two camps: the social activists, and the individual interventionists.

The social activists stressed organising people in their communities to address pressing issues evident in abundance. These included poverty, bad housing, inadequate sanitation, lack of education and limited employment prospects (Rowbotham, 1986, 1994). Many of their interventions were advocacy oriented. The individual interventionists were more concerned with introducing changes in individual behaviour. Poverty was seen to stem from poor morals, lack of discipline in spending habits, fear of hard work and unwillingness to learn. Moreover, they maintained that poor people's problems were exacerbated by the indifferent hygiene, large families, and criminal tendencies inherent in them (Rowbotham, 1994). This latter view was later popularised by Keith Joseph as Secretary of State at the Department of Health and Social Security when he defined it as the 'cycle of deprivation' transmitted from generation to generation (Coffield *et al.*, 1980).

These two trends have co-existed in social work, albeit uneasily, to the present day. Except for brief interludes such as the period when the Community Development Projects flourished, the dominant direction for the profession has been set by the individual interventionists. Differences of opinion occur within this grouping and, at times, the boundary between individual intervention and social action becomes more blurred. Nonetheless, the tension between these two divergent forms of intervention, and the dominance of the latter in social work *qua* social work, led community workers to disassociate themselves from the social work profession and create their own accreditation body and professional groupings (see

Baldock, 1982; Curno, 1978; Craig *et al.*, 1982; Ohri *et al.*, 1982; Jacobs and Popple, 1994).

A major success of the individual interventionists was to secure their position by bringing together various disparate groups to form the Charity Organisation Society (COS) in the late 19th century, thereby bypassing the social activists and those supporting the settlement movement. The COS established casework methodology as the major vehicle for carrying out social work intervention with individuals (Mowatt and Loch, 1961; Walton, 1975; Parry *et al.*, 1979). Focusing on individuals, this methodology contained a reformative element in that some social engineering was deemed necessary for resolving problems individuals encountered. These tended to be associated with society taking responsibility for items that could not reasonably be assumed by individuals, for example providing clean water and sanitation (Lewis, 1952; Chadwick, 1965).

COS was committed to establishing social work as a fully recognised profession with casework as its distinguishing methodology. It also acknowledged that several disciplines could contribute to the acquisition of academic credentials. Despite their fear of it as 'contaminating knowledge', these included sociology. Indeed, the first school of social work established in England was in the Department of Sociology at the London School of Economics (Bosanquet, 1900; Walton, 1975). Its individualist framework for intervention notwithstanding, COS sought high quality training within the academy as the way forward for the social work profession.

This aim has yet to be realised. It is still possible to obtain a social work qualification in Britain without training in a university-based programme. Unfortunately, as I argue later, programmes currently residing within universities and acting as standard bearers for the profession (HEFCE, 1995) are in danger of being closed by the government's threats to move social work training into the workplace. Probation has already had such proposals put forward in the Dews Report and the Home Secretary's response to it (Sone, 1995).

COS's other aim – launching a research-based profession, has met with even less success. Social work research is being carried out in university departments, by government bodies and independent institutes. But this is not necessarily being undertaken by people who either know, understand or support social work. Consequently, the definition of research problems and the methodologies chosen for their investigation have lacked a specific professional social work dimension.

A discipline with a specific remit

Social work continues struggling to establish its status as a discipline with a specific remit, despite having identified its own area of work. Securing its discipline status – by defining a certain area of knowledge (theory and practice) as uniquely its own – is critical to social work's goal of becoming an acknowledged profession with prestige and power. Some academics insist that social work is not a discipline (Sibeon, 1991; Davies, 1991) because, like a magpie, it collects bits and pieces from other subjects and adapts them to its own purposes. This view places unrealistic expectations on social work which are not applied to other disciplines. Sociology, psychology, economics, have their own knowledge base and draw on others without losing their status as disciplines. Sociology has had to argue quite hard to establish its position as a social science. Its victory is occasionally contested.

As discipline boundaries are becoming increasingly fluid, a question arises about the expected purity in drawing limits around social work's area of jurisdiction and competence. To what extent does posing this demand reflect men academics' intellectual arrogance in requiring standards of a discipline associated with women and 'women's work' which they would not dream of imposing on themselves? Moreover, disciplines are anticipated to have an impact beyond their immediate circle and reflect understandings which have relevance beyond the confines of a closed professional elite. Sociology has made its theoretical insights part of everyday analysis (Giddens, 1987). Social work has done likewise and lent many of its terms to the common lexicon – elder abuse, child protection, battered child, child sexual abuse, to name a few. Social work has its own theories and practice which have percolated into public consciousness and permeated its own areas of expertise.

As I demonstrated in the Introduction, the specific remit of social work is working with individuals, and groups and communities to enhance their contribution to society and ability to take control of their lives. Straddling both individual and societal relationships, this locates social work as a discipline, firmly within the social sciences. Developing the theories, methodologies and forms of practice for achieving this is a multi-faceted goal of social work as a discipline.

I argue that social work is both a discipline in its own right and an interdisciplinary one drawing on others to develop its own theories and practice. These focus on the 'person-in-the-situation' and forms of practice appropriate to intervening in other people's lives (Kendall, 1978). Social work theory and practice must be an integral part of each other (Parsloe, 1984). However, there is no simple relationship between the two. In some situations, theory development leads practice; in others it lags behind it. The differentiated impact on theory and practice emanates from the highly ideological nature of social work and the tasks practitioners are expected to perform. Research should be conducted to bolster developments in both theory and practice (Munday, 1972).

Since social work is about people intervening in the affairs of others with particular views about what life is about and how it should be lived, it is a highly political activity. Politics covers how individuals negotiate power with others regardless of the forms their relationships take. Social work is highly political in another aspect too. Society has a stake in what social workers do or don't do, making it political in a societal sense. This includes electoral politics as the expression of the vested interests of society at large, thereby giving any member of the lay public the right to express an opinion about social work. Being highly implicated in electoral politics, social work is vulnerable to political dictats in a way that other social science disciplines are not. Social work is also more politically vulnerable because it is a discipline which is associated with women, whose social power and access to resources are limited. Its structural weakness is further amplified by its failure to develop a powerful professional association which can defend its own partisan interests. For such an organisation to remain true to the principles of egalitarian social work, it would need to fully involve service users.

British social workers have formed their own professional organisations, but there has not been one which has commanded the support of the entire profession. This diversity has been a strength insofar as it has enabled a plurality of views about the social work task to persist. It has also been a weakness subjecting British social workers to more governmental control than would have otherwise been the case.

Professional power

Only one part of the social work profession, the probation service traditionally dominated by men, has sustained a powerful professional organisation over a lengthy period of time. The National Association of Probation Officers (NAPO) has represented its interests for over 80 years. NAPO has been able to exert a greater influence on the shape of the probation service by representing probation officers with one voice and lobbying ministers fairly forcefully. For example, it successfully challenged a retrospective reduction in grants to sponsored trainees. NAPO and other bodies with a stake in probation training have also unanimously rejected the Dews Report which seeks to uncouple probation training's link with higher education.

Social services workers have formed a number of different organisations. Some of these flourished only briefly. The British Association of Social Workers (BASW) and the trade union UNISON are now the key bodies for social workers. They have found it much harder to defend the interests of users, workers or trainees. It is unclear whether the recent merger of three trade unions NALGO, NUPE and COHSE as UNISON will improve social workers' bargaining position with employers. I suspect not. The number of social workers as a proportion of membership in such a union is small. It may prove difficult to defend the interests of social workers as a specific grouping in a general meeting.

Additionally, the fragmentation of social work in Britain is fairly complex. Certain areas of social work, for example community work, youth work and counselling, have organised their own organisations to advance their positions separately from social work carried out in social services departments under state auspices. Demarcation disputes between these groups can become rather heated. This was the case for community workers in the 1970s (Baldock, 1982). Community workers' commitment to grassroots organising and being part of the solution rather than the problem in working-class communities made them resist incorporation into a state activity which they associated virtually exclusively with social control (Handler, 1973).

Black people have felt aggrieved by the failure of the dominant professional associations to take on board their specific needs. They have, therefore, formed professional organisations to work alongside, but independently from, those run by white colleagues. Thus, in the mid 1980s, they created the Association of Black Social Workers and Allied Professionals (ABSWAP), the Association of Black Probation Officers (ABPO) and The National Association of Asian Probation

Officers (NAAP). These organisations promoted black perspectives and anti-racist initiatives in both training and practice in their own right, for example the formation of support groups for black workers and students (Dominelli *et al.*, 1995). They have also worked with white organisations to promote change and develop anti-oppressive policies and practice.

Who controls social work education?

The formulation of social work education and training following the Seebohm reorganisation of social services in the early 1970s, gave the government a direct say in training through a quango, the Central Council for Education and Training in Social Work (CCESTW) set up to accredit and oversee social work courses. The creation of CCETSW, the absence of a strong professional body to safeguard the interests of social work professionals, and the lack of input from a grassroots organisation run by users meant that the agenda for social work education and training was shaped largely by the dictates of the Treasury and the political aspirations of the party in power (Hall and Jacques, 1983, 1989). These interests were at times mediated by CCETSW for its own bureaucratic imperatives (see Pinker, 1986).

In the beginning, CCETSW's governing body encompassed a cross-sectional representation of those involved in social work education – users, employers, union officials, professional associations and academics. These posts were non-elected appointments made by the Secretary of State who received nominations from the relevant bodies. Those individuals who succeeded in being appointed had to pass political muster. Over time, CCETSW's structures became increasingly unrepresentative of the disparate interests in social work while the role of employers in its deliberations enlarged. The numbers of those with educational interests, particularly at university level, were reduced through successive restructurings of CCETSW after the Tories gained power in 1979. By 1994, a reorganisation of CCETSW had reduced academic (university) representation on its governing Council to two. Moreover, the Chair, previously held by an academic (a vice-chancellor), passed to a lawyer.

Meanwhile, the liberal model of education which underpinned the requirements for social work education came under attack (Ireland, 1985). And, the limited consensus around the content of social work education disappeared. Social services directors castigated the Certifi-

cate of Qualification in Social Work (CQSW) for being too preoccu-
pied with theory at the expense of practical skills.

The outcome of this struggle was determined by employers who
successfully introduced a more practical qualification – the Certificate
in Social Services (CSS), through colleges of further education. CSS
had a high employer input, focused on practical skills and provided
the model which the competency-based DipSW was to emulate. The
employers' victory on this count in the mid 1970s prepared the
ground for the demise of the CQSW which was controlled largely by
academics (Philpott, 1990; Sibeon, 1991). Although CQSW
students were spending 50 per cent of their time on placements in
employers' premises being taught by their employees, employers felt
irrelevant to the educational process (Lee, 1982). Academics, they
claimed, treated practice as incidental to the 'real' educational
enterprise. Few students ever failed academic work. Virtually no-one
failed a placement. Despite these criticisms, academics in the
vanguard of educational practice had established close relationships
with local agencies and consulted practitioners in course design and
assessment. For example, Warwick University had the Practice
Teachers' Collective through which practice teachers as a group were
able to influence course content and policy and nominate people to
sit on the examinations board. Being consulted and delivering part of
the programme, however close, is not control, and it was the latter
that employers sought (Lee, 1982). Moreover, practice teachers'
agendas did not always correspond with their managers'.

The status of CSS did not match the CQSW award, and it was
not long before a renewed onslaught against its educational
provisions was spearheaded by a coalition of interests including
academics and employers. Branding social work education as overly
theoretical, irrelevant to modern practice, and consumed by
leftwing ideologies, their refrain was echoed by Conservative
ministers demanding less theoretical and more pragmatic forms of
practice. The government also had another agenda – the privatisation of the welfare state and, within it, the personal social services.
This coalition demanded a revision of training provisions (see
Pinker, 1986, 1979; Harbart, 1985a,b).

At this point, it is useful to consider the different types of control
which are relevant in intellectual activities. These include administrative control, intellectual control, financial control, processual
control and personal control. The first of these deals with managerial

imperatives; the second with the exchange of ideas; the third with resourcing of various activities; the fourth with the involvement of social workers in organisational decision-making bodies; and the fifth with the degree to which individuals share or go along with institutional norms. Employers were keen to exert *control over the whole of the educational process* rather than at the margins. This required employers to exercise the first four forms of control and influence the fifth through training where the socialisation of future professionals occurs.

Employers assessed the final products coming out of the system, particularly those trained on 'radical' courses, as negative. They alleged that these students: challenged management; had only 'critical' ideas, no practical suggestions; wanted to 'throw money' at problems, thereby undermining 'clients'' sense of responsibility for their own well-being; spent too much time organising in unions instead of getting on with the job; and decried everything the organisation stood for. Many wondered why they bothered to be social workers if they couldn't handle things the way they were. Why indeed! In short, their critique implied a failure on the part of courses to pass traditional professional norms on to the next generation – a serious problem for professionals. Yet, a search for more relevant forms of theory and practice which engaged with the restricted opportunities 'clients' had to improve their life chances typified 'radical' courses responses to the more liberationist welfare agendas the new social movements were articulating (see Alibhai-Brown 1993).

This critique persists to the present day. An interesting feature of it is that employers do not substantiate their allegations with empirical evidence. My work with students over two decades demonstrates a contrary picture. Practice teachers generally look forward to working with students from 'radical' courses and see them as sources of inspiration. On graduation, these students find it relatively easy to obtain jobs, often in the departments in which they have completed their placements. Finally, when asked to provide 'hard facts', employers say that the practice of students from 'radical' courses varies little from that of students from non-radical courses. Except at the level of the institution where they can, as employers see it, be overly concerned with 'unrealistic' goals for improving policy, their microlevel practice can be fairly pedestrian. A contradiction, indeed. Employers' pronouncements, therefore, have consisted of rhetoric and long-term aspirations to wrest control of the educational agenda.

Naming their opponents constitutes an important prerequisite for mobilising others in defence of their interests.

The furore over the alleged decline of professional standards being occasioned by the spread of 'radical' ideas in social work became an important strategising ploy employers used in the power struggle over the heart of the profession. Undermining the credibility of such courses, even if much of it was rhetoric, divided social work academics who became too busy fighting each other to notice the realignment of the determining agents which was quietly taking place. Meanwhile, employers determinedly strengthened their position, gained more allies, including some professional academics, to their cause and continued the barrage against an already weak adversary. The employers' opportunity to become influential in the academic curriculum based in universities came when the CQSW was replaced by the DipSW at the beginning of the 1990s.

The employers' strategy was aided by several other social forces pulling in their direction. One of these was the privatisation of the welfare state including the educational sector. Another was the introduction of 'contract government' (Greer, 1994; Dominelli and Hoogvelt, 1994) which facilitated the creation of quasi-markets in the personal social services. The final force to be reckoned with was the globalisation of the economy which drove the other two developments (Sklair, 1991).

Attacking anti-oppressive stances in social work

Other, contradictory trends were also present. One of these, CCETSW's commitment to promote anti-racist and anti-oppressive practice as an assessed requirement, helped to sell the DipSW to sceptical academics. The struggle to make social work more responsive to the needs of those discriminated against on the grounds of class (Corrigan and Leonard, 1978; Bailey and Brake, 1975; Bennington, 1976), 'race' (Ahmed *et al.*, 1987; Cheetham, 1982; Dominelli, 1988; Ahmad, 1990) and gender (Brook and Davis, 1985; Dominelli and McLeod, 1989) had been a feature of social work education in Britain since the late 1960s, although its spread was slow and incremental. Black practitioners, interested in social work education and occasionally doing sessional teaching on courses, and white anti-racist educators had mounted sustained pressure on CCETSW to take anti-racist practice seriously and demanded its inclusion in both the academic and the practice curricula since the 1970s (see CCETSW, 1983). A similar approach had been used to advance gender issues, but this was less well organised and widespread (see Warwick, 1978; Hudson, 1985, 1987). Women had difficulty recruiting others to their gender agenda because many academics and practitioners found it hard to. believe that a profession dominated by women could have problems with sexism. Dominelli (1991b) refers to this as the 'problem of the presence of women', while anti-racist initiatives encountered the 'problem of the absence of black people'.

Those arguing for anti-racist social work did so knowing that racism was not being addressed on courses and that services delivered to black 'clients' were inappropriate. A series of reports had highlighted the systematic discrimination black people encountered whether seeking employment (as depicted in the PEP Reports: Smith, 1976; Brown, 1984), requesting assistance from education (Swann, 1985), housing (CRE, 1984), social services (ADSS, 1978) or probation (Taylor, 1981; Divine, 1992). They felt this situation had to be tackled as a matter of urgency.

The groups pressing CCETSW to develop an anti-racist policy included the:

- Mickleton Group, made up of black and white practitioners and academics;
- New Black Families Unit which led practice developments with black families in London;
- Association of Black Social Workers and Allied Professionals (ABSWAP) composed of black practitioners;
- Association of Black Probation Officers (ABPO) made up of black workers in probation;
- Black and In Care Group which promoted the perspective of young black 'clients';
- White Collective for Anti-Racist Social Work for white academics, practitioners and students supporting the development of anti-racist social work; and
- individual black and white academics and practitioners endorsing this cause.

Although white people were involved in this struggle, the activities of black people in the field sustained it over time. They not only mounted a critique of what was being done to black people in the name of service provision, but also developed alternative forms of practice at the local level (Livingstone, 1987; Lambeth, 1981; Gilroy, 1987; Ahmad, 1990).

Many of their initiatives blossomed during the expansion of anti-racist and anti-sexist measures promoted by the Greater London Council (GLC) under Ken Livingstone during the mid 1980s before the rightwing successfully launched a counter attack which culminated in the government passing legislation to abolish the GLC (Livingstone, 1987; Dominelli and McLeod, 1989). Thus, demands for progressive inputs into the social work curriculum were heavily influenced by research, developments in practice and 'client' experiences rather than the activities of anti-racist academics writing theories in remote ivory towers; a point missed by critics alleging 'political correctness' has dictated the anti-racist agenda in social work education (Dunant, 1994).

CCETSW's initial response to this foment was to facilitate workshops on anti-racism. Shortly afterwards, it set up a small internal group to examine the topic and liaise with practitioners and academics interested in it. In doing so, it set about amassing the 'authoritative' and 'allocative' resources which would subsequently enable it to influence the profession's socialisation processes. Moreover, these initiatives ran parallel with the production and dissemination of publications which raised the issue and suggested ways of moving forward. These drew on instances of good practice in both practice and academia (*Social Work Today*, 1979; Dominelli, 1988; Cheetham, 1982; Denney, 1983; Small, 1984; Ahmed *et al.*, 1987; Coombe and Little, 1986; CCETSW, 1983; Ahmad, 1990). Thus, traditional means of propagating ideas were used to innovate and revise the educational agenda.

The appointment of a new director committed to anti-racist social work at CCETSW in the mid 1980s provided the impetus for more rapid progress. A Black Perspectives Committee made up largely of black practitioners, but including black academics, was created to give intellectual leadership and direction to anti-racist developments. The efforts of the Black Perspectives Committee and later its Northern Curriculum Development Project gave the production of anti-racist course materials a major boost (Patel, 1994). Responding to pressures for constructive action, CCETSW included the requirement that students demonstrate an ability to work effectively in a multi-cultural society in Paper 30, the document containing the regulations governing DipSW. These provisions were strengthened when Annex 5 was added in 1991 (see Patel, 1994).

However, CCETSW made a major mistake in handling the issue which later proved costly for anti-racist social work. It obliged practitioners and academics, many of whom had little knowledge of anti-racist social work, having never had it in their own training, to implement the requirements of Paper 30 without preparation or training specifically geared to this purpose. As a result, the theories and practices which underpin anti-racist social work eluded them conceptually and practically. Even those committed to changing social work teaching in anti-racist directions struggled to meet the requirements (Patel, 1994). For many, this proved an impossible task. While financial exigencies and CCETSW's own uncertainty about precisely what would meet the anti-racist social work requirements dictated this way of proceeding, it created confusion, despair and hostility among substantial numbers of practice teachers and academics which those opposed to anti-racist social work subsequently exploited. That the commitment to anti-racist social work survived was due more to the determination of those on the ground to improve teaching practice by reflecting the needs of black 'clients' than CCETSW harnessing their energies. This episode also exposes CCETSW's own dependent status as a government agency (Jones, 1994a). It cannot act in ways consistent with the requirements of the profession if these go against the government's political agenda. And, in the case of anti-oppressive perspectives in social work, ministers at the highest levels opposed their presence in the educational curricula (Dunant, 1994).

Meanwhile, agencies and educational institutions also discovered they were ill-prepared for teaching the new ways of working advocated by anti-racist social work. Many white practitioners and academics, whose hearts were in the right place, had no inkling of what to do and so bungled their efforts. This enraged white colleagues who had neither an understanding of nor a commitment to such work. They complained anti-racist social work was a fad which wasted their time and produced poor practice. Students, black and white, became frustrated at the failure of courses to deliver the sensitive kinds of anti-racist practice which the theories had led them to expect. And, they worried that they would be unable to work with black and white 'clients' in ways consistent with both their aspirations and the anti-racist principles which their courses espoused (Grant, 1992; NISW, 1994; De Sousa, 1991).

CCETSW's failure to adequately prepare the ground for the vast body of practitioners and academics to teach anti-racist social work has been a key contributing factor to the backlash against it. The backlash was not long in coming. By the summer of 1993, the first cohort of DipSW students had barely finished their courses when a major onslaught against anti-racist social work education was articulated in the media. Hence, the link between anti-racist social work teaching and practice could only be tangential. Nonetheless, the connection was made in ways which reflected badly on the profession.

The media campaign was mounted on the basis of innuendo and the creation of a 'moral panic' (see Cohen, 1980). Resting its case on a Norfolk couple in which an Asian woman was allegedly refused an application to adopt a black child for being 'racially naïve' because she claimed to have never encountered racism, the media had a field day. Anti-racism was turned into a pejorative term which only 'lunatics' and ideologically driven dogmatists would endorse (Pinker, 1993). While the media's allegations regarding the Norfolk couple were later proved false, the die was cast (Philpott, 1990). The media packaged its 'righteous' outrage at the alleged decision with criticisms of ideologically driven social workers to demonstrate that the 'real' victims, of what was subsequently termed 'politically correct' social work, were 'clients' who received an appalling service. While not acknowledging their own ideologically driven position, opinion formers in the media relied on support from influential academics to make their allegations stick (see Phillips, M, 1993). Through this attack, the sensitivity with which anti-racist social workers sought to incorporate anti-racism into their practice was ignored and their efforts turned against them without adequate debate. From this followed the attack on Paper 30 and CCETSW for suggesting that 'racism was endemic in British society'.

Meanwhile, the term 'political correctness' passed into the social work lexicon as a handy label for disparaging the hard won opportunities for learning about anti-oppressive theories and practice. This attack undermined the efforts of those exposing 'the truths' as experienced by 'clients' and reflected in numerous pieces of research. It also succeeded in disguising the political and ideological agenda for social work education and training being promoted by the government and its supporters. For, if 'political correctness' symbolises a dogmatic and irrational approach to the realities of life as experienced by oppressed people, then those who resist any challenge to their perception that there are no widespread and systematic forms of oppression of which racism is one in this society, comprise the *truly politically correct brigade*. The rest of us are *politically incorrect* (Dominelli, 1993).

The backlash against anti-racist social work also gained allies by being muddied in the waters of anger against CCETSW for other reasons. Prime among these were its: indifference towards powerful key academics of the old school; failure to develop its support base inside academia; and inability to represent university-based academics' concerns in the rapidly changing social work arena. CCETSW undermined itself by creating deep resentment amongst professional academics by mishandling the appointment of external assessors for the DipSW. Seeking to establish national standards and exert more effective control over examiners and the assessment process, CCETSW rejected its previously *laissez faire* position for a more interventionist one. In the course of accrediting its own external assessors, CCETSW turned down the applications of many distinguished white social work academics who had played leading roles in its old CQSW policy-making structures, but whose interests in anti-racist social work were less proven. Consequently, CCETSW made enemies of some of its most powerful erstwhile friends.

The arrangements for teaching social work predicated in Paper 30 also raised other issues. For some academics, this included that of 'academic freedom' or the right of intellectuals to determine what teaching is appropriate (Pinker, 1986). Academic freedom is central to a tradition established by a particular kind of professional – the autonomous critical individual who has fought hard to get accepted and assert the right to question existing orthodoxies without fear of being sacked. An interventionist CCETSW was accused of undermining this sacred academic value (Pinker, 1986, 1993). It is ironic, therefore, that this argument should be used against a system of thought that challenges one existing orthodoxy – that Britain is not a pervasively racist society. It is more ironic in a context in which legislative fiat had abolished, in 1988, one of the key defences of academic freedom – the right to tenure.

Leading white male social work academics have opposed the requirement to introduce anti-racist social work into the curriculum, although their views have been most powerfully expressed in the media by white women columnists (Phillips, M, 1993, 1994; Dunant, 1994). Moreover, it transpires that one of them holds a powerful position on the Press Complaints Commission. A detailed investigation of such connections might lead to the development of innovative theoretical insights for the theory of the multiplicity of roles that people occupy and what conflicts of interests ensue from these.

DipSW introduced other sources of friction between academics and CCETSW. Eventually, some of these became shared by employers. A central feature of the DipSW is the delivery of training through a consortium partnership involving academic institutions and local employers. Had it built on good forms of practice existing under CQSW arrangements, this move might have received academic support. Instead, it introduced highly bureaucratic and labour intensive forms of control over course content without:

- the requisite resources for initiating these changes;
- ensuring that inadequate resourcing was not borne on the backs of highly stretched practitioners and overworked academics;
- securing the support of employers, academics and practitioners for its *specific* proposals; and
- assuring itself that its plans were understood, acceptable and capable of implementation.

Tactically, CCETSW's actions may have had a purpose. Overloading academics and practitioners, whose workloads had already been substantially increased in the minutiae of building structures and revising curricula, left them with little energy to examine broader developments, particularly the rise of NVQs and CCETSW's commitment to functionally based competences as *the* way to teach social workers. These developments, unremarked at the time, subsequently threatened the place of social work in universities and initiated another struggle for the survival of social work as a profession with status.

The cost of collaboration was a major concern. It carried a gap of 70 per cent which CCETSW expected financially starved agencies and universities to cover. This could not be sustained indefinitely without major upheaval. Academics and employers were united in condemning the excessive costs of collaboration and the demands it made on staff. The subject also rankled for being launched with minimal additional funding. Academics, practitioners and employers felt CCETSW was endorsing the provision of social work education on the cheap, having previously failed to secure funding for a three-year course. They were critical of the burdensome bureaucracy for promoting and monitoring the delivery of qualifying training, which in many agencies was no more than a small part of their overall training programme. They were frustrated by the serious national shortage of placements and CCETSW's seeming incapacity to remedy it. They were unhappy about participating in consortia that could take decisions about policy and practice, yet bear no responsibility for dealing with the consequences because they lacked legal standing. And, employers were thwarted in their hopes of making the workplace the site for qualifying training when the Employment Based Routes (EBRs) proved too costly for them to defend in cash starved authorities.

These changes indicate CCETSW was fulfilling the basic organi-sational role predicated by Weber (1968) and Michels (1962), that is, looking after its own interests. In doing so, it was enlarging its empire and amassing the resources it needed to safeguard its position as the body responsible for social work training and education. Thus, CCETSW has fought against proposals to establish an independent General Council for Social Care (Parker *et al.*, 1990) and compro-mised its stance on Paper 30's controversial elements to sanction the government's views. It has backtracked on the contested Annex 5 which covers the presence of systemic racism in society and disbanded the Black Perspectives Committee while at the same time, insisting that it is maintaining social work's 'value base' (Pierce, 1994). Few academics take this as a meaningful statement in the prevailing circumstances. Consequently, CCETSW has gained a breathing space. Meanwhile, some academics have formed a Forum on Social Work Education to examine the current malaise in the profession and seek alternative ways out of the crisis (see Jones, 1994a). Nonetheless, CCETSW's ability to survive as a quango says much about its ability to carry the government's agenda, particularly in promoting lower level social work qualifications through NVQs and bringing querulous academics to heel. This resolution of the problem is potentially unstable. Too many issues rooted in the real life experiences of 'clients', practitioners and academics have been sidestepped. Eventually, these will need to be addressed and new arrangements sought.

This power struggle and its attendant changes have to be understood in the context of a globalised economy, the privatisation of the welfare state and 'contract government'. 'Contract government' has shifted the lion's share of power in Britain's public sector away from policy-makers and professionals towards accountants and managers (Dominelli and Hoogvelt, 1994). Economic constraints have been driving change in social work practice and management structures (Clarke *et al.*, 1994). Thus, the privatisation of the welfare state has proceeded through financial incentives rather than a direct ideological attack on its principles (see Dominelli and Hoogvelt, 1995). The first of these economic directives was the Financial Management Initiative of 1982 which laid the ground for accounting principles to pave the way for privatisation. Through these, cash limits and other disciplines of the market have been imposed on the public sector. Initially, these policies affected health and education more than social services (see Broadbent *et al.*, 1993). In 1988, the Next Steps Initiative (NSI) established the infrastructure for 'contract government' – the means whereby government sheds jobs and tasks in the highly regulated public sector and passes them over to the deregulated private sector (Greer, 1994). Social work education and practice have not escaped its impact.

'Contract government' and social work

The globalised economy and the need for industrialised countries like Britain to demonstrate international competitiveness in the manufacturing sector, by competing against Third World countries having low wage rates and lacking public welfare and social services provisions, has led to demands for the privatisation of the welfare state (Dominelli and Hoogvelt, 1994). Privatising the welfare state has created sites for new forms of capital accumulation to develop, thereby deeply implicating the government in the restructuring of the economy. The vehicle driving the changes necessary for shifting public sector business to the private sector – altering the civil servant work ethic, reducing the power of professionals in the public sector and changing the organisational culture of local government bureaucracies, has been 'contract government' (Greer, 1994).

In it, the government creates a quasi-market in which the state, as principal, contracts out its activities to agents – firms in the private sector, freelance consultants, retiree returners to the labour market and former state employees who have been made redundant. Potential agents are asked to bid for the contracts which the state makes available (Dominelli and Hoogvelt, 1994). The successful ones provide the contractually specified services. The total amounts diverted to agents are substantial. In 1992–3, central government alone spent £565 million on external consultancies (Kettle, 1994).

Part of the contracting process aims to reduce costs, so the reproduction of the worker is not fully paid for. Workers now fend for themselves in areas that employers have traditionally covered – national insurance contributions for sick pay, unemployment insurance and pensions. The other part seeks to attract the private sector, so it must be lucrative enough for firms located within it to provide the necessary services. As a result, the savings which actually accrue to government are less substantial than anticipated. Kettle (1994) has estimated that out of £565 million the government spent on consultancies, it saved only £10 million. However, such measures enable the government to argue that it has effectively downsized by cutting back on staff it employs directly.

Social work has become subject to the demands of 'contract government' following the implementation of the National Health Services and Community Care Act of 1990 which requires the development of the 'purchaser–provider' split in service delivery (SSI, 1991a). The idea of market provisions for older people had been mooted in the Griffiths Report of 1988. In it, Roy Griffiths, the businessman leading the Commission producing the report, suggested that social services departments could benefit from the introduction of business methods. This marked a major shot in the move to split service delivery into two segments – one providing services and the other purchasing them. The government has proposed that the local authority acts as purchaser while voluntary and commercial agencies become providers. To ensure this happens, the government has stipulated that local authorities spend 85 per cent of their interim community care grant in the 'independent sector', the government's preferred appellation for profit-making and charitable agencies. In short, 'contract government' has enabled the state to pull out of providing direct services to consumers.

Besides laying the groundwork for privatised initiatives in social services by creating the purchaser–provider split, the government found in CCETSW a useful ally for encouraging the development of the 'competency-based approach to social work' education (see Mainframe, 1994). This training helps prepare practitioners for a market-driven environment. It also reduces the theoretical content of social work courses and reorients teaching towards more practical skills. Following this path creates a false division between theory and practice and ignores the dialectical relationships through which theory develops out of practice and in turn, changes practice.

The implications of competency-led social work practice are far-reaching. Decontextualised skills teaching would soon reach its limits and need to engage with theory. Competences avoid most of the critical debates that practitioners have to resolve in their work by spiriting them away. This magician's trick is pulled off because competences claim to quantify the unquantifiable. The social work task is moved away from relationship building and focused on the discrete delivery of a specified highly technocratised skill. To reach this point, CCETSW put out to tender a contract to define social work competences for revising Paper 30 in early 1994. The task of the consultants it appointed – Mainframe, a private agency, and the National Institute of Social Work (NISW) which delivers short courses in social work rather than degree programmes or DipSW qualifying ones – was to take practise skills and break them down into smaller and smaller constituent parts which could be performed by particular personnel trained to a specified level. I call the breaking down of complex social work skills into their constitutent parts under functionally based competences the technocratisation of social work.

Under 'contract government', the external agents establishing the competences for social work must undertake the following:

- specify the key purpose of social work
- get the potential providers to agree the key purpose
- identify the key roles or statements describing the main functions required for achieving the key purpose
- break down the key roles to a further level of detail that describe what needs to be done to achieve these
- specify the statements comprising the units of competence which stand as the national occupational standards
- break down the units of competence into elements of competence which are then qualified by performance criteria and range statements. Together, these form the assessable outcomes of performance employers use for evaluation purposes (Mainframe, 1994).

The assessable outcomes of performance depict the employers' expectations about the job and the standards employees are expected to achieve (Mainframe, 1994). This seems innocuous enough, but appearances can be misleading.

Competences provide the avenue through which employers exercise control over the content of the social work curriculum. This approach virtually eliminates a traditional preoccupation of university academics: whether or not students' can integrate theory and practice in their practical and academic work. The reduction of social work skills to elements of competence permits lower level awards to be accepted as legitimate qualifications for the job. Practitioners who have obtained Level One, Two or Three in National Vocational Qualifications (NVQs) can now undertake tasks previously performed by qualified social workers. This has led to further segmentation and fragmentation in the division of labour in social work. Competencies enable employers to drive down the costs of employing social workers even lower than that previously holding for a poorly regarded, low status women's profession. The status of social work in the money economy will decline further in consequence. Thus, the aspirations of white working-class and black women to enter a well-paid and satisfying occupation will be thwarted. Moreover, competences are the means whereby CCETSW can validate training almost exclusively in the workplace, thereby bypassing academics completely, unless employers hire them under highly specific contracts for which they will have to compete against others. Bidding has its advantages in reducing costs to the purchaser, but who pays for the unsuccessful bids (which can be numerous)? Does this not portray an enormous waste of effort which also needs to be accounted for if the exercise is to be fully costed?

The technocraticisation of social work through competency-based approaches has destroyed its basis as a profession which initiates change in individuals by establishing good working relationships between the professional and the 'client'. Meanwhile, complex processual issues have been lost in the fragmentation following the reduction of interactive skills to their simplest components. In the process, the role that social workers can play in lessening the alienation 'clients' feel towards the society they live in, has also been lost.

As for equal opportunities and anti-oppressive practice, competency-based social work is unlikely to meet its requirements. To begin with, process is an important feature of anti-oppressive practice. So is theory. Theory has a dialectical relationship to practice. Each develops out of the other. Looking at discrete skills in the way proposed by Mainframe's documents for the DipSW, encourages a crass checklist approach which fails to examine the practitioner's ability to combine a set of complex factors, including process, in finely balanced professional judgements which link disparate pieces of a 'client's' life into a meaningful whole. The 'client' can then use these to make decisions about alternative ways of responding to their life situations. Competency-based social work has little need for autonomous critical professionals whose central skill is to make sense of the disjointed set of 'facts' distressed people present for assessment.

Even this skill does not guarantee that practitioners will take all the necessary 'facts' on board. Gender, 'race' and other social divisions are often ignored when professionals exercise discretion. These are the shortcomings that anti-oppressive practice has sought to address. Moreover, anti-oppressive practice, of which anti-racist social work is a part, considers the whole person. That is why inputs, process, methods, relationships and outcomes are all important in the creation, development and implementation of anti-racist social work. And, it is why white people find it difficult to go beyond a tokenistic realisation of it. Individuals have to invest an extensive amount of work to develop their own consciousness and skills as anti-racist, anti-oppressive practitioners.

Finally, competency-driven approaches fragment and individualise many of the 'collective' values which social work espouses. By ignoring the social context of practice, competences allow the replication of pathologising ideologies which blame individuals for their failure to overcome structural inequalities.

This bleak situation in Britain can be contrasted to the more optimistic picture which emerges in The United States. There, the Council for Social Work Education and the National Association of Social Workers have established themselves as the professional bodies for social work educators and practitioners respectively. Thus, control of the training agenda rests in the hands of professionals and not government. Although these bodies are private organisations made up of members who fund the bulk of their activities, they have:

- achieved protected title status for social workers;
- enforced the registration of practitioners wanting to practice in social work;
- developed progressive codes of practice for different user groups; and
- monitored quality.

Moreover, they have established themselves in a mixed economy of provisions in which the state, the private commercial sector, the voluntary sector and the domestic sector, all play a large part in placing a variety of services before users.

Conclusions

British social work is engaged in a struggle over who determines its professional remit whether in education or practice. At the moment, CCETSW and the government have the upper hand. The extent to which a more open situation can develop in Britain depends largely on CCETSW's ability to maintain credibility not only with the government who funds its activities, but also with practitioners and academics. It is too early to predict the final outcome of the contest between them. But the struggle for a professionalism that reflects *education* and *training* interests will continue. Meanwhile, the voice of the users of the profession's services is conspicuous by its absence.

7

Education or Training? Power Struggles for the Heart of a Profession

Education or training or both? How should the student's learning experience be structured to produce a practitioner of quality, one who will do justice to the interests of both employers and 'clients'? How does social work reconcile the irreconcilable? These are perennial questions lying at the centre of the power struggle for the heart of the profession and its educational mandate. They also indicate the contradictory expectations placed upon social workers. Because there is a power struggle, any answer which is produced will be contested in the fullness of time. Compromise resolutions, which lack the consent of all participants, fail to incorporate their concerns, and cannot dissolve contradictory tensions, will prove inadequate.

In Britain, the controversy has been polarised to reflect dichotomous thinking that posits an antithetical relationship between theory and practice. In its more recent variant, those endorsing a practice position claim practical skills not theory are needed (Harbart, 1985a, b). They have labelled those who do not share their views the trendy ideological or 'politically correct' brigade (Appleyard, 1993). In reply, those on the opposite side of the divide argue that theory must inform practice for it to be useful (Jones, 1994b). The two positions may be summarised as follows: the former advocates training for the practical practitioner; the latter for the critical reflective practitioner. Students need both education and training to become effective professionals. The Central Council for Education and Training in Social Work (CCETSW) initially endorsed this idea. CCETSW's recent promotion of competency-based training which breaks with this tradition is to the detriment of the profession. The attraction of the competency-based approach is its capacity to focus solely on learning *outcomes*, ignore problematic inputs and discount the relevance of process in learning situations (CCETSW, 1991).

In this chapter, I examine the power struggle between these two opposing views of social work education and training at qualifying level, touching on the implications of the revised Paper 30. I seek to show that the division between theory and practice is false. However, the arguments which rage on either side of the dispute are essentially fundamental disagreements about the role and status of social work in society.

Education, training or both?

Education has been defined as an activity which aims to broaden a person's horizons through the acquisition of knowledge and skills (Ireland, 1985). Stimulating students' intellects is appropriate in tertiary level education, especially in the university setting. Most British universities' mission statements proclaim they prepare students for employment. While other subjects may not enjoy a similar advantage, social work, in training practitioners, is ideally placed to meet this expectation. But it suffers from not having a high academic status (Bailey and Lee, 1982).

Liberal education also seeks to develop the individual as a well-rounded personality through exposure to ideas and subjects that would not have otherwise come to mind (Ireland, 1985). Such an educational project requires time for students to engage with the materials presented and make up their own minds about what they accept or reject. Producing a critical thinker capable of making independent judgements is at the centre of the educational process. In transferring this model to social work, the development of the critical or reflective practitioner tallies with its aims. This project requires students to integrate theory and practice at both intellectual and emotional levels. It also asks that each owns the understandings that flow from their doing so by making their practice consistent with their theoretical stances (Ireland, 1985; Lishman, 1991; Richards, 1987; Phillipson *et al.*, 1988). The charge that education is overly concerned with theory is fallacious. Theory is used to inform and extend practice and vice-versa.

The permissiveness of the educational framework is likely to encourage students to be critical of what they see and challenge the status quo. Students who do so are likely to be branded politically motivated ideologues by their opponents who use ideology as a derogatory label to suggest their position is non-ideological because it concurs with the prevailing one. Educated students acquire a potential to break new ground in both the educational setting and social work practice by examining new ways of doing things. Unfortunately, unremittant questioning of customary practices is unacceptable in organisations charged with ensuring continuity in the status quo or, as Davies (1985) terms it, 'maintenance'.

Training has had a more limited and specific remit. It teaches people in ways that quickly bring them to specified standards of efficiency. Training instructs rather than educates. It is a more practical and technical approach to learning. Practical skills are emphasised and theoretical skills downplayed. Theories are not considered important enough to have space in the timetable. It is not that there are no theoretical underpinnings to the skills which are promoted (see Howe, 1987); simply that these are not made explicit or overtly developed. The technical capacity to do the job, as defined by those in authority (employers), not critical thinking, is valued. People who are simply trained are less likely to question the status quo or become innovative thinkers seeking new horizons and methodologies. However, they may be highly inventive in solving specific problems related to day-to-day technical tasks (Ireland, 1985).

The polarisation of social work education and training along these two fault lines is unhelpful. Academics arguing for an educational approach are largely not in favour of the technicist orientation of competency-based approaches. The employers and CCETSW, lined up behind the latter position, have the willing support of government. The real losers in this debate are students, the users of the personal social services and the profession itself.

Davies and Wright (1989) claim students differ in their views about the importance of theory, but that most have little time for it. Evidence suggests this oversimplifies the matter. A number of admissions tutors on postgraduate programmes believe that the bulk of their students welcome theory. Learning about different theories is cited as a key reason for their choosing to attend MA courses. If candidates hold positive views about theory when they are being interviewed, what accounts for the negative opinions uncovered by Davies and Wright (1989) later in their educational career? Could it be that they have subsequently been turned off theory? If so, Davies and Wright's findings say more about the way in which courses handle 'theory' than students' predisposition against it. I have found that students complain about theories on their courses, not because they are averse to them, but because they want 'theories relevant to practice'. This is not an unreasonable expectation on a professional course. But it is rarely what courses offer. Courses' lack of time to fully explore a range of theories in practice-relevant ways and social work educators' limited background in theory development contribute to this state of affairs. Yet, despite the shortcomings of teaching, practitioners need to be able to theorise and conceptualise what they are doing (Kendall, 1978). They must also be skilled in what they do. They need both education and training. Social work programmes need to turn out competent reflective practitioners capable of integrating theory and practice and examining the connections between the two.

The socialisation of social workers

Critical to both education and training is the expectation that the students will acquire the habits recognised and accepted by the profession (Heraud, 1979). This requires students to demonstrate that they have been socialised into the ways of the profession. But what is the nature of their socialisation process and how does it come about?

The socialisation process is guided by the ethics and values which are the hallmarks of the social work profession. These include a commitment to valuing others, helping people make decisions about their lives, 'client' self-determination, empathising with the predicament of others and addressing the social factors which increase people's vulnerability (Hollis, 1964; Perlman, 1957; Compton and Galaway, 1975).

Socialisation into the profession begins with the selection process for admission to a qualifying course and continues throughout the qualified worker's career. During the admission process, a form of gatekeeping takes place through the selection criteria which identify candidates 'suitability for social work'. The criteria are subjective in so far as selectors are required to make judgements about an individual applicant on the basis of what the application portrays about how they work, have worked, or expect to work with 'clients' and colleagues, their understanding of social work practice and aspirations for their future career. The relevant information is gleaned from the prospective student's personal statement, references and what applicants say about themselves and their work when interviewed.

Resourcing shortages and pressures on staff time have led a number of British courses to dispense with interviews and rely solely on written documentation. Such responses indicate another site in which external circumstances rather than professional imperatives dictate the nature of the socialisation process in dependent professions. This contrasts sharply with business studies courses which have funded recruitment procedures through self-generated income by charging what the *market will bear*. Unlike public sector employees whose training needs are constrained by cash strapped training budgets imposed by governments, private sector employees can tap into financial resourcing based on paying the full market price for a course.

Since selection criteria are defined and can be reproduced by different interviewers, they carry a certain amount of objectivity. They are not arbitrarily imposed on the basis of individual preferences. However, insofar as the criteria are *interpreted* by interviewers, they are subjective. Thus, they are subjectively objective. An applicant's experience can be one of a biased application of the criteria, particularly if they are rejected for a place.

Course selectors vary as to how they determine suitability. Some simply focus on the overall impression the candidate conveys, using as key considerations: the applicant's sensitivity to others' woes; an appreciation of the limits of a social worker's authority; a degree of flexibility approaching problems and others; and the ability to conceptualise and reflect on their previous work experience.

Some courses have formally specified criteria in a checklist which itemises questions selectors ask during interview and provides the framework for evaluating the application. The latter is more common on courses selecting candidates on the basis of documentation rather than interview. Tight selection of students and competition for places means that marginal applicants will be rejected at this stage. If selection is sufficiently rigorous, few social work students should fail their courses. Could this explain another feature identified by Davies and Wright (1989) – that few social work students 'fail'?

Some CQSW courses had initiated an exploration of a student's commitment to social justice in determining suitability for social work as part of good practice. DipSW increased the numbers doing so in compliance with Paper 30. Consideration of these values during the selection process also signifies a course's response to feminist and black activist critiques of social workers adding to the oppression of 'client' groups by not addressing sexism and racism in their practice.

Having been accepted for a course, a student's suitability for social work is checked out throughout their educational career – in both the academy and the field. However, academics do not anticipate the socialisation of students into the profession in any complete sense when they graduate from a course. Professional socialisation is projected not as a one-off event, but as a continual process of learning and unlearning as practitioners reflect upon experience and accumulate knowledge throughout their working lives. Further education and training is required by social workers as a regular part of their work at all levels of the labour hierarchy. Such provisions are even more necessary in a discipline whose legal parameters and contours of practice are constantly changing in light of new legislation, government agendas, innovations in practice emanating from either the academy or field, and 'clients'' calls for improvements in service delivery. The socialisation process maintains stability in the profession over time and space. In social work, it has to be fluid enough to respond to a constantly changing constellation of demands. Employers' insistence that courses produce qualified workers who can walk into a job without further assistance ignores this reality.

A student's socialisation experience on courses is affected by: their interaction with other students – their peers, staff (clerical, administrative, academic and practitioner); the theories they are exposed to; the practice models which are presented; and their placements where they encounter employers, 'clients', students from different courses and practitioners other than practice teachers. The contribution each of these makes to the overall balance is difficult to ascertain, for the research data which might guide us to the answer has not yet been collected. However, our teaching experience and knowledge about theories of interaction between people provide some clues. On the informal level, peers are likely to exert considerable influence on each other's thinking. Formally, however, the educational process is driven by assessment requirements which may prevent its tallying with the needs of individual students whose capacity to learn and assimilate material usually proceeds at their own pace (Ireland, 1985; Davies, 1979) rather than according to a course schedule predetermined by others – teachers, rules of the educational establishment, employers' expectations and a government quango (CCETSW), which is at one remove from them. This arrangement creates a tension students must manage if they are to complete their studies within a course's specified parameters. Working within these constraints is part of the socialisation process. Social work professionals are constantly having to juggle insufficient resources and lack of time in which to do things in their daily work.

Until the DipSW, teaching on placements largely followed the apprenticeship model: students watched and learnt by example. The assumption was that the practitioner, a knowledgeable and competent professional, would know what was expected of students acting in that capacity. By watching others, asking questions and doing, the student would come to understand agency constraints and employers' demands. By being attentive, conscientious and hard working during this process, they would pick up the necessary knowledge and skills.

The apprenticeship model is more akin to training than education. Moreover, this approach focuses largely on learning by assimilation. The student assimilates office routines and passes the placement, or they do not and fail. For the delivery of a standard product at the end of the process is an expectation of professional training. The socialisation process in the practice setting involves a considerable degree of not rocking the boat or an uncritical acceptance of office routines and policies. A student might want to question them, but fear of failing or being considered a 'trouble-maker' has meant that the majority of them keep their thoughts to themselves. This has proved to be particularly true for black students and others who are perceived as 'difficult' (NISW, 1994; De Souza, 1991). The socialisation process is ultimately geared to producing a known, predictable and uniform outcome (Barnes, 1985). In this paradigm, black students are penalised for being 'different' by raising questions and demanding alternative results to the ones set by a powerful white establishment which decides what is or is not acceptable (De Souza, 1991; NISW, 1994). As the politics of training and professional socialisation are hidden or seldom openly discussed, the issue is not raised in these terms on courses.

On the informal level, students discuss their concerns with other students, using their networks to survive the socialisation process. Occasionally, students relying on role distancing to survive, might mention their fears to tutors – usually at the end of the course, when they feel they have safely passed the assessment hoops. Otherwise, these issues tend to surface formally when a placement goes drastically wrong. Black students, whose needs are greater given their marginalisation for being different, have raised the need for formal support groups, though few courses actually provide these.

Fortunately, other models of practice learning exist. Even in pre-DipSW days, placement supervisors followed an educational model and encouraged students to reflect upon themselves, their work and their agency, challenging poor practice as appropriate. These students could rely on their supervisors' support in their endeavours and could use their experiences as learning materials. Students who chanced on such nuggets considered themselves 'lucky' in what otherwise seemed a lottery for good practice experiences.

High quality practice teaching was left to the individual practitioner's views about what constituted a good learning environment. Many practice supervisors were not supported in their work by either agency or line managers. Student supervision was seen as an additional extra, which they did for love by organising their time to produce some 'spare' capacity for carrying it out. Practice teaching was and is undervalued and unappreciated except by students, most of whom speak favourably of their practice experiences, despite concerns about teaching processes and placement allocation methods. Indeed, for many students, the placement 'makes' the course (Claytor *et al.*, 1994).

Predictability is an essential feature in the socialisation of competent professionals. Under CQSW, practice teaching arrangements were generally ad hoc, unsystematic and could not guarantee the end results. Dissatisfaction with this method of proceeding was widespread among practice supervisors, students, employers, academics and government. For, regardless of the divisions and different ideological standpoints they held, all agreed that proceeding with this haphazard model of organising social work education and training was unacceptable. Complaints about its unreliability as a measure of professional preparedness or capacity to socialise students into the appropriate ways of practising were intensified by the worry of colleagues not formally involved in assessing students' work, that 'unsuitable' students might 'pass'. Their concerns were expressed in the rubric that social work courses had 'too low a failure rate'.

However, as black students have pointed out, this picture of training opportunities obscured their reality. Most black people got selected out at the admissions stage when their practice experience if not mainstream social services, probation or (white) voluntary sector was disregarded. Black applicants doing voluntary work with black 'clients' in black communities were most affected (NISW, 1994). Once on courses, black students disproportionately failed academic assignments and placements (NISW, 1994; De Souza, 1991). For De Souza, these results signalled white educators' failure to appreciate the use of black perspectives, writings and experiences in written and practical work. Consequently, innovative contributions which indicated black students' ability to reflect upon and use biographical knowledge to push boundaries outward, was marked down and devalued. In other words, they failed to get through a socialisation process which emphasises the sameness of the final product, not its uniqueness.

Black students began commenting on the professional socialisation process as it was unfolding for them. They criticised it for its inability to accept the validity of socialisation processes which challenged the racist nature of course practices, but were penalised for questioning activities which reduced black 'clients' chances of receiving the services they required and were entitled to. Part of the socialisation process in social work aims to get students to understand themselves and their experience and to apply self-knowledge in social work relationships (Compton and Galaway, 1975). Devaluing black students' use of self-knowledge penalised them for having socialisation experiences which differed from those of the majority of white students.

Black students' critique exposes the normative basis of the sociali-sation process and its social control dimensions in a way that white students have been unable to do. It is unclear how far white students either grasp or are conscious of the dynamics to which they are being subjected. Critiques of the apprenticeship model also reveals the numerous formal and informal levels on which power operates in the education and training process. While the majority of students feel unable to overtly challenge and articulate their sense of powerlessness in it, compliance as part of their submission to assessment procedures enables the system to continue. Thus, they are implicated in creating and recreating those forms of domination which oppress them as students preparing to enter a profession which is defined in particular ways by powerful others.

The contract they sign as students implies their acceptance of the prevailing terms and conditions. Resistance to the constraints imposed on them ranges from a non-threatening, formally going along with things despite their reservations for the sake of getting a qualification which accesses their 'meal ticket', to overt challenges and outward shows of discontent. Moreover, education provides an outlet for their idealism while retaining their capacity for independent thought at the private or informal level. Nonetheless, students' views about course content are amplified and developed in the public arena where their concerns interact with those being articulated by other actors including practitioners, employers, academics and users.

More is expected of social work students than those taking university courses without professional training. Academics generally perceive social work students as a critical group. They are labelled 'a difficult lot' who always 'moan about the teaching they get', even though its quality is no worse than that provided to other students and their participation in course decision-making structures much higher (HEFCE, 1995). However, given the intractable nature of many problems social work students address in practice, the limited amount of time in which they have to develop their understanding intellectually and emotionally, and the strain on teaching resources, it is not surprising that their expectations about what they should be taught and how, are high.

Social work courses, in asking for constant feedback and evaluation from students are setting expectations that the course will be amenable to change through their critiques and actions. The disillusionment which sets in when their aspirations are not met, is predictable. Insofar as students examine courses in collective groups, the dynamics that unfold in this setting give a fuller hearing to those who are dissatisfied with their situation. Social work students' sympathies for 'underdogs' and general reluctance to publicly contradict their peers, even if they disagree with them, for fear of being labelled disloyal, allows the concerns of dissatisfied students to receive a disproportionate airing over satisfied ones. This gives rise to a process I call the *amplification of discontent*. It accounts for the discrepancy many social work educators experience between the views students supply anonymously in individual questionnaires and those they articulate in a course group review.

Accrediting practice teaching

DipSW gave CCETSW the opportunity to tackle unsystematic approaches to practice teaching by demanding the accreditation of practice teachers and agencies (CCETSW, 1983, 1991a, 1989). Encapsulated in Paper 26.3 the accreditation process became one avenue CCETSW used to exert greater control over professional socialisation processes in practice teaching and paralleled those applying to academic courses. It aimed to ensure uniformity and predictability of outcome, regardless of the setting in which a student trained or the personality of the practice teacher, by targeting practice teachers through accreditation and the practice teaching award and agencies through the agency approval process. The former focused on improving the quality of individual practice teachers' contributions to students' learning opportunities. The latter addressed recalcitrant employers who were not providing the infrastructure required for practice teachers to perform their job adequately and students to learn in the best possible environment. Being confident about the type of social workers that is produced, and knowing that they have the skills 'to do the job' is an important and necessary part of the profession's socialisation process. However, there is a fine balance to be struck between encouraging innovation and conformity in students. Currently, the competence-based approach which fosters a mechanistic reproduction of knowledge and skills threatens to enforce unreflective conformity.

The new arrangements introduced by DipSW also formally recognised practice teachers' need for training in practice teaching by inventing the practice teachers' award to replace the ad hoc arrangements courses previously provided. DipSW also required that a practice teacher's assessment of marginal students be examined by another practitioner through the second opinion process. This reduced practice teachers fears about deciding to fail a student on their own. In addition, the second opinion process was charged with ensuring that power disparities caused by 'race' and gender were addressed by matching that person with the student whose work was being re-examined. This innovation sought to address the worries that black students and women had about being judged adversely because they challenged racist and/or sexist practices in agencies. The second opinion procedure was a costly one, and the Review of Paper 30 during 1994–5 threatened to abolish it (*Community Care*, 1995). This highlights another aspect in which developments in a dependent profession are dictated by external exigencies rather than professional requirements. This proposal is being resisted. As social interaction reflects negotiated interplays between actors of unequal status, the outcome may be the survival of some form of second opinion procedure (*Community Care*, 1995).

These changes have introduced significant improvements in practice teaching (Claytor *et al.*, 1994). The learning experience has been systematised so that less depends on the 'accident' of getting a 'good' practice teacher. The accreditation process has ensured that practice teachers receive (some) recognition for their work and formal training. These stipulations have empowered practice teachers to demand more from their agencies. Practice teaching can now be claimed in their workload, although the actual time the job takes remains seriously underestimated. Having minimum standards set by CCETSW has enabled social workers to say 'no' to practice teaching without the appropriate backup. Resisting managers' pleas despite inadequate resourcing for such work had been harder under previous arrangements.

The DipSW system has its own discrepancies. It is grossly underfunded. The lack of suitable placements has reached crisis proportions. The visibility of practice teaching in a climate of severe pressure on resources has led to its being costed and evaluated like other activities social services departments conduct. Agencies have decided they cannot afford to support it to the extent that they would like and, rather than sacrifice quality, many have decided to reduce places. Courses have been subjected to having factors outside their control determine admissions policy. Despite CCETSW's strong stance, and the existence of research backing its demand for adequate funding, the government has refused to release additional monies. The Treasury's commitment to keeping public expenditure in check has squeezed those professions relying on it for funding hardest. Being Treasury-dependent, lacking a powerful lobby working on its behalf and being poorly equipped to mobilise public opinion in defense of its position, social work is particularly vulnerable to government vicissitudes and policies.

Assessment as part of the socialisation process

The assessment of academic and practice work is a crucial part of the professional socialisation process. It is the point at which students are deemed competent and accepted into the profession, or rejected for not meeting the required standards. Assessment procedures also highlight disparities in power between teachers and students. Students have commented on how they feel they have to 'toe the line', present or write their work in ways acceptable to the course or agency in which their studies occur rather than follow their own inclinations. They are painfully aware of the constant intrusion assessment makes into their education and training. In today's social work courses, like those of yesteryear, the pedagogic processes students engage in are assessment driven. Assessment concerns overshadow teaching and distort student's experiences of it.

Paper 30 made the requirements for courses and practice teachers more explicit than previously. CCETSW also introduced the idea that examiners needed socialising into the appropriate mind-set by creating its own national list of external assessors. These it chose and trained to replace the external examiners universities had formerly appointed to examine both professional and academic awards. DipSW arrangements required two external assessors appointed by CCETSW from its approved list per course. Through this means, CCETSW sought a more uniform system of quality control and a change in the demographic make-up of the external examiners at its disposal. Its approved list of external assessors consisted of roughly equal numbers of practitioners and academics. It included significant numbers of black practitioners and black academics, another group which had been marginalised and rendered invisible under the former system. Practitioners became officially involved in the assessment process – for the first time as assessors *formally* monitoring academic work. As external assessors for the DipSW, practitioners held the same assessment powers as academics. Many practitioners on the CCETSW approved lists had never examined before. They found being thrown in with experienced academics challenging, disconcerting and deskilling (Patel, 1994).

However, CCETSW's restructuring of the external examiner system proved problematic. Universities were reluctant to concede power over assessment to an external body. Their regulations were inimical to the inclusion of those outside the university system. Practitioners and black people found themselves marginalised because DipSW courses carrying university awards required their own external examiners. The integration of social work qualifications and academic awards on university courses in pre-DipSW days had led to the same pieces of work being accepted as assessment material for both sets of award. Most academics were reluctant to relinquish this integration which represented their commitment to linking theory and practice. They sought piecemeal solutions to CCETSW's failure to ground social work qualifications within an academic framework. For example, the London School of Economics, disentangled the DipSW from its Masters programme. Other courses opted to have their external assessors appointed as external examiners so that only one verdict would be given on a piece of work. These arrangements do not always solve the tensions ensuing from one piece of work having to comply with two sets of requirements which at times could be antagonistic.

Under DipSW, the two systems sat uneasily side by side: university regulations had priority over professional ones in matters regarding academic awards; CCETSW's in professional awards. These two systems could rub alongside each other if assessed pieces of work did not occasion controversy between markers. Disputes could produce bizarre situations. A piece of work acceptable academically for its sociological content could be rejected for inadequate coverage of practice and vice-versa. The former could happen if a student's work indicated a comprehensive understanding of the theories under consideration, but failed to integrate these with developments in practice. Such situations could arise more readily in the assessment of pieces of work for the specialist areas of practice. These are mandatory written pieces of substantial length which integrate theory and practice (CCETSW, 1989). These are marked by both academic tutors and practice teachers. Disagreements between them could result in the practice teachers' verdict being overturned further up the marking chain, thereby making them feel that their work had been undervalued.

Problems are exacerbated when universities fail to appoint one of the external assessors as external examiners, either because course numbers only justify one, or because one of them, usually the practitioner, does not meet academic criteria of appointment. These regulations set up differences and inequalities within the examination process. Many of those deselected for not meeting academic requirements, like being an academic of at least senior lecturer level, were black. These conditions continue the under-representation of black people in the examination system, thereby perpetuating institutionalised racism in universities. The extent to which such a situation prevails is difficult to judge as this question has not been systematically researched. It is possible to challenge this form of exclusion because the criteria used by the universities lead to indirect discrimination. This outcome is illegal according to the 1976 Race

Relations Act. Despite this record, universities have seldom utilised section 5(2)(d) of this Act which enables them to recruit appropriately qualified black people and address their under-representation in both the examination and teaching processes.

CCETSW staff's moves to tighten the socialisation of external assessors through regular workshops and meetings indicate that the looser forms of socialisation prevailing under the earlier system of accrediting courses was no longer acceptable for the demands now being made. The previous system was inappropriate to a context in which employers demanded the curtailment of academics' autonomy and that social work training reflect their concerns. Moreover, CCETSW now charged external assessors with monitoring courses more thoroughly and extensively. Monitoring took the form of lengthy reports based on prescribed questions or topics. These were collected and analysed by CCETSW's Quality and Standards Committee which attempted to ensure that social work courses adhered to the requirements Paper 30 sought to make national standards. These arrangements intensified CCETSW's administrative control of academics. They also signified that the balance of power in determining the nature of social work education was shifting away from academics.

An additional contradiction was CCETSW's move away from prescribing inputs – course content and pedagogic methods, to focusing more specifically on *outcomes*. Before the review of Paper 30 in the summer of 1994, there were 106 outcome competences for students to reach. Covering these within a two-year timetable is problematic. Courses are of insufficient length for students to grasp these in a substantive way. The shift away from content prescription meant that CCETSW *no longer required* students to be knowledgeable about the cognate disciplines informing social work – sociology, social policy and psychology. The contribution of cognate disciplines in an educational context which teaches practitioners how to work with the 'person-in-the-situation', is not essential in training technically skilled practitioners who cover only a limited range of work.

Whilst CCETSW's position reflected a smart move from the competency point of view, it was disastrous for the development of proficient practitioners who knew enough about the way in which human beings and societies operate and interact with each other to intervene effectively in practice. A lack of this complex understanding is particularly undesirable when it comes to taking action in complex cases of mental illnesses, sexual abuse, child physical abuse and neglect, and elder abuse (see Gordon, 1988; Davies, 1979; Phillipson and Walker, 1986).

Despite their shortcomings, systems theories had at least advocated a greater understanding of the different systems operating in 'clients'' lives (see Pincus and Minahan, 1973). The competence-based approach neglects this and feeds a current major criticism of social work intervention in complex situations involving a range of people and agencies; procedural form has taken over process. This has produced defensive work promoting agency interests rather than dealing adequately with issues raised by 'clients'. Fortunately for DipSW students, most university courses have retained their teaching in the cognate disciplines of psychology, social policy and sociology. This has further exacerbated tensions around the untrustworthy nature of social sciences perspectives which encourage critical thinking in students and intensify overcrowding in a curriculum with space for only a superficial coverage of a great many subjects. But it underscores the government's lack of commitment to developing the social work profession. It persists in refusing to fund a three-year qualifying course despite constant agitation in its favour by CCETSW, professional academics, practitioners and employers. This exposes another site in which external bodies distort professional imperatives and reveals the relative powerlessness of social work professionals *vis-à-vis* their political masters.

The requirement that each DipSW student specialise in a particular area of practice (APP) aimed to overcome the failure of generic training to get students to specialise systematically in one field. However, students could use their interests to specialise informally under CQSW by following options and placements which concentrated on work that they wanted to do after qualifying. DipSW also changed the assessment process by requiring that the substantial written piece submitted for the APP Unit was marked by practitioners and academics and focused on practice developments. It also sought to ensure that students had the skills employers deemed appropriate.

DipSW increased CCETSW's and employers' control over the socialisation of social work students. Their influence covered the criteria for selection, assessment process, course structure, placement structure and placement provisions. Exerting such control by promoting competence-based social work was an important strategy in shifting the locus of power away from academics (Dominelli,

1995). The struggle to get competences as the basis for teaching social work was conducted through a restructuring of training, not a head-on fight for the heart of the social work profession. This went by default. Reorganising training for competences also encompassed the restructuring of the CCETSW Council and disbanding of the Black Perspectives Committee. But these two events may have been unintended consequences of the struggle to assert bureaucratic controls favouring employers' interests over the profession.

Developments in Britain are moving in different directions from those in continental Europe. There, the harmonisation of social work qualifications is taken seriously. The European Union's (EU's) First Directive on Professional Training stipulating a three-year minimum period in an institution of higher education for professional training to be recognised across frontiers prompted countries failing to meet its requirements to comply (Cannan *et al.*, 1992). Italy, for example, is busy moving social work education into the university setting to secure its status and transferability across national borders.

In the United States and Canada, qualifying training is already enshrined within the university system. Basic training occurs at the Bachelor level which typically includes two years of courses across a common faculty-wide base thereby giving students exposure to social work's cognate disciplines, followed by two years of social work specific training including practice placements. Students specialise through a Master's Programme of, usually, two years' duration. Others go on to complete doctorates. Social work teachers are increasingly required to hold a doctorate to become assistant professors. This form of training strengthens the hand of academic professionals in the socialisation process and raises social work's status more in line with traditional professions. It has also given men greater control as men dominate the highest rank of full professor in North American schools of social work (CASW, 1992; Dominelli, 1986c; NASW, 1992).

The American and Canadian systems also have the effect of lessening government's potential to take *the* critical role in developing social work education and training. The power struggle over the heart of the profession is therefore played out primarily with professionals as the key adversaries. Service users play a very limited role. Having responsibility for controlling the profession and socialising practitioners lodged in a professional organisation results in interprofessional conflict being managed through peer rather than bureaucratic control. Control by professionals has not simply reproduced conservatively oriented professionals in either the United States or Canada. The Council for Social Work Education (CSWE) in the United States and the Canadian Association of Social Work (CASW) carry the duty of accrediting courses. Both have included a commitment to anti-oppressive practice in their ethics and value base and expect this commitment to be reflected in teaching. Indeed, one course was recently given provisional rather than full accreditation because it had failed to give sufficient attention to First Nations issues. Additionally, although the dominant mode of social work in the United States remains strongly clinically oriented, courses are more vibrant and diverse than is the case in Britain. Much of the diversity which existed here prior to DipSW has disappeared under it (Jones, 1994b). The British situation reflects the strength of bureaucratic controls in producing a more uniform product.

Social work's commitment to social justice is more readily accepted in some countries than others. For example, South Americans have schools of social work devoted to liberationist ideologies; therapeutic ones are also well represented. The International Association of Schools of Social Work recognises that social work must be actively involved in making life better for society's marginalised groups in its mission statement. Moreover, its definition of social work is an inclusive one encompassing social development. Why is it that Britain is at odds with trends elsewhere?

Part of the answer is that Britain is at the forefront of globalisation (see Dominelli and Hoogvelt, 1994). Being subject to a centralised highly ideological government is another. The British government's direct control of the massive resources encompassed by the state (40 per cent of the Gross Domestic Product) and its determination to privatise all state activities regardless of the wishes of those involved, give it the edge in restructuring the welfare state in accordance with its ideological leanings. Consequently, it can free up public resources to promote capital accumulation in the private sector (Hutton, 1995). The realisation of this project requires changing education and training to suit commercial demands.

Holding direct powers over professionals in education and training gives the British government greater freedom to implement its policies than is possible in countries where professional interests and groups outside the governmental process have more room to manoeuvre. Successfully challenging the direction social work is taking in Britain becomes an overwhelming task. Given the current state of (dis)organisation among its professional elite and consumer groups, it is unlikely that effective resistance will be mounted. Yet, the government, as the elected representative of all its peoples, should be playing greater attention to the needs of marginalised groups. Appeals to a higher moral authority than that currently evident in market-oriented Britain is essential in cushioning vulnerable 'clients'. Given uncertainty and instability in the job market, anyone could lose substantial independent resources and become a 'client' of the personal social services. Welfare provisions, therefore, have to cater for the needs of all citizens. Social work training and education has to reflect this goal if practitioners are to offer the best possible practice, thereby incorporating this objective into the professional socialisation process.

Conclusions

DipSW has been the vehicle through which CCETSW has technocratised social work education and shifted the balance of power away from professional academics and practitioners on to employers. Bureaucratic controls have superseded professional ones as relationship building in social work becomes supplanted by practical competences endorsed by government and employers. These changes reflect a move away from training as an educational process concerned with socialising professionals into the best traditions of the profession towards the technical transmission of approved skills.

8

Professionalism, Working Relations and Service Delivery

The victory of the Charity Organisation Society (COS) in shaping the social work profession gave it a highly individualistic casework oriented approach drawing on scientific principles contained within the medical model emulated by the 'founding mothers'. This defined the professional–'client' relationship within hierarchical parameters in which the worker knows best. Meanwhile, professional power and might were to be tempered through professional ethics and values which demanded respect for the person and a due emphasis on 'client' self-determination (Butrym, 1976). Nonetheless, a strong moralistic tone underpinned these aspirations. It became particularly evident in work with 'unmarried mothers' (Sidel, 1986; Richardson, 1992). The obligations imposed on workers were complicated by inadequate resourcing for doing the job properly and a firm belief in the personal failings of 'clients' to organise coping strategies against exigencies threatening their well-being.

These created a contradictory situation rendered more complex by the influx of middle-class women who sought to inculcate middle-class values into working-class 'clients'' heads (Jones, 1983). Of equal importance, though identified as a failing much later, was the profession's neglect of significant social divisions including 'race' (Dominelli, 1988; Ahmad, 1990), gender (Dominelli and McLeod, 1989; Hanmer and Statham, 1988), disability (Morris, 1991; Oliver, 1990), age (Phillipson, 1982), and sexual orientation (Weeks, 1981; Richardson and Hart, 1981).

Although the professionalisation of social work was rooted in the voluntary sector, its values, ethics and ways of working were later absorbed by the welfare state. Its incorporation into local authority corporate state structures has been labelled 'bureau-professionalism' for being concerned with realising the burgeoning ideal of professionals and a major impediment in broadening access to welfare provisions (Parry *et al.*, 1979).

In this chapter, I examine the implications of these trends in defining the worker–'client' relationship, the type of work state social workers do, and the nature of working relations.

Worker–'client' relationships

The dominance of middle-class professionals has promoted particular definitions of social work which have not always been in keeping with its ethics, value base or the aspirations of poor working-class people at the receiving end of their ministrations. A key force driving social workers' professionalism in its early days has been the classist 'moral superiority' and ideology claiming middle-class ways are best.

This ideological bent has decried working-class values and undermined an appreciation of their survival skills. The condescension projected by this outlook exacerbates derogatory definitions of working-class lifestyles among those practising in poverty stricken areas. Within this framework, working-class people are pathologised and blamed for their predicament. These parameters also set the scene for individualising their situation without recognising that structural factors like low pay and appalling housing conditions contribute to their woes. Thus, the systematic political and economic marginalisation of working-class people remained obscure, although Marxists and socialists claimed at the time that this was a predictable outcome of a capitalist system of exploitation (Marx, 1965).

To establish middle-class hegemony over 'clients' excluded from mainstream economic and social life, middle-class social workers require their implicit consent to the superiority of middle-class lifestyles. Acceptance creates a powerful form of social control which implicates the subordinated class. In social work, it provides the basis for dividing 'clients' into the 'deserving' and 'undeserving' poor. The former subscribed to the middle-class world view, emulating its prescriptions in their own behaviour; the latter did not. Moreover, this division drew working-class people into collusive relations legitimating a rationing of resources between them and their policing each other. This further reinforced the internalisation of the dominant ideology. Material advantages accrued to those encompassed by the 'deserving' category who, in absorbing the dominant ideology, were less inclined to see society from the point of view of 'undeserving' poor people, thereby limiting their desire to express intra-class solidarity. Instead, 'deserving' poor people pathologised those below them in the pecking order. The constricted structural opportunities confronting working-class people became unimportant considerations to be overcome by sheer force of personality and hard work. These dynamics also shaped inter-class relationships by affirming the dominant ideology. Meanwhile, middle-class people (re)entrenched their position and continued to draw social work into their ambit.

Social relations organised along these lines created a form of social citizenship which was partisan and exclusive rather than inclusive. Those inside its remit received the 'benefits' provided by 'civilised society'; those outside it got their just deserts. If nothing came their way, the 'undeserving' poor had it within their power to alter their condition. They simply needed to get a job (marriage for women) and look after themselves. Poor Law legislation also ensured they would be severely punished if they ignored the obligation to fend for themselves (Chadwick, 1965). Though divisive, this differentiated system proved an extremely powerful way of formulating and regulating relationships among people with limited access to different 'allocative' and 'authoritative' resources.

The fragmentation of working-class people was extended and covered more social divisions than those based on intra- and inter-class stratification. Sexism, racism, heterosexism, ageism, disablism, mentalism, adultism and other forms of hierarchical relations created other 'insiders' and 'outsiders'. These, too, provided important loci for middle-class dominance and privilege. White middle-class people with their 'superior' lifestyles and more comfortable surroundings stood as 'role models' for the lower classes to follow. Some working-class people resisted this paradigm, but their resistance was marginalised by the dominant groups. Legal sanctions declared certain forms of opposition and association illegal and denied those deemed 'unfit' access to social power, positions and resources. Ostracism and exclusion structured the binary dyads encapsulating relations of domination which privilege one group over another, including the casting of white people as 'deserving' and black people as 'undeserving' (Fryer, 1987).

Social work was strongly implicated in the assertion of middle-class hegemony over working-class people. White middle-class women philanthropists went into working-class communities as real 'role models' of this 'superior' way of life. Drawing on women's genuine commitment to help others, this approach became an even more powerful hegemonising force. This practice further disaffirmed the position of working-class people roused many feelings of resentment and injustice (Rowbotham, 1994).

This shift in the relations of power between working-class and middle-class people was not predetermined. It entails an actively constructed process encompassing the activities of middle-class and working-class people interacting with each other to create, enforce and perpetuate it. Working-class people went along with its evolution if they did not take an active decision to the contrary. Establishing ideological hegemony over 'clients' requires more than the use of discretion in power relationships. Their acquiescence, active or passive, is essential for social control to reinforce middle-class morality and ration welfare benefits amongst potential claimants.

The impact of ideological hegemony is apparent in the harsh treatment of unmarried mothers (Sidel, 1986; Richardson, 1992). Publicly espoused Victorian middle-class morality and regard for marriage was not shared by all working-class people who had a history of common-law relationships eschewing sanctification by either church or state. A variety of patterns for organising intimate relationships also prevailed within black communities (Collins, 1991). Moreover, white middle-class Victorians betrayed their ideals. Men used women as prostitutes and engaged in extra-marital affairs (Briggs, 1968). So, a certain amount of hypocrisy covered the stigmatising of unwed working-class mothers. But, it proved a strong means of controlling the sexuality of all women in approved directions and rationing resources to 'deserving' women, especially widows (Sidel,1986; Richardson, 1992).

Having women do social work is interesting from a gendered analysis of social control. Women in working-class neighbourhoods pressing home the message of middle-class superiority was advantageous in bringing the 'soft' arm of social control into play (Parry *et al.*, 1979). Middle-class women entered these areas without physical confrontation in mind. The written word, moral sophistry and 'role models' were less intimidating weapons for waging a class war aimed at undermining working-class strengths. High rates of illiteracy, different cultural standards and norms, and socially disparaged alternative lifestyles hindered working-class people's fight on middle-class terms and terrain. Moreover, their limited political and economic power ill-equipped them for obtaining other 'allocative' and 'authoritative' resources. Meanwhile, the state held legal and practical means for coercively enforcing bourgeois social relations. Women social workers did not have to assume this task directly. They could call on other agencies such as the police and courts to do so on their behalf.

Having women social workers enforce a middle-class view of the world had another useful by-product; it divided women and prevented the growth of solidarity between them on either an inter- or intra-class basis. Had this not happened, women's interactions with each other might have been more supportive and egalitarian (see Barker, 1986; Torkington, 1981). Anecdotal evidence suggests this is happening in the delivery of services today. Working-class women, for example social care assistants, are more likely to treat working-class clients without the moral superiority characterising middle-class social workers and engage in more meaningful relationships with them.

CASE STUDY

For two hours a week Raj, an Asian woman, assists with the personal care of 80-year-old Gladys, a white working-class woman, after a serious operation has left her temporarily immobile. Raj has been *instructed by her employer not to do housework.*

Gladys, an independent woman who does things for herself, is embarrassed to involve Raj in her personal hygiene. She wanted social services to help with the housework. This had been denied by social services as the home help budget had been exhausted by the time Gladys requested it.

On her first day, Raj quickly completed the few personal tasks Gladys had identified and, having another hour left, asked what else she wanted her to do. Gladys replied she did not have any personal care needs but would appreciate assistance with dusting. The house looked a mess and desperately needed it. In explaining her need, Gladys told Raj how she hated to see the place like this and that it was 'driving her batty'.

Raj looked sad, saying this was a task she was not authorised to undertake. Gladys looked so crestfallen and upset, Raj took a cloth and cleaned the furniture. Gladys was delighted. Raj felt her appreciative warmth and was pleased.

From then on, Raj did the dusting without being asked. Neither woman spoke about it nor did they report this change. Over time, Raj did less personal care and more housework. The two women developed a close relationship, looking forward to their two hours of work together.

Raj's work was formally monitored. Gladys's evaluation was always positive; Raj never complained about working with a 'client' who demanded more than her entitlements.

The behaviour of these two women indicates how they work by relating to the whole person rather than a category. Their doing so facilitates Raj's willingness to go beyond the stipulations in her job description to provide a service the user defines as necessary to improve her life circumstances.

Home helps and social care assistants are often asked to do tasks outside their contract. They respond in the affirmative by fitting many of these into their schedules to *improve the quality of 'clients' lives.* I call this provision *extra-contractual care.* Despite injunctions from employers to the contrary, these relationships transcend simple, physical tasks to become a complex web of interaction in which human beings relate to each other as whole persons with needs. These bonds form the basis of a 'labour of love' (Graham, 1983) and enable employers to exploit the goodwill of staff who do extra work without pay and do not complain about the gaps in service provision and delivery because they fear dismissal if their extra-contractual care becomes officially known.

'Clients' collude with workers' breaking their contracts by not reporting the extra work being done in order to get what they want and not jeopardise the job prospects of their carers. The interaction between home helps and 'clients' has mutually beneficial elements. Home helps get the satisfaction of 'doing the job properly' by making someone's life better and draw on bonds of solidarity – their capacity to empathise with others' predicament, ability to form satisfying working relations, and skills in negotiating a position with which both feel comfortable.

Women workers enter these relationships not only because they need the money or the job – the elements provided through the contractual care – but because they want to exert control over, and retain autonomy in, their work. It may be easier for them to be responsive because the work draws on skills and feelings like empathy with which they are familiar. Moreover, they are used to 'doing what needs to be done' at home by 'getting on with the job' of caring for others. In asserting themselves in this way, they are defining the boundaries of their profession and its working practices. They are also creating their profession – its meaning and validity in the process. In becoming self-identifying professionals, 'doing good' becomes central to their methods of working and is an important avenue through which they validate themselves. In this respect, the strategies home helps use do not differ from those women social workers employ when using discretion to overcome bureaucratic constraints and become self-defining professionals – if only for a brief moment. In other words, they transcend bureaucratic authority to achieve professional power through personalised caring relationships.

Besides being primarily middle-class women, social workers have also been white. Their interactions with black 'clients' have emphasised white supremacy or the moral superiority of the white 'race' (Ahmad, 1990; Lorde, 1984). Supremacist attitudes and ways of organising social services have disempowered, depersonalised and pathologised the few black 'clients' who have come to their attention along gender, 'race' and class lines (Bryant *et al.*, 1985; Wilson, 1978).

Until the government formally assumed control of social services through the welfare state, the voluntary nature of social work meant that overall co-ordination was haphazard, even under COS (Mowatt and Loch, 1961). The spread of different charities with a national scope has enabled competing ideologies about the nature of social workers' relationships with 'clients' to surface. Thus, a concern with social justice and a critical examination of the system which produces deprivation and poverty on a massive scale exists alongside views emphasising the weakness of poor people's moral fibre.

However, advocates of social justice analyses have not achieved a hegemonic position. The forms of practice they have developed have been limited to small geographic areas or particular 'client' groups. Moreover, in the interplay for the heart and soul of social work, limited funds have prioritised clean water, sanitation and housing in stemming the spread of contagious diseases and social unrest from the slums (Stedman Jones, 1971). Curtailing these eventualities was more relevant to middle-class people's short-term goals than responding to poor people's need for unfettered access to other essentials in life.

The motifs of assumed moral, cultural, economic, social and political superiority and ability of white-middle class people to impose their world view on working-class people (black and white) have been sustained in contemporary society. The welfare state has led to an articulation of this project on a public as well as private dimension. Moreover, the current privatisation of welfare provisions has rearticulated and reimposed ways that encourage the development of the private commercial sector. These endorse models of care which pathologise 'clients' and privilege privately purchased individual facilities over public collective ones (Culpitt, 1992). Furthermore, the promise of replacing poor quality state services with better quality private ones has imposed white middle-class aspirations on working-class people and promoted socialisation processes for internalising middle-class mores. Consequently, working-class people have accepted the state's right to use its formal powers and institutions to reward those adhering to the dominant middle-class way of life and penalise those who do not. In furthering their effort, middle-class elites had media assistance in consistently praising their lifestyle while demonising poor people's (Morris, 1994).

Working relations under state welfare

State intervention in postwar social work enabled 'bureau-professionals' to recast these old motifs in a new form. The new arrangements resulted in greater bureaucratic controls over the workers, substantial managerial involvement in defining professional tasks, controlling workers performance, and a formal delineation of services available for 'clients'. The process can be termed the 'statisation' of social work. State control which favours privatisation undermines the position of autonomous professionals exercising independent judgements in work with 'clients' and exacerbates the tension between service provision and accessibility. Policies moving away from universal publicly funded services have increasingly excluded 'clients' from the welfare state's remit and jeopardised their citizenship status. These also substantially alter the nature of working relations and 'client'–worker relationships.

The Citizen's Charter has been mooted as an empowering feature. However, it enshrines citizenship in bureaucratic legalistic formulations by operationalising rights in published complaints procedures which neither empower 'clients' nor enhance their contact with professionals. For the quality of their interaction gets squeezed by resource constraints and calls on 'clients', the most powerless social group in the welfare equation, to take their responsibilities seriously. Litigation, another form of user comeback on professional incompetency is usually too expensive to be pursued by most 'clients'. Cash limits on 'legal aid' have eroded this possibility, although even a 'successful' outcome can leave the taste of ashes in the mouth. Moreover, many 'complaints' are not matters for expensive litigation. They are small, endlessly repeated put-downs or one-off occurrences which disempower them. These include being made to feel they cannot challenge the social worker's opinions or that their words are given insufficient weighting. These indications of poor practice cannot be easily resolved through court hearings.

The state has also subjected professionals to a new labour discipline (see Tissier, 1994b). Reduced professional autonomy and the fragmentation of their work into limited discrete tasks has led to their proletarianisation. Reducing middle-class social workers' area of professional discretion has made them more dependent on working within the state apparatus in (state) employer sanctioned ways and imposed restrictions on practice innovations favouring the cause of welfare disenfranchised people. The state can reject as partisan practitioners' activities which support users at its expense. The state's willingness to curb professional power favours managerialist control and curtails their ability to organise at the grassroots (Dominelli, 1990; Loney, 1983).

Professionals' resistance to such constraints is circumscribed by the tough time they would have mobilising internal support and an unwillingness to risk reprisals from their employers. If social workers' activities foster empowerment which challenges the status quo, however minimally, the *in*visible professional boundary whose presence is not normally overtly articulated, becomes visible and contested. Professionals can proceed a step too far in pursuing 'client' self-determination. Having transgressed the limits of 'acceptable' professional behaviour as far as employers are concerned, the struggle becomes one about the power to determine not only the role of professionals, but also how to manage the aspirations of marginalised people. Managerial imperatives backed by enormous 'allocative' and 'authoritative' resources are more likely to win in a state-dependent profession.

Nonetheless, the state has substantially expanded the numbers of social work employees and opened opportunities for women joining the labour force. Until the 1980s it had been, not a mean-spirited employer, but an important ally in raising both the levels of pay and status of the profession. The statisation of social work attracted more white men into its ranks. This picture was to change as the forces of globalisation and privatisation impacted on the welfare state.

The privatisation of the welfare state has created a quasi-market in social services (see Price-Waterhouse, 1990). This development has been characterised by contractually specified bureaucratic controls and management (Culpitt, 1992, Le Grand and Robinson, 1984). The quasi-market is causing a regendering of the division of labour. The higher paid, higher status managerial ranks in large bureaucracies concerned primarily with purchasing of services are occupied by men. The lower paid, lower status provision of services, including those in small-scale voluntary projects and private firms, are the realm of women. The advance of large international firms in service provision and the growing nationalisation and international-isation of large voluntary organisations also contributes to this reorientation of the labour hierarchy. Moreover, an extrapolation of current trends suggests that service provision and labour relation-ships will become increasingly driven by market discipline and considerations at the expense of the human needs. In this scenario, women, alongside poor people having lesser access to 'allocative' and 'authoritative' resources, will find it difficult to shift the framework in more egalitarian directions. So will voluntary organi-sations, for their remit as providers will be constrained by contract specifications imposed by purchasers.

The New Right's neo-conservative welfare agenda has established a new hegemonic relationship endorsing residual notions of welfare. In it, entitlement becomes a privilege borne on the sufferance of society's morally superior 'white male middle class' (Murray, 1984, 1990, 1994). Self-sufficiency and individual responsibility, as the cornerstones of a new relationship between society and the individual, privileges those with unfettered access to social power and resources. In a racially stratified and gendered society, this approach is exclusionary. The 'moral panics' New Right ideologies foster around single parent women who have never been married, delinquent youth, and the so-called black 'underclass' are sympto-matic of the restructuring of old welfare dilemmas (Dominelli, 1993; Morris, 1994; Walker and Walker, 1987). The New Right uses 'moral panics' to mobilise public opinion in favour of disenfran-

chising welfare recipients of limited rights. Their failure to successfully complete this project rests on the contingent reality produced
by their opponents.

Reasserting control over social developments by (re)creating a
hegemonic order in their favour is a critical part of white men's
backlash. Getting the state on their side is central in restructuring
social relations. This has required the New Right to take over the
state apparatus by winning electoral control and using its period in
power to alter the way it had been configured: putting its
sympathisers into key decision-making positions, making organisational cultures consistent with market dictums and reversing the
state's previous social agenda. The latter had included within it, the
promotion of social justice and rights for working-class people via its
commitment to tackle poverty, black people in the struggle to end
racial discrimination, and women demanding gender equality
(Dominelli, 1991b; Walby, 1990). Having successfully redefined the
role of the state, the New Right continues to undermine those rights
despite substantial resistance to its doing so. The gains reclaimed
through this struggle reveal how, in social conflict, no side can claim
'the last word'. Victories will be temporary as both those holding
social power and those excluded from it regroup their 'authoritative'
and 'allocative' resources to (re)contest each other on new terrain.

These events indicate that the 'new social movements' have
mobilised more general support for their causes and moved the state
into responding to demands for equality. Although expectations have
never been fully realised, legislative changes and practice innovations
within the welfare state have promoted a social change agenda which
requires the abolition of all forms of structured inequality.

Men and the welfare state

White men want to reverse gains obtained by white women and
black people because they believe the state 'has gone too far' in
supporting their demands for equality (Omi and Winant, 1986) and
insist on reinstating their historical, taken-for-granted privileges.
Their commitment to overturning social equality began in the 1970s
but picked up momentum under Margaret Thatcher in Britain,
Ronald Reagan in the United States, and Brian Mulroney in Canada.
There were many exchanges of ideas among New Right ideologues
and politicians in these countries as they learnt from one another's

experiences. The New Right amassed information, not always accurately reflecting reality, to refashion gendered and racialised stereotypes to undermine practices aimed at reducing structural inequalities (Morris, 1994; see Murray, 1994 for example).

The New Right's attack on non-traditional family formations had white men claiming their rights as husbands, fathers and workers had been trampled upon by white women and black people so that they now formed a disadvantaged minority (see Gairdner, 1992). They complained that: alimony gave women divorcing their partners a meal ticket for life; courts automatically awarded mothers custody without considering the suitability of fathers; and unqualified white women and black people were preferred over qualified white men in the job market. However, the empirical evidence does not affirm this analysis.

Individual white men may have lost taken-for-granted privileges linked to excluding white women and black people from competing for jobs by their being spuriously labelled incapable of working in top posts, or good primarily at doing domestic tasks. But, to maintain that men experience gender and racial oppression of the kind white women and black people do, confuses reality for fantasy. In a fairer competition for social resources, white men, previously privileged at the expense of others, will lose those privileges. However, this simply amounts to playing the game by men's own rules. Individual competition and merit still determine the criteria for assessing eligibility to social resources. Current research does not uphold the claim that unqualified black men and women are getting jobs being denied to qualified white men. The bulk of top jobs remain the prerogative of white men. And a restructuring of the labour force is producing lower paid casualised jobs rejected by them (Walby, 1990).

Studies undertaken from a variety of political complexions dispute the New Right's charges. These have demonstrated that: *men* (not women) are more likely to abuse their power over women and children within family relationships by abusing them physically, sexually and emotionally (Finkelhor, 1984); high status, well-paid posts are held mainly by white men, not white women or black people (Walby, 1990); women experience a drop of 75 per cent in income on divorce while men see theirs rise by 47 per cent (Ruth, 1989); and women not men, perform the bulk of unpaid domestic work in the home and simultaneously hold jobs in the waged labour market (Walby, 1990). While the backlash indicates the 'blame the victim' philosophy, it also relies heavily on using one-off examples to argue for a non-existent general trend. Thus, it involves an individualistic framing of the problem to be addressed and the solution to it.

The sociological problem becomes one of disentangling the position of individual men from their social grouping when the two are intertwined. Doing so requires an examination of the power relationships holding collectivities together, questioning assumptions about the values embodied in the social relations men support, and understanding how men can do well as a social category while individual men suffer. This analysis will expose the scarcity factor as a major culprit in their failure to personally acquire the 'authoritative' and 'allocative' resources they require. It also exposes how scarcity becomes a kind of social control which keeps both men and women in their place.

To argue that white men *need* these social resources is another point. Of course, they do. This claim holds for white women and black people too. But, as long as society is organised according to market driven allocatory principles, people will lose out. Individual merit in this context becomes an allocatory device for rationing scarce goods. Changing this equation of inequality requires doing more than arguing that women should return to the kitchen sink while men get on with running the world – an unfeasible proposition in the current historical conjecture.

White men have taken the lead in restructuring hegemonic relations of domination. Some white women have supported their stance because relations of domination and subordination do not exist out there in the abstract, except as 'ideal types'. Each individual man and woman has to personally engage in their creation and recreation. In the process of doing this, men and women acting as agents in a social drama will make decisions which best meet their personal interests, value system and world view. These may be partly derived from their social position. But, whether men and women will act according to stereotype as the 'ideal type' model dictates, or challenge it, is not predetermined. Oppression is a socially constructed not biologically driven phenomenon. Thus, men and women do not create and recreate relations of domination and subordination through their physical attributes, as essentialist theoreticians would have us believe, but do so in negotiation with others through purposive action geared to meeting specific objectives which they define.

Individually, men and women can make choices in any direction. Their ability to exercise that choice depends on their access to social resources. This is the point at which social structures and organisations and the positions individuals occupy within them become important. The constraints people encounter will be shaped by the social position they occupy collectively as well as individually. As society is currently organised, men have the edge over women as the (re)definers of reality and (re)allocators of resources. But there is nothing immutable in this being the case. It can be changed through purposive collective action, hard as this may be to achieve. White women, such as Jean Rook in Britain and Phyllis Schlaffy in America (Ruth, 1989) have, as individuals, the 'allocative' and 'authoritative' resources necessary for exercising a choice and have done so in ways that justify men's attacks on women's demands for further equality (see Schlaffy, 1977). In this, they have used their influential and well-resourced positions. And, they have drawn on the fragmentation which occurs in oppressed groups because individuals act to realise particular ends. That they may not succeed in achieving these is due to contingent realities which are created by other people acting to preserve their counter interests. Contingent realities may or may not coincide with their specific aims. If they do, success is theirs. Success or failure depends on the 'authoritative' and 'allocative' resources swung behind a specific position.

The oppression of women makes white middle-class women's experience of life substantially different from their male counterparts. However, the privileged lifestyles of white middle-class women differentiate their interests from those of white working-class or black women, except at the most abstract level of gender oppression. While this level of abstraction is useful in certain situations, it tells us little about the position individual women might adopt on a given issue. A similarly complex picture emerges for other social divisions. In the United States, members of the black middle class have revealed a more complicated racial configuration. Professional middle-class black men like Shelby Steele (1990) argue black people's fear of success, not structural deterrents, is the major barrier to black people seizing opportunities for advancement secured through the civil rights movement.

Arguing the general situation on the basis of individual experiences, Steele, Schlaffy and Rook have framed the problem to treat the individual as *independent* of the social structure. Feminists conceptualise individual experiences and social structures as *interdependent*. The structural transformations being wrought in the nation-state through international economic realities and demographic changes are being disregarded by the New Right. Yet, these provide powerful actors with the means for perpetuating structured inequalities independent of individual volition or the actions of marginalised people. For example, Britain and the United States have been losing out in the restructuring of manufacturing industries, often initiated by American and British firms responding to competition from Japanese industry. 'Downsizing' caused by structural change, not white women or black people, has deprived skilled white working- class men of well-paid jobs.

Well-paid manufacturing jobs with their attendant unstigmatised welfare benefits in the West have been relocated to the 'Tiger Economies' of the East where lower environmental controls, cheap labour and minimal publicly funded welfare facilities have given employers a freer hand in exploiting workers and the environment. The current situation mimics Victorian Britain before a powerful labour movement challenged the might of employers to have things their own way. As social workers' and probation officers' caseloads reveal, the loss of blue-collar jobs has had the greatest impact on skilled working-class men and young people who can no longer hope to land employment once they leave school (Oakley and Williams, 1994). These changes present Western countries and social workers with a challenge. Social workers' 'client' groups may alter substantially to incorporate more men. Social workers and probation officers will need to find socially useful and attractive fulfilment for young people in place of drugs and crime. But this will only happen if practitioners as those who know can convince the general public, policy-makers, politicians and opinion formers in the media, that *society acting through collective decision-making mechanisms for the good of all its members* assumes responsibility for realising this aim.

The New Right's conceptual framework ignores the low-paid, part-time nature of job opportunities now available in the British and North American economies. These are taken primarily by women whose responsibilities in caring for others limit their availability for the labour market (Coyle; 1984, Walby, 1990). Women are not competing for men's posts because men reject casualised low-wage employment. Economic changes have bypassed men. Meanwhile, the growth in the numbers of the working poor indicate that waged earnings have dropped to such an extent that more and more *employees* are *poor* (Walby, 1990).

Even middle-class professionals ensconced within the interstices of the welfare state are experiencing lowered standards of living. Salary levels have failed to keep up with the costs of living, particularly housing. Yet home ownership forms a crucial element in defining their lifestyle (Wistow *et al.*, 1994; Carter *et al.*, 1992). They also face greater job insecurity through rapid organisational changes and the casualisation of work. For example, in the constant restructuring of British social services departments, social workers are forced to apply for their own jobs and sign new, more limited employment contracts. Posts may be split or job-shared to allow employees greater flexibility, but the majority of workers opting for these, including those at managerial level, are women. The rising costs of living and the greater pressures on families to live lifestyles portrayed by media stars has consigned the one-earner family to the dustbin of history. More and more families need two incomes to enjoy modest lifestyles (Walby, 1990). An increased emphasis on consumerism exacerbates these pressures. These transformations have affected social workers too, even though their salary levels have never attained the heights reached by doctors and lawyers. Low salaries also make front-line jobs less attractive to men.

Structural changes have affected different groups of people differentially. White middle-class professionals have realised that their jobs no longer assure them of comfortable lifestyles or certainty in employment. These changes have impacted dramatically on white women with dependent children, older white women and black people across the lifecycle who bear the brunt of poverty caused by both a changing labour market and cuts in welfare benefits and services (Walby, 1990). Yet, the gendered or feminised nature of poverty (Scott, 1984) has been used by the New Right to blame women individually for their plight. Arguing that there are jobs for the taking, New Right governments in Britain and the United States are compelling women with young children to enter paid employment or lose benefit (Oakley and Williams, 1994). The New Right's analysis ignores realities such as the jobs available do not allow women to earn incomes which would keep families above the breadline.

The New Right could have defined the problem to be addressed as one of low wages rather than women's character defects in an effective ploy of victim blaming. My argument is not that women are 'victims' of forces beyond their control. Women will make rational choices based on opportunities open to them in particular circumstances. For them, managing on less money than they have already would be an irrational choice. While they are 'victims' of an economic system which gives them access to only low-paid dead-end jobs, women will respond by using the resources at their disposal to actively limit their victim status. Rejecting these jobs by staying on benefit assures them of a more comfortable survival than would have otherwise been the case. Maintaining a higher income is a rational choice. Women are victim-survivors and not mere victims.

The right to family life is a privilege New Right ideologies accord only to white middle-class people (Levitas, 1986). This is consistent with a belief in the 'moral superiority' of their ways. Under their tutelage, racialised discourse has reached new twists, especially in the United States where disproportionate numbers of single parent families headed by black women are on welfare. The term 'underclass' has been reconstituted to describe black people's situation and imbue it with racial and gender hostility (Morris, 1994). Black people's position in Britain is substantially different. They constitute a smaller proportion of the overall population. The black middle class is small. The numbers of black people on welfare are minute. Yet, Charles Murray (1990) is peddling racialised 'underclass' discourse on our shores. More worryingly, he has many white British people across the political spectrum buying into his vision.

New Right theorists have created the concept of a 'culture of welfare dependency' (Murray, 1984; Glazer, 1988) to insist that individuals on welfare, especially families headed by white women and black people, wilfully refuse to look after themselves by relying on 'state handouts'. These enable them to lead more affluent lives than the working poor on whom such writers have bestowed the 'deserving' mantle. The New Right offers one way of defining the situation. It is irrelevant given the problem of low pay and structurally reproduced inequalities. However, it is potent in creating 'moral panics' which justify their removal from the welfare rolls as the 'undeserving' poor.

Placing the emphasis on individuals taking responsibility for their predicament reinforces the pathologising of individuals caught in structurally created poverty traps. Putting the spotlight on them and their failures bypasses the system and the role it has played in creating inequalities in the first place. It also ignores the role structures play as resources enabling actors to amass other 'allocative' and 'authoritative' resources in protecting their interests across space and time. Moreover, views pathologising individuals feed into people's feelings of powerlessness when confronting forces whose workings they do not understand. These legitimate simplistic solutions fostering 'illusions' of 'doing something about the problem'. The interplay between different levels of reality facilitates New Right politicians' mobilisation of popular opinion against the welfare state by manipulating alleged abuses of their 'nanny state' in Britain and 'welfare' in the United States.

The New Right has succeeded in redefining the welfare agenda to a considerable degree in Britain, despite the presence of a significant proportion of the population opposing it. This has been possible because it has attracted working-class voters who had previously voted Labour to gain electoral control (Hall and Jacques, 1983, 1989) and access to a new set of 'allocative' and 'authoritative' resources. These voters had experienced structural changes which increased insecurity and instability in their own lives. Gender-hostile and racialised discourses legitimated the scapegoating of white women and black people in an understandable if morally reprehensible action taken to assert their own power and control. The surprising feature is the Left's failure to see this coming and mobilise opinion against it. The Right has not only defined its own politics, it has also set those which Labour, in the absence of an alternative vision to galvanise its mass base, has to follow. Claimants, welfare provisions and caring professionals have lost out in this process.

Despite this gloom, white women and black people have continued to struggle for their rights. Social work has become a crucial site in which white women and black people press their claims to equality and social justice. A good deal of their ability to survive attacks on their limited gains lies in the strength they have derived from having implemented many of their principles in practice. Campaigns against them have ranged from the abolition of the Greater London Council (GLC) which promoted anti-sexist and anti-racist initiatives and offered municipal socialism with its more solidaristic approach as a foil to the individualistic Thatcherite one in the early 1980s, to personal attacks on them as 'outsiders'. Black women's efforts in developing resources responding to their specific needs illustrate how black communities have supported their continued presence when others have sought to undermine them (Bryant *et al.*, 1985). Such solidarity has defended black children's nursery and play provisions closure (see Wilson, 1993; Bryant *et al.*, 1985). Similarly, white women have found it easier to protect resources they developed to cater for women's health care needs (Oakley and Williams, 1994; Foster, 1989). Other GLC initiatives, which the state has refused to support, have been adopted by the voluntary sector, for example lesbian support groups (Whitlock, 1987).

Social work's white middle-class disablist heterosexist definition of bureau-professionalism has failed 'clients'. It has been challenged by a variety of social movements including feminism, black activism, the disability movement, and gay and lesbian movements. These groups have presented alternative visions of what they want in service provision and professional–user relationships. They have also implemented their theoretical ideas in practice. Although their efforts have not realised their dreams for the personal social services, they have developed services responsive to user defined needs and facilitated more egalitarian professional relationships which users evaluate as being of a superior quality to those espoused by state bureau-professionals (Foster, 1989; Dominelli and McLeod, 1989; Mama, 1989).

Organising the bureau-professionals

Dreams to create a strong profession were revived post-Seebohm when generic teams held out the hope of uniting disparate specialisms in a common cause. Moreover, the overall strength of the trades union movement in 1970s Britain encouraged sympathetic academics and practitioners to argue the relevance of collective organisation to social work. NALGO, NUPE and COHSE enjoyed rising social worker membership. The British Union of Social Workers (BUSW) was formed in opposition to BASW to flex union power (Joyce *et al.*, 1987). Though shortlived, the sense of optimism which then prevailed increased the confidence with which social workers felt they could challenge the state by mobilising class interests (see Corrigan and Leonard, 1978; Bolger *et al.*, 1981; Joyce *et al.*, 1987).

By organising within trade unions, social workers highlighted a contradiction: powerful professional tensions between the interests of workers and those of 'clients' which erupt when these conflict. Discussions about strike action crystallised one of these moments. During the late 1970s and early 1980s, workers who sought to improve their terms and conditions of employment found it difficult to reconcile this desire with their commitment to serving 'vulnerable clients'. The media had fun exposing the dilemmas inherent in their actions. While media pundits derided social workers and the divisions between them, strikes went ahead (see Joyce *et al.*, 1987). Some workers took this opportunity to raise questions about the nature of the services on offer and how to enhance their quality. Concerns about pay and conditions have been accentuated during the period that men entered social work in increasing numbers. Whether or not this has been coincidental remains to be established. Research scrutinising the gender dimensions of these conflicts has yet to be conducted. Gender does not feature prominently in the text which describes industrial activism in social work (see Joyce *et al.*, 1987).

Social workers' interests have not always been pitted against those of users. For example, BASW, COHSE, NAPO, NALGO and NUPE have been influential in securing policies promoting the development of anti-oppressive services. As the struggle to end gender and racial inequalities in social work unfolded, union organisations themselves became the targets of initiatives seeking to eliminate oppressive policies and practices. However, the thrust for developing the relevant strategies has come from white women and black people organising within these organisations in autonomous special interest sections and mixed groups to challenge racist and sexist policies and practice (see Joyce *et al.*, 1987). As a result of their efforts, the empowerment of users has become a legitimate part of trades unions' agendas. Thus, BASW, NAPO, NUPE and NALGO have played major roles in legitimating, developing, promoting and monitoring equal opportunity policies both within their own organisations and their employing agencies.

Given a preoccupation with accessing equal opportunities for individuals or supporting individual complaints, trades unions may be criticised for not going far enough and for focusing on procedural rather than transformational change. However, these have marked a significant shift away from the previous gender-blind and colour-blind policies which have masqueraded under the cloak of neutrality in social work.

These organisations' task now is to engage in collective advances which address structural inequalities around gender and 'race'. In the United States, these constitute 'class actions' which, at the time of writing, are fraught with division and uncertainty. The dynamics of the backlash undermine attempts to establish egalitarian relations.

The defeat of labour activism and privatisation of welfare services have intensified the difficulties organisations and individuals seeking to end oppressive working relations have to surmount.

The obstacles to progress are compounded by features endemic to social work. White middle-class bias continues to bedevil it and has profound implications for the development of provisions. Values and forms of social organisation which are not white middle-class ones remain defined deviant and pathological. Services continue oppressing people rather than contributing to their empowerment. Facilities which oppressed groups have created for themselves stand outside the mainstream in exacerbated marginalisation. Their inability to mainstream these have reinforced the failure of white people to reconceptualise services to be more in keeping with black people's aspirations or men to respond effectively to women's agenda.

Unpacking the dynamics which 'paralyse' white people wanting to implement anti-racist practice helps progress their commitment in that direction. White people need to undertake this task with each other sensitively, drawing on training as a form of consciousness-raising which guides their understanding and behaviour rather than transmitting preconceived knowledge. In moving forward, white people have to consult with black people to ensure they are not colluding with each other to reinforce racist dynamics. A similar process should be followed in addressing other forms of oppression, including sexism.

The following example depicts how training as consciousness-raising engages with the complex interaction between 'race', gender and authority. Traditional social work values – empathy, 'client'-centredness, proceeding at the pace of the individual, are essential in the work done by the white woman trainer and white male 'student'. White people need to maintain their dignity and find something of worth in themselves before they can value the contributions of others different from them. Reflecting on the connections between their social position and personal experiences of it as individuals unlocks white people's capacity to empathise with others. The white facilitator's key concern is helping white 'students' understand their own role in reproducing racism and working to eradicate it. She works closely with a black facilitator whose prime responsibility is to assist black 'students' develop a strong sense of identity as black people with specific needs in surviving racism and transcending its limitations. The facilitators regularly check out their proposed ways of proceeding with each other.

'Students' in the case study are divided into autonomous peer groups according to 'race'. In these, they initially begin to examine and work on their own personal agendas. Autonomous peer groupings enable students to explore their own specific needs in a relatively safe environment. Reducing power differentials is important in creating an open climate. Each 'student' takes responsibility for letting others know what they need to 'feel safe' and agrees the ground rules which will guide both content and process in their interaction, recognising that each person experiences 'safety' in relative terms. The groups may be subdivided further, along other social divisions, for example gender. The size of the groups should be sufficiently small to allow 'students' to spend ample time addressing their personal needs before engaging with others on problems of mutual concern. Having completed the personal agenda-setting task, black and white 'students' work together as a mixed social work team to focus on practice issues: becoming capable of working in anti-racist ways with 'clients', black and white; and following anti-racist principles in relationships with colleagues. Their common objective is to empower themselves in working in anti-racist ways and feel confident in doing so.

CASE STUDY

Alex is a white working-class student who has struggled hard to get to university. He wants to do well and prove himself. But, at the same time, he does not wish to achieve his laurels at the expense of others. While on the course, the issue of racism is raised by both black and white students on it. Alex's sense of justice makes him feel that he should support their anti-racist initiatives, but he feels disempowered and unable to work out what the 'correct' line is.

Although the course avows that creating new orthodoxies is not the aim of anti-racist social work, and that each student needs to work out which positions they are willing to support for themselves, this makes little difference to Alex. He feels pressured to develop ways of working with 'clients' which are more sympathetic to their needs as they see them. While his own value base makes this an acceptable way of proceeding, he feels 'stuck' as to how to put such commitment into practice.

In sessions where Alex is encouraged to examine his personal agenda – what he wants from working in anti-racist ways, what frightens him about it, what he hopes to gain from becoming anti-racist and similar questions, it becomes clear that several obstacles block his ability to work in the ways he wishes. One of these is his fear that as a white working-class man who has struggled to get this far, he will be unable to forge ahead and get his 'just deserts', that is, what he deserves given his skills, knowledge and qualifications. Moreover, he worries that education, his avenue to upward mobility, will become a barrier to it. He, too, wants out of his 'white ghetto'.

His other concern is his being a racist individual; a hopeless case. Since he cannot change himself, he feels anti-racism lies outside his grasp. Whatever his commitment, he interprets past failure to act in anti-racist ways as proof that it is impossible for white people to achieve such status. At the same time, he does not feel personally responsible for the racist nature of the country's institutions, nor its racist past. However, he acknowledges the exploitation of black people because they are black.

The white woman trainer believes that the crucial issues this young man has identified need to be addressed directly. To do so, it is important to accept his commitment to anti-racist practice as genuine. The problem is how to overcome the structural and personal blocks to realising this. Both dimensions have to be addressed for progress to be made.

To begin with, the facilitator feels that Alex needs his sense of self as a person with something useful to offer others in the social work relationship to be validated. The struggles and sacrifices he has made as a working-class male to get to this point in a system which is not geared to meeting his needs to be acknowledged. Sadly, the system makes him feel ashamed and unworthy of the things he has achieved thus far – that he is 'not quite good enough'. Thus, the middle-class bias of the system he engages with needs bringing out for him to examine.

The trainer feels it is important for Alex to use this experience and knowledge about himself to develop empathy with other oppressed people. While class oppression is not the same as the oppression of women or black people, it is a significant form of oppression in its own right and needs to be tackled. It, too, leaves scars on the person and subjects individuals to structural inequality. Class oppression shares certain features with other forms of oppression: the exclusion of those defined as 'others' from socially acquired power and resources; blocked aspirations, despite talents and qualifications. Alex's internalised feelings of inferiority and the sense of powerlessness based on class oppression can be extrapolated to other forms of oppression. So can his desire to break out of it.

Moreover, the facilitator makes the point that structural inequalities are socially created. Racism is socially constructed, therefore racist attitudes, behaviours, and actions have their base in society. Alex is racist, not by nature but because the social relations he engages in on a daily basis encourage this form of behaviour to maintain a particular distribution of power and resources. There is nothing about his behaviour that cannot be changed. He is no more racist by his biology than white women and black people.

His understanding and experience of class is used by the trainer to help Alex broaden his understanding of 'race' issues. Just as he rejects being defined 'inferior' because he is a working-class man, women and black people similarly reject the stereotypes applied to them. Such action is acknowledged as a valid and valued form of resistance to oppression.

Looking at the interconnections between personality (the personal) and social organisation (the structural) are important to Alex's intellectual understanding of what is happening. But he also needs to connect at the emotional level. Emotional understanding is critical to his being able to integrate theory and practice and move from his specific situation to the wider picture.

Another crucial aspect is enabling Alex to value himself. This requires Alex to undertake more work on himself; examine his motivations for doing things; highlight his expectations about himself; and seek ways of becoming comfortable and confident about his ability to consider complex and difficult matters such as racism and sexism. He discovers to his surprise that having the approval of others, particularly his peers, is important. So is his need to 'feel OK' about himself. Reaching this level of self-awareness led to a series of discussions about what he likes in himself, what he does not and why.

This work is significant in getting Alex to realise that he is not a hopeless case; that he is not totally worthless. Like most other people, he has characteristics which he wants to keep and others that he wishes to reject. Having identified which these are makes it easier for Alex to work to enhance his positive atttributes and eliminate those he feels bad about. Self-affirmation is an important ingredient in initiating change in individuals (Steinem, 1990). He becomes more at ease with himself and less worried about what others says about him. Hence, he is better prepared to deal with those barbs which undermine his sense of confidence and initiate behaviour he feels ashamed of. It also strengthens his resolve to stand up for those values he deems important. Equality and social justice are cornerstones of his value system.

While much progress had been made, Alex remains concerned about 'the scarcity factor'. He worries that in the competition for jobs, he will lose out if he tries to stand up for his beliefs. In his view, social work only pays lip-service to empowering 'clients'. People like him can easily be labelled 'troublemakers' to be denied jobs and the opportunity to earn their living.

At this stage, the trainer is able to say that this is indeed a danger that he has to consider. Like everything else, working in anti-racist ways carries risks when undertaken in a world that is either indifferent or hostile to its development.

Not working in anti-racist ways also carries risks. Aside from his not being true to his own value system, other people – black people – pay the price for his inaction. Alex's experience of class oppression is used to help him understand how he pays the price as a working-class person for middle-class privilege.

On a historical basis, working-class people have died to make the advances he now enjoys, including making access to university possible. Black people have also died and are dying everyday in their struggle against racism. However, it is clear that, as a white person, he can choose whether to take up the anti-racist struggle or not. But in making his choice, it is important that he assesses the risks he takes in both directions and the price his (in)action exacts from black people.

The trainer brings in her experience at this point. She has taken risks in resisting racism, experiencing periods of unemployment and rejection for having done so. She has maintained her integrity by knowing that power is not so monolithic that only racists can get their way. There are jobs espousing anti-racist commitments which he could apply for. These help pay the bills and have the advantage of making progress in eradicating oppression. There is so much work which needs to be done on this front that to talk about a scarcity of work, or competition from others, overestimates the scarcity factor. However, she agrees that, in the longer term, a fundamental restructuring of the labour market is required.

She feels it is important to raise demands for racial equality in all public fora and join with others embarking on similar ways forward. In addition, she feels that anti-racist practice, as good practice, better equips Alex to work with white 'clients'. It is important to acknowledge that they get a poor deal from the personal social services and that a fundamental restructuring of social services would improve service provision for them, too. Such work requires forming alliances and working with others.

This case study demonstrates how critical it is for trainers to respond to each person's reality as they see it. There is little point in classifying their responses as merely racist or false consciousness and leaving individuals to their own devices. Besides being dogmatic and unhelpful, these responses alienate potential allies in the anti-racist struggle and deny them the possibility of making choices other than those they customarily make. Given that white socialisation processes do not foster egalitarian relationships between black people and white people, it is not surprising that white people's reaction to addressing the issue is one of confusion, failure to see their own contribution to racism or inability to make connections between different kinds of structural inequalities which keep people in their place and render them more easy to both exploit and be exploited.

People's multiple identities have to be explored. Individual people can be both oppressed and oppressing. Making connections between these roles facilitates people learning how to use their experience of oppression along one dimension to develop the skills of countering it along others. Their deepened understanding of different forms of oppression can be the outcome of transferring skills from one area to another. Transferability of skills is useful in extending good practice.

This case study highlights the importance of paying attention to process. Doing so requires sensitive work, some of which is undertaken on a one-to-one basis. Working in this way is time consuming and resource intensive. This is a major impediment to the spread of anti-racist social work in the current political climate. There are techniques and resources which can defray this resource shortage, for example student-directed groups, videos, computer-assisted-learning packages. *They do not make up for the lack of access to a skilled facilitator who draws on a wealth of knowledge and experience in responding to the specific problems presented by a particular student.* Moreover, students who struggle with their own reactions to racism and being labelled racists should be treated with respect and dignity as, without this, it is not possible to change their behaviour. People may mouth the right rhetoric, but they will lack the skills for moving from one learning situation to another in a way that is consistent with anti-racist practice. The importance of having ends and means working in harmony and compatibility with each other cannot be overstated, especially in situations in which individuals have embarked on a process of painful personal change. This is a message both feminists and black activists have emphasised (Collins, 1991).

Conclusions

Social work's professional ethics emphasise its caring dimensions. However, their implementation in practice is constrained by organisational, legislative, economic and political priorities. These may thwart practitioners' aspirations to provide services that either 'clients' want or their professional judgement dictates. At times, social workers' own needs as employees may conflict with those of service users. While none of these dilemmas is easily resolvable, social workers have used anti-oppressive theories and practice to deliver services more appropriate to 'clients'' needs. Training, as consciousness-raising, assists this task.

9

Strategies for Change

Social work occurs in an organisational context with the care and control dilemma as a key element. Social work is essentially about striking a balance between caring for and empowering people or controlling them. Changing organisational structures which legitimate its activities and methods is a major concern of anti-racist feminist social work.

Handling the legal, statutory and organisational constraints within which social workers negotiate work with 'clients' requires sociological social work and user-oriented evaluations of existing services to assess user satisfaction. As part of the evaluation process, users and workers have to collaborate in formulating possible strategies for improving services and changing arrangements to suit emerging circumstances.

Managers are marketing the incorporation of quality control mechanisms such as British Standard (BS) 5750 or Total Quality Management (TQM) in social work bureaucracies as an innovative move in empowering users (Wistow *et al.*, 1994; Clarke *et al.*, 1994; Dobson, 1994). Their procedures have bureaucratised the evaluation process, making their claims more rhetoric than substance. These quality control mechanisms go for the lowest common denominator in service delivery rather than the best possible standards. In an individualised service, these have to be tailored to the specific needs of each individual. However, BS5750 and TQM aim at a uniform or standard product which ignores the unique and focuses on the common. Their mechanisms reduce the 'voice' of consumers and disempower them in the name of enforcing 'rights'.

A key danger which arises is that bureaucratic quality control measures obscure the different starting points of marginalised groups and hold back development by establishing the same minimum standards for everyone rather than eliciting responses appropriate to user-defined needs. These are likely to entrench existing inegalitarian social relations and ensure that those in privileged positions gain more than those whose lives are mediated through social disadvantage. For example, a residential home for young adolescents seeking funding for its activities is required to introduce quality control mechanisms as a condition of an award. This includes meeting specific targets, achieving a given ratio of key workers to residents. When a (white) inspection team arrived, the quality control mechanisms were in place and the staff–resident ratio attained. The inspection team left feeling everything was now in place for delivering the best possible service. None of its members learnt that a request by three young black residents for black key workers had been ignored. This information came to light only when a relative visiting one of the three black youths asked how serious their key workers were in addressing racism.

This chapter explores user involvement in evaluating the personal social services and considers how this can be strengthened by understanding their position of structural powerlessness and aspirations for better provisions.

Case study materials covering a range of settings will be used to indicate that change should be embraced rather than resisted in the interests of enhancing the quality of users' experiences. Achieving such possibilities nationally draws on active local networks and support groups which provide many small-scale prefigurative illustrations of 'good practice' in the field. Movement in their direction invites the sharing of information through communication links which promote debate and action across the country, within the profession and outside it.

Empowerment in 'client'–worker relationships

Social workers have cherished 'client' self-determination as a value through the years. But it has not been fully observed in practice. Nor has there been an evaluation of its relevance and prevalence. Most traditional social work methodologies contain within them a vision of the 'expert' professional being in control of the situation and using his or her definitions of 'client' need to promote personal change in socially acceptable directions (see Hollis, 1964; Perlman,

1957). As a result, 'clients' felt disempowered and unhappy at receiving interactions which did not meet their needs (Kadushin, 1959; Solomon, 1976; Bailey and Brake, 1975; Doyal and Gough, 1991). After years of these experiences, users organised on their own behalf and demanded that social work practice be altered to meet their aspirations (Dominelli and McLeod, 1989; Corrigan and Leonard, 1978; Morris, 1991; Oliver, 1990; Hanscombe and Forster, 1982).

A range of 'client' groups have grasped the initiative by establishing action groups within social services to pursue their interests: young people who set up the National Association of Young People in Care; women in management; women carers; black people; gay men; lesbian women; people with disabilities; people with learning impairments; and older people. Each of these groups have created social movements from which they draw strength and develop prefigurative examples of practice which model new provisions.

Each of these groups has similar complaints of the official services on offer and accuses professionals of being:

- remote
- bureaucratic
- unresponsive to their needs
- unaccountable, and
- speaking for them.

Users have rejected welfare provisions for being elitist and having priorities other than theirs. Moreover, they are fed up with being disempowered by the very people who ostensibly attend to their needs. Thus, they have created alternatives which carry their confidence and which they control.

Social divisions

Social work's failure to address social divisions in its practice has ignored the different realities that structured inequalities shape for each 'client' group. This has lowered the quality of services provided and made them irrelevant to users' needs (see Ahmad, 1990). Traditional assumptions emphasise 'sameness' among users: all 'clients' are the same; their needs are the same and can be met through the same provisions. This unsubstantiated universalising of social existence has delivered inappropriate services to people whose status and access to resources are below the norms used to evaluate need and establish provisions. These norms have been defined as racist, classist, heterosexist, ageist, disablist and mentalist (see Corrigan and Leonard, 1978; Phillipson, 1982; Ahmad, 1990; Morris, 1991; Fernando, 1988). Consequently, services sink to the lowest common denominator and meet the needs of limited numbers of 'clients' seeking them.

Knowing that services have not been developed with them specifically in mind, 'clients' avoid them. Help from social services is usually sought in dire circumstances, as the last resort. Such dynamics perpetuate the creation of services accessed not 'as of right' but as residual services carrying considerable stigma. Consequently, self-referrals are few. Most referrals are made by other professionals, particularly doctors and health visitors who encounter potential 'clients' in an unstigmatised health service.

The high number of referrals from the medical profession has legitimated the transfer of the professionally popular and prestigious medical model of intervention to the social services setting with minimal alteration. The social worker stands as the expert telling 'clients' how to ameliorate their situation. However, 'clients'' realities are such that social workers come across as punitive professionals to be avoided at all costs; or 'do-gooders' who could listen sympathetically to their tale, but be powerless to act. Either way, consumer satisfaction with services delivered has been relatively low. Nonetheless, those who successfully establish professional friendships with their social workers have valued these for the support they have offered. The bulk of 'client' problems stem from extreme poverty and lack of other material resources. But this is one area in which the social worker's ability to intervene is limited. Consequently, 'clients' accuse social workers of 'keeping a lid on things' or patching them together with 'sticking plasters' – palliative measures at best (Bolger *et al.*, 1981).

The task of social workers commanding resources or holding their own *vis-à-vis* other professionals has been made substantially more difficult by the profession's low status. For example, social workers have felt powerless influencing decisions taken by consultants, psychiatrists and others of standing in medicine (Heraud, 1979).

There has been a general lack of clarity about social workers' role. This has not helped enhance their popularity or encourage the use of their services. Strategies for organisational change have to develop 'client'-centred services. The example below illustrates how organisational constraints impede the realisation of such work.

CASE STUDY

Naseera was a visually impaired young Sikh woman of fifteen. She had been in care for two years in a predominantly white establishment in a rural area where few black people lived. During that time her needs as a Sikh child with a desire to continue seeing relatives and former friends, who resided in an urban area at some remove from the Home, had been given scant attention.

The residential workers at the Home had little time to devote to individual residents. Their energies were consumed with taking care of day-to-day duties and keeping the administration ticking over. Moreover, Naseera was a quiet, well-behaved young woman who did not need much intervention on their part. They wished the Home was full of people like her and not the more rebellious and aggressive young white women in their care. They noted that Naseera had few friends among the residents, but put it down to 'her being different from the others' and left it at that.

This example should not be happening while Section 22(5)(c) of the Children Act of 1989 says that social workers must take note of a child's ethnicity and religious needs. Observing this requirement is vital for young people who cannot advocate for their rights or have no-one to do it for them.

The case study verifies Goffman's (1961) analysis of closed institutions. Instead of 'client' needs driving what takes place within its walls, staff are so hard pressed that 'getting by' becomes the order of the day. 'Clients'' needs are neglected and much harm can stem from that. For Naseera, no cognisance has been taken of her as a black woman placed in a white environment a long way from home. Her dietary, religious and ethnic rights have been cast aside. Even the social worker's decision to place her here has to be questioned. It seems wholly inappropriate. A better match between Naseera's needs and the placement is required even if places for black women are in short supply.

This case illustrates how institutional, cultural and personal racism are taken for granted and unremarked upon. The colour-blind approach it portrays reveals that the service aims for the lowest common denominator and leaves individuals who are 'different' at the receiving end of inferior and inappropriate services. It is no comfort for Naseera to know that white women's needs are also neglected. Nor would she be pleased that a quality assurance exercise has vindicated the agency without meeting her requirements. Bad practice can occur through omission as much as commission.

Naseera has not complained about the poor service. This does not justify its existence, but highlights how bureaucratic forms of quality assurance fail to pick up on poor practice. It is not always easy for 'clients' who feel vulnerable and/or powerless to give accurate evaluations of the services received. Few people will complain if they feel alternatives are unavailable to them. Nor will they cast doubt on services which they perceive as all they can expect. They will also not complain if they feel grateful not to be 'out on the streets'. In these circumstances, even direct questions seeking their views prompt a neutral or slightly positive response like 'fine'. If an evaluation fails to address the relative powerlessness of the 'client' being asked to express an opinion, it may produce meaningless responses for evaluative purposes. 'Clients" failure to voice dissatisfaction or express opinions about services gives no grounds for assuming that the situation is satisfactory. Doing so capitalises on their relative powerlessness or passive resistance and denies a fundamental principle of good professional practice – probing beneath surface appearances to discover what is really going on (Perlman, 1957; Compton and Galaway, 1975; Coulshed, 1988).

An external observer with a black perspective would have criticised Naseera's treatment at several points had he or she been asked to evaluate it. The observer would draw attention to the prevalence of the 'equal treatment' paradigm: every resident is deemed to be the same and have the same needs. The norms being used to judge these are the dominant white middle-class norms. These guarantee minimum standards for everybody. If these do not meet the specific needs of the 'client' concerned, they exclude those they aim to serve and do more damage than good. In Naseera's case, these entail: her separation from family and friends; the submerging of her identity as a young Sikh woman with a culture and tradition inalienably her own; and a dependency on adults with whom she has little in common and who do not respond to her as an individual *in* a social situation, who brings another social setting with her.

The methods used for evaluating services can be ideologically driven and reveal little of 'clients'' feelings about services or the extent to which their 'rights' to appropriate ones have been upheld. Classical texts on this subject treat evaluation as a neutral bureaucratic or technical activity which professionals can undertake, fully confident in their analytical outcomes. Bringing in external consultants or observers can identify shortcomings not easily evident otherwise and act as catalysts in improving standards of practice.

Quality control

The drive to inculcate market discipline in the British personal social services began in earnest in the 1980s with the introduction of the Financial Management Initiative (FMI). Since then, managers have been asked to pay strict attention to quality control and ensure that monitoring mechanisms operate effectively. Some managers have opted for British Standard (BS) 5750, others have gone for Total Quality Management (TQM) (Claytor *et al.*, 1994; Dobson, 1994).

These standards have been developed in industry but are increasingly being used in social services. Although these mechanisms have yet to be fully evaluated within the social services setting, there are reasons for questioning the imposition of approaches developed to deal with commodities on to a sector providing services to people.

First, the relationship between the producer and the consumer is different. In social work, the consumer does not simply want an item of consumption, but something that will improve their quality of life. Thus, a provision has to address more than one function or purpose. A teapot will be used primarily to make a pot of tea. But in Naseera's case, the quality of her whole life experience is at stake. Moreover, the commercial relationship assumes that the consumer exercises choice regarding the product when deciding whether or not to buy it. In social services, the situation is more complicated. There may not be another provider. Here, whatever the consumer thinks is irrelevant, except insofar as their knowledge can place non-financial pressures on providers to develop other provisions in future. There is no guarantee, however, that this will happen. Or, consumers may not have the cash to purchase the superior services they really want. They may buy inferior products because they cannot get into debt rather than because they are being offered what they want or need.

Finally, in the social work relationship, it is not always clear who the 'client' is. Naseera is obviously a 'client'. How far her wishes have been taken into account is unclear. But what about her relatives, should they not express an opinion about what happens to her? What about close others, are they not as important as other professionals who have an interest in her short life? What about groups who are advocating on behalf of black people or even those in the disability movement? Do they have a role in determining the kinds of services provided for people like Naseera? The government and politicians whose interest is much more removed from direct service provision feel they must have *the* final word. Yet, they are seldom at the receiving end of the policies and practices they advocate. These queries indicate how difficult it is to establish who the 'stakeholder(s)' in social services are. All those mentioned have reasons for inclusion. The fact is, there are many stakeholders in the social services remit. Reconciling their differences may not be easy.

By contrast, a Home committed to anti-racist principles would have strategies addressing service provision and delivery, employment practices and 'client'–worker relationships. It would employ significant numbers of black workers, including Asian Sikhs, throughout the organisation. These workers could be role models for Naseera and encourage her to talk about her feelings, herself and her own identity. Their presence would also enable her to talk about such issues without having to challenge unspoken assumptions about white supremacy. Additionally, provisions for Naseera to observe her own religious and dietary preferences would be available. There would also be pictures depicting positive images of her culture and peoples throughout the Home. Both black and white residents would be encouraged to learn about valuing each other and respecting their differences. For this stance to have been reached, both residents and staff would have had to address the negativity white people associate with difference. Audre Lorde defines these as the 'fear and loathing' which devalue difference and ascribe inferiority to it. This prompts white people to react to difference by ignoring it, copying it (if dominant), or destroying it (if subordinate). For these reactions to be transcended, white people need to learn to relate to black people as equals – a precondition for creative change to occur (Lorde, 1984).

White staff would engage in the process of creating an anti-racist environment in the Home. Facilities and resources would be released to facilitate interaction between Naseera and her friends and relatives, for example travel grants for them to visit. Finally, a Home really committed to user empowerment would have decision-making structures which enable staff and residents to meet together to discuss policies and practice. Staff would seek to attract a number of black residents to the Home. Its administrators and workers would have to consider ways of encouraging more black people to use its facilities so that Naseera would not be the only, probably token, black resident on their committees. The Home would also have to be proactive in developing links with black communities, from further afield if there are none in the locality, to ensure that its depiction of black cultures reflected the vibrant reality of today and not some ossified picture in a white person's head. Such links could also be used to develop more culturally sensitive anti-racist policies and practices. Moreover, workers would seek avenues through which Naseera and her family could be involved in making decisions about her future and the care she receives on a day-to-day basis.

Working along these lines enables the Home to make strides in meeting the needs of black users. Much would remain to be done within both the Home and broader society. Agency policy and practice has to be reviewed regularly to ensure that it responds to the need of both black and white users to develop their full potential. Being in care should not be a matter of warehousing people, whoever they are. Nor should day-to-day administrative tasks take over the process of working with young people and encouraging them to become fully fledged citizens. Meeting this objective requires workers to consider what must be done, not only with regard to residents' daily care, but also in preparing them for their future.

An investment in today's young person pays dividends for society tomorrow. Society is a social creation that is greater than its constituent parts, each of which is interdependent. Changes in the broader society have to encompass legislation tackling personal, institutional and cultural racism more widely, including that present in immigration policies, the criminal justice system and social security (Ahmad, 1990; CCAB, 1983; Layton-Henry, 1985). Finally, this example reveals how improving practice with black people ameliorates services for white residents. Young white people also have a right to maintain contact with families and friends and affirm the positive aspects of their culture. As we see below, work with white people should also observe best practice guidelines.

Joan was a 30-year-old white woman of English origins involved in an abusive marriage with a 35-year-old (white) Englishman named John for over ten years. She had one child, a son Damian, aged four. Damian had been conceived one night when her husband raped her after a drunken episode.

Joan's life revolved around her relationship with her son. As a result, her jealous husband made life more difficult for her by intensifying the ferocity of his attacks. One night, he came in drunk, assaulted and threatened Joan with a knife. The neighbours, hearing her screams, rescued her before John could use it. They restrained him until the police arrived. Joan took this opportunity to leave with Damian.

She went to a women's refuge. Life at the refuge was difficult. Joan needed privacy, but none was available because it was so overcrowded. She found it difficult to collect her thoughts and decide what she wanted to do with her life.

Damian found life there tough too. He was shy and withdrawn and did not mix easily with other children. He always seemed in a state of fear. Fortunately, the refuge workers and other women went out of their way to make Joan and Damian feel welcome.

A number of support services were provided for them. These included having a child development worker work with Damian to make him feel comfortable in his new environment, deal with the trauma he had experienced and improve his sociability skills. He responded well to the attention he received and slowly started to come out of himself and make friends. He also began attending playgroup in the mornings, a move Joan would not have contemplated while she was at home. She would have been too ashamed of the bruises to show her face in public.

For the first time in her life, Joan concentrated on her needs. This she found extremely difficult. But, she received support from other women and a feminist counsellor in the refuge. Slowly, she gained confidence and began to participate in its activities, attending group meetings, going on outings, taking Damian to playgroup, and generally sorting herself out.

Eventually, she sought career help and advice to gain skills to make her employable, and put herself on a council housing list. She dreaded this move as it meant that she would be going into a new area where she knew no-one. However, several woman in the refuge had become close friends and they promised to keep in touch. Although they were all aware that it might be difficult to keep their promise once she left, they all felt that just knowing that they could make friends with those whom they valued, and who in turn valued them, would make it easier for them to make new ones. While at the refuge, Joan decided to file for a divorce. Again, the workers helped her complete the paperwork and attended sessions with her lawyer.

The refuge was run along feminist lines. Its principal aim was to help Joan gain control of her life and make decisions for herself. Its philosophy was implemented by encouraging women to become fully involved in decisions about how the refuge was run and helping them address their own individual needs. The experiences of other women who had also been assaulted provided ready material which could be shared as each woman saw fit, to enable each of them to develop skills and confidence. A number of the workers had been assaulted by male partners. Thus, they were able to make direct connections with the women and speak to them as 'victims' who had gone beyond the role of 'survivor' to control their own lives and offer positive role models for women in the refuge. Their presence inspired others and demonstrated that the powerlessness they felt while being abused could be overcome.

Providing women with the space to run their own lives and make their own decisions forms part of feminist praxis. Relationships between the women workers and women coming to the refuge are more egalitarian than is the case in most social work relationships or in refuges run by social services. Men are not allowed to work in feminist refuges because it is feared that they will violate the space women need to recover from being abused by them (Dobash and Dobash, 1991, 1980). The women workers do not assume the role of 'expert', although they have acquired expertise in dealing with other agencies, such as social services and the police, by working in the refuge movement. Their main concern is to pass skills on to abused women so that they can empower themselves and control their own lives.

Feminist refuges have problems: under-resourcing is chronic; overcrowding is rife. Lack of provisions to fully support women and children seeking solace places even greater pressure on the limited facilities that exist. Resources aimed at retraining women who wish to gain employment skills, assume other lifestyles and obtain housing need to be more fully developed. Finance to develop child support services consistent with feminist principles and provide feminist counsellors to work with both women and children to address the trauma caused by their cruel treatment is lacking (Chaplin, 1988).

In addition, feminist praxis for working with men who have assaulted women requires urgent development. There are a few such projects in Britain, for example CHANGE in Edinburgh (Fagg, 1993). These are under-resourced and struggling to survive. They are fairly new and have to be developed more fully. More research following up men undergoing treatment in these centres is necessary to measure long-term behavioural change. Central to the work being done is their resocialisation so that men can feel OK about themselves without having to exert power and control over others (Dominelli, 1992b). Working with men to develop their skills in relating to women as equals rather than as subordinates is an important part of working with them (May and Strikwerda, 1992; Dominelli, 1992b). This approach requires a reformulation and rethinking of masculinity. Some men's groups have been pursuing these lines, for example the Working with Men Collective in London (Fagg, 1993).

Working with women therefore has implications for working with men. Feminist theory and practice is not limited solely to women, even though women are its starting point. Moreover, as work along feminist lines has developed in the past two decades, it is becoming more and more clear that changing men – their role in society, expectations about women, their relationships with others including men, and the ways in which they seek to maintain them, must be redefined to be in keeping with equality as the framework within which gender relations are conducted (Dominelli and Whitehead, 1994).

Another area of difficulty those working in feminist refuges have addressed and sought to handle more effectively is how to work in anti-racist ways and make their facilities more relevant to black women. The record of white feminist refuges to date has been found wanting by black women. They have had to create their own refuges to have their ethnic, cultural, religious and dietary needs taken on board (Guru, 1987).

Although (white) refuges have adopted anti-racist policies, they continue to fail black women and have not succeeded in gaining their confidence in using them. These refuges have also been unable to attract sufficient numbers of black women workers to impact on the overall make-up of the refuge workforce. A single black woman worker can often feel like the token woman that makes the refuge look good. Her experience is one of the constant affirmation of white values at the expense of her own (see Guru, 1987; Wilson, 1993). Similar occurrences prevail in the lives of black women seeking safety in them. Racism shapes black women's reality giving them problems which do not affect white women. For example, black women are concerned that racist stereotypes about violent black men distort the justice process if they lodge a complaint against a black assailant (Mama, 1989). Or, they may find that their allegations are treated less seriously than white women's because the police assume violence is a 'normal part' of relationships between black men and women (Wilson, 1993; Collins, 1991). Or, the immigration system may come down on black families leading to their deportation (Mama, 1989; CCAB, 1983).

Moreover, some refuges have addressed anti-racism in ways that antagonise white women who have not normally thought about their relationships with black people. They carry racist stereotypes and unquestioned assumptions about black people into the refuge. These can lead to tense situations which need to be handled with care, for they may make black and white women, already traumatised by the violence they have endured, feel 'picked on' again. This is illustrated below.

CASE STUDY

Sandra was a white woman who went to a refuge with her 6-year-old daughter, Betty. The refuge had an anti-racist policy, but had only one black worker, a woman of Afro-Caribbean descent. There were two black women in the refuge – a woman who had come to Britain from Jamaica ten years earlier, and another who had emigrated from Egypt six years ago. When Sandra and Betty got to the refuge, they found they had to share a room with Djamila, the Arabic-speaking woman and her 4-year-old daughter, Aysha. Both women had tried to create space for each other and keep their interaction to a minimum, but friction still resulted.

Of greatest concern was Betty taunting Aysha about her 'foreignness' and calling her abusive names. Djamila protested both to Sandra and the workers, saying that the anti-racist policy the refuge took pride in was being flouted and she was having to deal with racist abuse as the mother of the victim.

The refuge workers' group discussed the issue and talked to Sandra and Betty, highlighting the need for them to adhere to the policy and desist from abusing black people. They reminded Sandra that if the racist abuse did not stop, the anti-racist policy, with which she had agreed to comply when she came in, would result in both of them having to leave. They also offered to work with Betty so that she could both appreciate herself as a white (English) child and value the identity of the black child.

Sandra was very offended by their suggestions. She claimed the child was only repeating what countless others thought and her father had verbalised on many occasions. She did not see the need for any specific action to be taken on this. She did tell Betty not to call the black child names, but did not enforce this instruction. It was not long before Betty was at it again, upsetting Aysha greatly in the process.

Once more, Djamila protested. This time, the workers brought the issue to a group meeting of all the women and workers to decide how to uphold the policy which had been accepted by all of them when admitted. During the meeting, at which both Sandra and Djamila were present, relations became very tense. Sandra felt that the importance of the issue was over-exaggerated. Children often say abusive things to each other as part of the growing-up process. Djamila felt more offended than ever and said that Sandra's trivialisation of the issue only made matters worse. She did not want to punish Sandra or her daughter, but she did not want to be subjected to racial harassment and had to insist that such behaviour stop.

The majority (though not all) of the women took Djamila's side. Moreover, they felt Sandra had been given ample opportunity to deal with the issue and get support in doing so. Her denial of its importance, or that it was even an issue, meant that she was not keeping her commitment of adhering to their anti-racist policy and relating to black women as equals. They felt that unless Sandra promised to take the issue seriously and work on her daughter's racism and her own, she should leave. Sandra decided to do just that. Djamila, the workers and women who had supported her felt very sad at this outcome.

This case study indicates how difficult it is for white people to change their racist views of black people in simple straightforward ways. It also highlights how women who share similar forms of oppression in abstract terms have social divisions which keep them apart and make their daily experiences of it highly dissimilar. These complexities provide irrefutable reasons for feminists to take racism seriously and seek creative solutions in addressing it. White women *must* have the opportunity to change their racist views about black people. Meanwhile, the process through which the issue is approached and the discussions about it have to facilitate behavioural change in individuals. For, at the end of the day, racist behaviour is unacceptable and must be treated as such.

Conclusions

Strategies for change must address individuals, institutions and the dominant culture if new, less oppressive forms of practice are to be realised. Social movements provide resources social workers can access to learn about innovations in practice; purchase services; develop support networks for themselves and their 'clients'; get feedback on proposed changes to service delivery; and campaign for better services. Working through these, social workers can begin to alter practice to make it more consistently anti-oppressive.

10

Conclusions: Sociological Social Work as a Model for Practice

Radical social work *à la* Bailey and Brake (1975) and Corrigan and Leonard (1978) has failed to produce lasting social work paradigms which promote anti-oppressive practice. People at the receiving end of appalling welfare services, therefore, have had to develop more meaningful theories and practice.

To what extent can professionals in social work respond to the agenda disenfranchised and dispossessed peoples place before practitioners and academics? This chapter examines this question through the use of case study materials and concludes by assessing the possibility of an affirmative answer. I argue that a new sociology of social work can be created. Anti-racist feminist sociological social work can provide the breakthrough that social work theory and practice need to do this. This book attempts to initiate a debate along these lines.

The radical social work movement which focused largely on class failed to adequately connect macrolevel theory with microlevel practice. The primacy it gave class over other social divisions failed to pick up on reality as experienced by many 'clients'. Consequently, its practice was deemed inadequate, particularly by white women and black people.

Forms of practice developed by these two groups using feminist and black perspectives have responded more appropriately to their needs. A prime reason for this has been that both approaches have relied on oppressed people themselves to develop the relevant forms of practice. Scholars and practitioners who have supported them have tried to develop different views of their roles in the struggle to end oppression. They have placed themselves at the service of oppressed people, facilitating their access to public arenas so that they can speak about their oppression from their *own* experience and not have experts use vicarious knowledge to usurp them. The voices of those at the receiving end of oppression, struggling to transcend it have a greater legitimacy in identifying what will lead to liberation. Many of these scholars and practitioners had another feature in common with oppressed people: they have been oppressed. Thus, they can share the skills they have acquired in resisting oppression. Drawing on their experiences, including their abilities to overcome adversity, they can provide positive role models for others. Moreover, they have access to communication channels which groups oppressed by poverty do not. Thus, they can raise issues in fora otherwise exempt from their influence.

White feminists and black scholars have also sought new 'paradigms' for practice. I place the word 'paradigm' in quotes to distance it from its association with the natural sciences. This imbues the term with meanings which block the exploration of experiential experiences and forms of knowledge which conceptualise social interaction in alternative ways. The new 'paradigms' are inclusive of the range of social divisions which shape people's realities. These forms are being created and recreated by and through social interaction among people without a fixed definition of them. There is only a fluid one which is constantly changing, although its external contours retain many familiar features which allow its designation as a particular kind of phenomenon. Constant movment and growth are reasons why feminists refuse to provide a blueprint for their alternative visions of society, satisfying themselves intellectually and emotionally with a set of principles which are continually (re)examined and (re)thought as they are being used.

Key principles put forward by feminist scholars and oppressed peoples as critical for caring professionals to observe working in empowering ways alongside oppressed people are:

- redefining professionalism so as not to add another layer of oppression to those 'clients' already carry
- asking 'clients' what they want and listening to them
- recognising that people lead lives which straddle both public and private domains
- providing users with the information they need to deal with things for themselves
- challenging personal, institutional and cultural forms of oppression.

These principles can provide new 'paradigms' for practice which address both macrolevel and microlevel concerns, that is, *the individual in his or her social context.* They also provide the key for proceeding to develop a sociological social work that posits new theories and forms of practice which relate to the complexities of the modern world. A world in which shrinking borders, technological innovations and the growth of giant bureaucracies of international scope exacerbate the oppression felt by those on the margins of society on a global scale (Midgley, 1981; Macpherson, 1982; MacPherson and Midgley, 1987; Phillips, 1993). Within this context, the workforce is increasingly becoming internationalised. Workers at both the top echelons of the labour hierarchy and those on its lower rungs are moving around the world in unprecedented numbers in search of jobs. This mobility raises with greater urgency the need to transcend the borders of the nation-state to think about the welfare needs of people on an international basis (Phillips, 1993). The interdependency between people this exhibits encompasses the world.

With extensive migration becoming commonplace, people's ability to move anywhere without losing their rights to welfare provisions makes access to the personal social services an international matter. It is important that portability in these rights is guaranteed and that all nations become committed to meeting the needs of people, whoever they are, wherever they are, and wherever they may have come from.

Sociological social work – a new 'paradigm'

Sociological social work examines the welfare needs of individuals within the society in which they live. Society is a social formation created by people who have organised their social relations to distribute power and resources in particular ways. It is local and specific while at the same time, general and universalising. Sociological social work therefore focuses on relationships which encompass individuals, society, the state and broader world. And, if it is to address issues of oppression, must be directly concerned with social justice. These dimensions make sociological social work a highly political professional activity. Its politics are out in the open rather hidden. However, for those wishing to use political power to keep under wraps the dynamics whereby social policies and welfare provisions exclude rather than include people, sociological social work will continue to be a subversive activity or 'contaminating knowledge'.

Sociological social work's commitment to exploring the situations and needs of oppressed people is unlikely to be popular with powerful groups governing society. They have vested interests in ensuring the continuation of the status quo by keeping social work engaged in controlling people rather than their liberation. By following their dictates, social work becomes a mechanism whereby powerful groups can block demands which question social work's existing parameters – its role in society and the nature of its task. Although not a monolithic group who act in predetermined ways, those governing society seek to (re)assert control over their lives, fashion reality in ways more to their liking, and react to challenges in ways consistent with their perceived interests. Social relations of domination are constantly being (re)created through the actions of those who are oppressed and those who oppress. These relations are not fixed and immutable. Challenging (or accepting) the existing configuration of social relations through (re)action underpins people's capacity to change (or not) what they find. Like the waters of a flowing river, social relationships are constantly being (re)enacted in (new) forms under (new) constellations which draw on the contributions of both oppressing groups and oppressed ones.

Diversity among ruling elites and subjugated groups needs to be constantly explored and examined by those attempting to shift the balance of power in new directions by inspiring non-oppressive social relations. The condemnation of sociological knowledge as 'contaminating knowledge' can be expected. It exposes the comfortable position that powerful elites occupy and demonstrates how their power, position and privileges rest on the backs of people whose mobilising capacities are engaged in a struggle for bare survival.

In these circumstances, sociological social work can be profoundly revolutionary. It can challenge governments which allow economic priorities to drive social policy and welfare responses, and argue for human needs to become the power engine fuelling the development of new forms of welfare. Taken within a global context, it can promote the welfare needs of people throughout the world. Moving in this direction requires that the market orientation of the personal social services be transcended.

Implementing this vision will not happen easily or overnight. Much detailed work has to be done nationally and internationally, in and through government policies, social work institutions nationally and internationally, and inter-governmentally via bodies such as the United Nations and international non-governmental organisations. The European Union may provide a prototype of how such issues can be addressed.

Each practitioner can work towards the realisation of such a vision. By working in his or her own particular agency to make connections between one form of oppression and another, considering how each of these contribute to the 'diswelfare' of people and seeking to overcome it, they can contribute to developing new 'paradigms' which promote an egalitarian and socially just society for all rather than replacing old privileged elites with new ones. Creating the 'good life' for all does not mean aiming for the lowest common denominator if the diversity of human beings is to be acknowledged within the structures established for its fulfilment. But, it does suggest that those who are extremely wealthy will see a diminution of their wealth in favour of those who are extremely poor – on an international basis. Moreover, the close connection between humankind and nature will require a detailed consideration of ecological issues. The exploitation and rape of nature is no more acceptable in an interdependent world than the rape and pillage of peoples.

Some of these concerns have been raised, for example, in feminist organising around the peace movement at Greenham Common in England in the mid 1980s (see Dominelli, 1986b; Cook and Kirk, 1983). Here, women took action initiated locally and raised it to the national and international levels in a powerful way which challenged British, other European and American government policies on nuclear armament. The methods used by Greenham Women were also characterised by more egalitarian forms of organising which relied on each individual woman using her own life experience and confidence to engage in direct action which confronted state definitions of reality. Moreover, each woman was free to decide for herself her degree of commitment to any particular action in the collective effort. In these ways, feminists' desire to enact egalitarian relations in their practice was maintained (Cook and Kirk, 1983; Dominelli, 1986b).

The following case studies indicate how feminist practice might be promoted through sociological social work undertaken with 'clients'. Most will focus on one level – the interpersonal – as the starting point from which more generalised action might emanate. To begin working along these lines, the practitioner has to ask several sociological questions:

- Who will benefit from the work I do?
- Who will I work with?
- How will I work with them?
- How will I ensure that 'clients' are fully involved in defining the questions to be addressed?
    - How will these be addressed?
    - What work needs doing individually? together?
    - How will we achieve our goals?
- How will I recognise the forms of oppression that I will both encounter and reproduce in my own work?
- How will I challenge the various forms of oppression I will encounter in this work?
- How will I deal with how I am oppressed myself and how I oppress others?
- What rights do I have as a worker in such situations?
    - What rights belong to those with whom I am working?
    - How do our rights and obligations interact?
- How will I link up with others to challenge practices that are beyond the scope of one individual?
- Where do I go for support when I get stuck?
- How do I look after my own needs as well as those with whom I am working?
- What agencies should be or are working in this area?
    - When do I work with them?
    - How do I work with them?
- Do I need to initiate organisational change?
    - Who do I do this with?
    - How do I do it?

The example which follows illustrates the complexities which social workers can easily fail to address if they do not use a sociological social work approach.

CASE STUDY

Janush was a 81-year-old white man of Polish descent who lived alone on a small pension in a tatty rented flat. The landlord wanted to get rid of all his older sitting tenants on protected rents in order to convert their suites into bedsits for young people so that he could make more money out of the property. Janush steadfastly refused to move.

Janush had come to England as a refugee when the Communists took over Poland. Although he had been an engineer there, the only job he could get here was on an assembly line in a food factory. His knowledge of English was poor. In his old age, he had become forgetful and accident-prone. One day, he accidentally set fire to himself and the flat.

While he was in hospital being treated for his burns, a white English social worker was assigned to his case. She did not speak Polish, but did not seek assistance in communicating with him, accepting without question the lack of translation facilities and Polish-speaking workers in the office. The landlord kept telling her he wanted Janush out in case he put other tenants' lives at risk, although he had no family to go to.

The landlord refused to talk to Janush and would not have him back. The social worker accepted his definition of the situation and did not discuss it with Janush. She sought sheltered accommodation for him, but was unable to find him a place. She put him on a waiting list, but it was very long. In the meantime, the hospital needed his bed so he was discharged into bed and breakfast accommodation.

Once there, Janush became even more confused. He had to vacate the premises during the day. Breakfast was included, but there were no facilities for other meals in the lodgings. Janush forgot to eat regularly and wandered the streets day-in and day-out in all weathers. He could often be seen crying as he walked. His health deteriorated further.

He also became a nuisance to the bed and breakfast owners. He would constantly turn up for non-existent meals, demand to be let in during the day, shouting and banging loudly on the doors when he failed to attract their attention. This behaviour could go on at length. The white English neighbours began to complain about the noise and 'stupid foreigners on welfare' lowering the tone of their community. Attempts to engage him in discussions about his behaviour led nowhere. He understood very little of what was said to him. And, with his poor English, little of what he said back was understood by others. Calls to social services went unheeded. Those who took them kept saying there was nothing they could do since he was on a waiting list for sheltered accommodation.

This case reveals several structural problems that social workers have to consider if they are to respond appropriately to personal distress. It also indicates how older people can come to the attention of social services departments, have a demonstrated need and fail to get it met.

A social worker using sociological social work which addresses social divisions and issues of social justice as they arise would look at this case on several levels and make an assessment of what had to be done on this basis. Their theory and practice would draw on a broad knowledge base: sociology, psychology, social policy, economics, history, psychiatry and social work.

Structurally, the case covers several social divisions which interact with each other to produce inappropriate responses to Janush. The approach of the agencies responsible for his welfare contributes to his diswelfare. He is worse off for having had social work intervention than when fending for himself. That this situation should arise is an indictment of the services British society provides to vulnerable people.

The structural problems and social divisions which need to be addressed in this case are:

- poverty
- ageism
- racism
- under-resourcing.

Janush is a poor white working-class man who, having worked hard all his life, has contributed to British society in the best way he can. He has cared for himself as long as possible. In old age, he has become unable to fully do so and receives little assistance from the services allegedly created to look after him. The case is replete with classist, ageist and racist responses to his plight. It also exposes the chronic under-resourcing of services in health and social care which undermines attempts to keep people functioning effectively in the community. Thus Janush, the individual, is neglected and goes down a spiral from which it would be hard for him to extricate himself without assistance. Let us examine these issues one by one.

Classism

The landlord's response to getting Janush out was based on his desire to maximise profits from his housing investment. In accepting his excuse for not wanting Janush back at face value, the social worker colluded with the landlord's infringement of Janush's human rights. Although the safety issue was important, other responses could have been initiated if the social worker had not colluded with the landlord's definition of the situation and the lack of resourcing. But even within the constraints of what was available, arrangements could have been made to provide Janush with forms of support aimed at reducing the risks of his accidentally burning himself or others, such as attending a day centre with Polish-speaking social workers, home help services, meals-on-wheels. Janush's Polish origins, working-class status, poverty and isolation should have been the base line for an assessment for services. These should not be treated as givens which can be ignored.

Ageism

Ageism appears in a variety of guises. Janush's life is not valued because he is old and poor. He has not been given resources which a younger person might have demanded as a right – the right to be heard and listened to, by involving a Polish-speaking social worker for a proper assessment of his needs to be made. Both the hospital and social services failed to pick up on this. Moreover, they infantilised or treated him as a child; a dependent older person whose needs did not have to be discussed thoroughly with him (see Leonard, 1984). The landlord wanted to get rid of him to house younger people to exploit the opportunities provided by the removal of protected rents from the statute books. This action exacerbates intergenerational conflict by pitting Janush's needs against younger people's. The bed and breakfast owners treated him as a 'tiresome old man' who was a 'foreigner' to boot.

Racism

The overlaps between age, class and 'race' are evident. Janush is discriminated against racially for his Polish origins. His needs as a Polish-speaking person living in England are ignored. His require-ments as a member of a specific ethnic group have been accorded minimal priority and enabled racism as a form of rationing to continue without being publicly acknowledged. The lack of translation services can be interpreted in this light. This forms the basis of the institutional racism being perpetrated against him. Moreover, his citizenship and human rights are being neglected with impunity. The social worker's responses also indicate personal racism by colluding with the absence of the services necessary for doing her job properly. Personal racism and institutional racism create the context in which good practice becomes impossible to enact.

Inadequate communication exacerbates the problems Janush encounters. Yet, understanding what people need and obtaining information from them through adequate communication is a key social work skill. It does not mean that the communication *must* be in English. No-one has explained Janush's entitlements to him or given him a picture of the services available. The assumption that one set of provisions is adequate for all 'clients' represents cultural racism – that white Anglo-Saxon ways are best. The social worker's personal racism has been exacerbated by institutional and cultural racism. Both of these have been (re)enacted and reinforced by her personal racism and highlight the links between them. The racism of the bed and breakfast owners and their neighbours is more overt. Their responses to Janush's plight also draw on personal, institutional and cultural forms of racism. In their respective order, these are: personal prejudice against 'foreigners'; catering for the needs of vulnerable people in an inappropriate manner; and devaluing the life of older people who are excluded from decision-making processes for a variety of reasons including racism.

Under-resourcing

Health and social services have institutionalised ageist, racist and classist practices by not providing appropriate facilities for older people of Polish descent. In not taking these issues up, the social worker colludes with these and provides Janush with an appalling service which places him at risk of further abuse. This form of institutional abuse is different from the forms of individual abuse care givers perpetrate on their charges. The social worker fails to think imaginatively about how she can react to his needs even in her own terms by not considering better forms of support for him in his own home. Instead, she colludes with the landlord's desire to evict him. Thus, Janush's plight as an isolated and confused older person is exacerbated by her actions.

Addressing the chronic under-resourcing of the personal social services is both a political and a professional issue. Social workers can tackle this in their practice by identifying for line managers the difficulties it creates in delivering high quality services to individual 'clients' and putting pressure on them to take this up with senior managers and politicians. They can also pursue the issue collectively through their professional associations and trades unions. Or, they can initiate campaigns in alliance with users to engage the public in debates about welfare priorities. Taking action at both the professional and organisational level assists the performance of their work on the interpersonal level.

Personal distress

Janush's life has been made more miserable than it needed to be through lack of appropriate interagency collaboration and has placed him at considerable risk of further abuse and human rights violation. Yet, there is no-one to challenge this aspect of policy and practice or advocate on his behalf.

A worker committed to sociological social work would consider all these issues and address them organisationally within the agency and interpersonally in the 'client'–worker relationship. This means raising demands for provisions such as interpreters and translators, community-based support services and housing for older people. It might even include challenging the idea that older people should be put into ghettos for older people, and looking for alternative forms of housing which do not separate the generations – as black voluntary organisations working with black elders have done (Patel, 1990; Farrah, 1986). Janush's loneliness would also be addressed.

Conclusions

Working in anti-oppressive ways requires sensitivity, awareness of, and a commitment to, ending relations of domination and subordination. It also needs change to take place at the personal, institutional and cultural levels to shift social relations away from reinforcing human misery and degradation. Anti-oppressive practice aims to end oppressive hierarchical relations and replace them with egalitarian ones facilitating individual and group fulfilment. Moving towards this requires people to think not in dichotomous terms, but of the interconnections between people and nature and among people. This seems a tall order for social work professionals and academics charged with their education and training. But it sets feasible goals which, if met, bring rewards to 'clients', practitioners, academics and society. Sociological social work supports this task by furnishing a vision of the competent, reflective practitioner confidently drawing on critical analytical knowledge and practice skills – essential tools for working with people in non-oppressive ways. It is small wonder that powerful, privileged groups condemn sociological understandings in social work as 'contaminating knowledge'. Their response provides every reason for being proud of embarking on a journey to remove the shackles of oppression which distort and destroy the humanity that is the right of every individual to experience. Social work has a critical role in enabling each person to develop their full potential in a social setting. Sociological social work from an anti-racist feminist perspective is one means through which professionals committed to egalitarian social relations can engage with the process of their doing so.

Bibliography

Abbott, P and Wallace, C (1990) *An Introduction to Sociology: Feminist Perspectives*. London: Routledge.

Abramovitz, A (1991) Putting and End to Doublespeak About Race, Gender and Poverty: An Annotated Glossary for Social Workers', in *Social Work*, **36**(5): 380-384, September.

Adamson, N, Briskin, L and McPhail, M (1988) *Organising for Change: The Contemporary Women's Movement in Canada*. Oxford: Oxford University Press.

Adamson, O, Brown, C, Hanison, J and Price, J (1976) Women's Oppression Under Capitalism in *Revolutionary Communist*, Number 5, 1-48.

Ahmad, B (1990) *The Black Perspective in Social Work*. Birmingham: Venture Press.

Ahmad, B (1992) *A Dictionary of Black Managers in White Organisations*. London: National Institute of Social Work.

Ahmed, S (1978) Asian Girls and Cultural Conflicts, in *Social Work Today*, August.

Ahmed, S (1982) Social Work with Minority Children and their Families, in *Ethnic Minority and Community Relations*. Open University Course, No E354, Unit 16.

Ahmed, S, Cheetham, J and Small, J (1987) *Social Work with Black Children and their Families*. London: Batsford.

Alfred, R (1992) *Black Workers in the Prison Service*. London: Prison Reform Trust.

Alibhai-Brown, Y (1993) Social Workers Need Race Training, Not Hysteria, in the *Independent*, 11 August.

Anderson, P (1976) *Considerations on Western Marxism*. London: New Left Books.

Appleyard, B (1993) Why Paint So Black a Picture, in the *Independent*, 4 August.

Armitage, A (1975) *Social Welfare in Canada: Ideals and Realities.* Toronto: McClelland and Stewart Ltd.

Armstrong, J (1977) *Analysis of the Inner Area Partnership Scheme Applications.* Paper for Leicester Community Work Training Unit Management Meeting. Leicester: CWTU.

Asante, M S (1987) *The Afrocentric Idea.* Philadelphia: Temple University Press.

Association of Directors of Social Services (ADSS) and the Commission for Racial Equality (1978) *Multi-Racial Britain: The Social Services Response.* London: ADSS/CRE.

Attlee, C R (1920) *The Social Worker.* London: Library of Social Service.

Baert, P J N (1989) *Unintended Consequences: (Un)Awareness and (Re)production.* Paper for the British Sociological Association Annual Conference, 1989, Plymouth.

Bailey, R (1982) Theory and Practice in Social Work: a Kaliedescope, in Bailey, R and Lee, P (eds) *Theory and Practice in Social Work.* Oxford: Basil Blackwell.

Bailey, R and Brake, M (eds) (1975) *Radical Social Work.* London: Edward Arnold.

Bailey, R and Lee, P (eds) (1982) *Theory and Practice in Social Work.* Oxford: Basil Blackwell.

Baldock, P (1982) Community Work and the Social Services Departments, in Craig *et al.* (eds) *Community Work and the State.* London: Routledge & Kegan Paul.

Baldwin, N *et al.* (1993) *Resident's Rights: A strategy in Action in Homes for Older People.* Aldershot: Avebury.

Banks, O (1981) *Faces of Feminism.* London: Martin Robinson.

Barker, H (1986) Recapturing Sisterhood: A Critical Look at 'Process' in Feminist Organisations and Community Action, in *Critical Social Policy,* **16**:summer, 80–90.

Barnes, B (1974) *Scientific Knowledge and Sociological Theory.* London: Routledge & Kegan Paul.

Barnes, B (1985) *About Science.* Oxford: Blackwell.

Barrett, M (1981) *Women's Oppression Today.* London: Verso.

Barrett, M and McIntosh, M (1982) *The Anti-social Family.* London: Verso

Barrett, M and McIntosh, M (1985) Ethnocentrism and Socialist Feminist Theory, in *Feminist Review,* (20).

Beaumont, B and Walker, H (1981) *Probation Work – Critical Theory and Socialist Practice.* Oxford: Basil Blackwell.

Becker, H (1966) *Outsiders.* New York: Free Press.

Becker, S (ed.) (1991) *Windows of Opportunity: Public Policy and the Poor.* London: CPAG.

Beechey, V (1980) On Patriarchy, in *Feminist Review*, (2).

Bell. S (1987) *When Salem Came to the Boro'.* Harmondsworth: Penguin.

Benn, M (1983) Isn't Sexual Harassment Really about Masculinity?, in *Spare Rib*, No 156, July, 6–8.

Benn, M and Sedgley, A (1984) *Sexual Harassment.* London: Tavistock.

Bennington, J (1976) *Local Government Becomes Big Business.* London: Community Development Projects.

Benston, M (1969) The Political Economy of Women's Labour, in *Monthly Review*, **21**(4):September, 13–27.

Bhavani, K K (1993) Talking Racism and the Editing of Women's Studies, in Richardson, D and Robinson, V (eds) *Introducting Women's Studies.* London: Macmillan.

Bhavani, K K and Coulson, M (1986) Transforming Socialist Feminism: The Challenge of Racism, in *Feminist Review*, (23), 81–92.

Black Assessors (1994) DipSW Consultation a Sham, in *Community Care*, 13–18, October.

Bolger, S, Corrigan, P, Dorking, J and Frost, N (1981) *Towards a Socialist Welfare Practice.* London: Macmillan.

Bonny, S (1984) Who Cares in Southwark? London: National Association of Carers and their Elderly Dependents.

Bosanquet, H (1900) Methods of Training, in *Charity Organisation Society Occasional Papers*, Third Series, No 3.

Bottomore, T B (1964) *Karl Marx: Early Writings.* New York: McGraw-Hill.

Bourne, J (1984) Feminism and Black Women, in *Race and Class*, **XX**(4), winter, 45–60.

Bourne, J (1987) Homelands of the Mind: Jewish Feminism and Identity Politics, in *Race and Class*, **XXIX**(1), summer, 1–24.

Bowl, R (1985) *Changing the Nature of Masculinity: A Task for Social Work.* Norwich: University of East Anglia Monographs.

Brandwein, R (1991) in Mehta, V and Yasas, F (eds) *Exploring Feminist Visions.* Puna: Streevani.

Brewer, C and Lait, J (1980) *Can Social Work Survive?* London: Temple Smith.

Bridges, L (1975) The Ministry of Internal Security: British Urban Social Policy 1968–1974, in *Race and Class*, **16**(4):376.

Briggs, A (1968) *The Other Victorians.* London: Jonathan Cape.

Brittan, A (1989) *The Power of Masculinity.* Oxford: Blackwell.

Broadbent, J, Dietrich, M and Laughlin, R (1993) *The Development of Principal–Agent, Contracting and Acceptability Relationships in the Public Sector: Conceptual and Cultural Problems.* Sheffield University.

Brook, E and Davis, A (1985) *Women, the Family and Social Work*. London: Tavistock.

Brown, C (1984) *Black and White Britain: The Third Policy Studies Institute Survey*. London: Heinemann.

Brownmiller, S (1976) *Against Our Will: Men, Women and Rape*. New York: Bantam Books.

Bruegal, I (1989) Sex and Race in the Labour Market, in *Feminist Review*, (32) summer, 49–68.

Bryant, B, Dadzie, S, and Scafe, S (1985) *The Heart of the Race: Black Women's Lives in Britain*. London: Virago.

Burden, D S and Gottlieb, N (eds) (1987) *The Woman Client: Providing Human Services in a Changing World*. London: Tavistock.

Burgess, R (1994) Black Managers in the Probation Service. Unpublished MSc dissertation at the University of Reading.

Butrym, Z (1976) *The Nature of Social Work*. London: Macmillan.

Callahan, M (1994) Stereotypes of Women in Social Work. Unpublished PhD Thesis. Bristol University.

Canadian Association of Social Workers (CASW) (1992) Women in Social Work Education, in *CASW Bulletin*, summer.

Cannan, C, Berry, L and Lyons, K (1992) *Social Work and Europe*. London: Macmillan.

Carby, H (1982) White Women Listen! Black Feminism and the Boundaries of Sisterhood, in CCCS, *The Empire Strikes Back*. London: Hutchinson.

Carers National Association (CNA) (1992) *Speak Up, Speak Out*. London: Carers National Association.

Carter, P, Chan, C and Everitt, A (1992) *Practice*. Newcastle: Northumbria University Publication.

Carson, R (1963) *Silent Spring*. London: Hamish Hamilton.

CASE CON: A Magazine for Radical Social Workers in the 1970s. Various Issues.

Central Council for Education and Training in Social Work (CCETSW) (1976) *CQSW Cognate Disciplines*. London: CCETSW.

Central Council for Education and Training in Social Work. (CCETSW) (1983) *Social Work for a Multi-Racial Society: Report of a Working Group. Paper 21*. London: CCETSW.

Central Council for Education and Training in Social Work (CCETSW) (1989) *Requirements and Regulations for the Diploma in Social Work. Paper 30*. Revised in 1991 and 1995. London: CCETSW.

Central Council for Education and Training in Social Work (CCETSW) (1991a) *Requirements and Guidance for the Approval of Agencies and the Accreditation and Training of Practice Teachers. Paper 26.3*. London: CCETSW.

Central Council for Education and Training in Social Work. (CCETSW) (1991b) *One Small Step Towards Racial Justice: The Teaching of Anti-Racism in Diploma of Social Work Programmes.* London: CCETSW.

Chadwick, E (1965) *Report on the Sanitary Conditions of the Labouring Population of Great Britain.* Edinburgh: Edinburgh University Press.

Challis, D J and Davies, B P (1986) *Matching Resources to Needs.* Aldershot: Gower.

Chapeltown Citizens Advice Bureau (CCAB) (1983) *Immigrants and the Welfare State.* London: Blackrose Press.

Chaplin, J (1988) *Feminist Couselling in Action.* London: Sage.

Cheetham, J (1982) *Social Work and Ethnicity.* London: George Allen and Unwin.

Chodorow, N (1978) *The Reproduction of Mothering.* Berkley: University of California Press.

Cixous, H (1981) Castration or Decapitation?, in *Signs: Journal of Women in Culture and Society,* 7(1):41–55.

Clarke, J, Cochrane, A and McLaughlin, E (1994) *Managing Social Policy.* London: Sage.

Claytor, A, Dominelli, L and Sibanda, S (1994) *Practice Teaching Evaluation Project: Final Report.* The University of Sheffield.

Clegg, S R (1989) *Frameworks of Power.* London: Sage.

Cloward, R and Piven, F (1972) *Regulating the Poor: The Function of Public Welfare.* London: Tavistock.

Cloward, R and Piven, F (1977) *Poor People's Movements: Why They Succeed and How They Fail.* New York: Pantheon Books.

Cloward, R and Piven, F (1982) *The New Class War: Reagan's Attack on the Welfare State and its Consequences.* New York: Pantheon Books.

Coffield, F, Robinson, P and Sarsby, J (1980) *A Cycle of Deprivation? A Case Study of Four Families.* London: Heinemann.

Cohen, R, Coxall, J, Craig, E and Sadiq-Sanster, A (1992) *Hardship Britain: Being Poor in the 1990s.* London: CPAG.

Cohen, S (1980) *Folk Devils and Moral Panics.* 2nd edn. Oxford: Martin Robertson.

Cohen, S (1992) *Imagine There's No Countries: 1992 and International Immigration Controls Against Migrants, Immigrants and Refugees.* Manchester: Greater Manchester Immigration Unit.

Collins, P H (1991) *Black Feminist Thought: Knowledge, Consciousness and the Politics of Empowerment.* London: Routledge.

Comer, J P and Poussaint, A P (1975) *Black Child Care.* New York: Pocket Books.

Community Care (1995) Change Urged for Second Opinions, 2–8 February, 3.

Commission on Racial Equality (CRE) (1984) *Hackney Housing Investigated: Summary of a Formal Investigation Report.* London: CRE.

Community Development Projects (CDP) (1977a) *Gilding the Ghetto.* London: CDP.

Community Development Projects (CDP) (1977b) *The Limits of the Law.* London: CDP.

Community Development Projects (CDP) (1978) *Final Reports.* London: CDP.

Compton, B and Galaway, B (1975) *Social Work Processes.* Homewood, Ill.: The Dorsey Press.

Comte, A (1838) *The Philosophy of Auguste Comte.* London: Bell.

Cook, A and Kirk, G (1983) *Greenham Women Everywhere: Dreams, Ideas and Action from the Women's Peace Movement.* London: Pluto Press.

Cook, D and Hudson, B (1993) *Racism and Criminology.* London: Sage.

Coombe, V and Little, A (eds) (1986) *Race and Social Work.* London: Tavistock.

Cordery, J and Whitehead, A (1992) Masculinity and Sex Offenders, in Senior, P and Woodhill, D (eds) *Gender, Crime and Probation Practice.* Sheffield: PAVIC Publications.

Corrigan, P (1977) The Welfare State as an Arena of Class Struggle, in *Marxism Today*, March.

Corrigan, P and Leonard, P (1978) *Social Work Under Capitalism.* London: Macmillan.

Coulshed, V (1988) *Social Work Practice: An Introduction.* London: BASW/Macmillan.

Coulson, M, Magas, B and Wainwright, H (1975) The Housewife and Her Labour Under Capitalism: A Critique, in *New Left Review*, **89**:Jan–Feb, 59–71.

Coyle, A (1984) *Redundant Women.* London: Women's Press.

Coyle, A (1989) Women in Management: A Suitable Case for Treatment, in *Feminist Review*, (31), 117–25.

Craig, G, Derricourt, N and Loney, M (1982) *Community Work and the State.* London: Routledge & Kegan Paul.

Culpitt, I (1992) *Welfare and Citizenship: Beyond the Crisis of the Welfare State?* London: Sage.

Curno, A *et al.* (eds) (1981) *Women in Collective Action.* London: Association of Community Workers.

Curno, P (ed.) (1978) *Political Issues in Community Work.* London: Routledge & Kegan Paul.

Curnock, K and Hardiker, P (1979) *Towards Practice Theory: Skills and Methods in Social Assessments.* London: Routledge & Kegan Paul.

Dale, J and Foster, P (1986) *Feminists and State Welfare.* London: Routledge & Kegan Paul.

Dalla Costa, M and James, S (1972) *The Power of Women and the Subversion of Community.* Bristol: Falling Wall Press.

Daly, M (1973) *Beyond God the Father: Toward a Philosophy of Women's Liberation.* Boston: Beacon Press.

Daly, M (1978) *Gyn/Ecology: The Metaethics of Radical Feminism.* Boston: Beacon Press.

Davies, M (1981) Social Work, the State and the University, in *British Journal of Social Work,* **11**(3):275–88.

Davies, M (1985) *The Essential Social Worker: A Guide to Positive Practice.* 2nd edn. Aldershot: Gower.

Davies, M (ed.) (1991) *The Sociology of Social Work.* London: Routledge.

Davies, M and Wright, R (1989) *Skills, Knowledge and Qualities in Probation Practice.* Norwich: University of East Anglia Monograph.

Davies, P (1979) The Organisation of State Social Work: Skill, Professionalisation and Management Control. Unpublished MA dissertation. University of Warwick.

Davis, A (1982) *Women, Race and Class.* London: Women's Press.

Davis, A (1989) *Women, Culture and Politics.* London: Women's Press.

Day, P, (1981) *Social Work and Social Control.* London: Tavistock.

Day, P (1987) *Sociology in Social Work Practice.* London: Macmillan.

Dearlove, J (1974) The Control of Change and the Regulation of Community Action, in Jones, D and Mayo, M (eds) *Community Work One.* London: Routledge & Kegan Paul, pp. 22–43.

De Beauvoir, S (1974) *The Second Sex.* Translated by Parshley, H M. New York: Vintage Books.

Delphy, C (1984) *Close to Home: A Materialist Analysis of Women's Oppression.* Translated by Leonard, D. Amherst: University of Massachusetts Press.

Denney, D (1983) Some Dominant Perspectives in the Literature Relating to Multi-Racial Social Work, in *British Journal of Social Work,* **13**(2):149–74.

Denney, D (1992) *Racism and Anti-Racism in Probation.* London: Routledge.

Derrida, J (1987) *The Postcard: From Socrates to Freud and Beyond.* Translated by Bass, A. Chicago: University of Chicago Press.

De Sousa, P (1991) Black Students, in *One Small Step Towards Racial Justice.* London: CCETSW.

Devore, W and Schlesinger, E G (1981) *Ethnic Sensitive Social Work Practice.* St Louis: C V Mosby.

Dinnerstein, D (1977) *The Mermaid and the Minotaur: Sexual Arrangement and Human Malaise.* New York: Harper Colophon Books.

Divine, D (1992) *Black Probation Officers and Confirmation: A Report.* London: CCETSW.

Dobash, R and Dobash, R (1980) *Violence Against Wives: A Case Against the Patriarchy.* London: Open Books.

Dobash, R and Dobash, R (1991) *Women, Violence and Social Change.* London: Routledge.

Dobson, R (1994) Quality Street, in *Community Care*, 17–23 November, 24.

Dobson, R (1995) Balancing Act, in *Community Care*, 6–12 April, 16.

Doel, M and Marsh, P (1992) *Task Centred Social Work.* Aldershot: Gower.

Dominelli, L (1977) Criticism of *Social Work under Capitalism*: Personal Communication to Peter Leonard and Paul Corrigan. University of Warwick.

Dominelli, L (1982) *Community Action: Organising Marginalised Groups.* Reykjavik: Kwenna Frambothid.

Dominelli, L (1983) *Women in Focus: Community Service Orders and Female Offenders.* Coventry: University of Warwick.

Dominelli, L (1984) *Working with Families: A Feminist Perspective.* Paper presented at the BASW Annual Conference at Nene College, Northampton, April.

Dominelli, L (1986a) The Power of the Powerless: Prostitution and the Enforcement of Submissive Femininity, in *Sociological Review*, Spring, 65–92.

Dominelli, L (1986b) *Women Organising: An Analysis of Greenham Women.* Paper presented at the IASSW Congress in Tokyo, 2 August.

Dominelli, L (1986c) Women in Social Work Education: An International Picture, in *IASSW Newsletter.* Vienna: International Association of Schools of Social Work.

Dominelli, L (1988) *Anti-Racist Social Work.* London: BASW/Macmillan.

Dominelli, L (1989) An Uncaring Profession: Anti-Racist Social Work, in *New Community.*

Dominelli, L (1990) *Women and Community Action.* Birmingham: Venture Press.

Dominelli, L (1991a) *Gender, Sex Offenders and Probation Practice.* Norwich: Novata Press.

Dominelli, L (1991b) Race, Gender and Social Work, in Davies, M (ed.) *The Sociology of Social Work.* London: Routledge.

Dominelli, L (1991c) *Women Across Continents: Feminist Comparative Social Policy.* London: Harvester/Wheatsheaf.

Dominelli, L (1992a) More than a Method: Feminist Social Work, in Campbell, K (ed.) *Critical Feminisms.* Milton Keynes: Open University Press, 83–106.

Dominelli, L (1992b) Sex Offenders and Probation Practice, in Senior, P and Woodhill, D (eds) *Gender, Crime and Probation Practice.* Sheffield: PAVIC Publications.

Dominelli, L (1993) Gender, Values and Offending: Where to Next?, in Senior, P and Williams, B (eds) *Values, Gender and Offending*. Sheffield: PAVIC Publications, 57–68.

Dominelli, L (1995) *The Competences Revolution*. Paper given at the Conference on the Role of the Academy in Social Work Education at Keele University, 15 May.

Dominelli, L (1996) Deprofessionalising Social Work: Equal Opportunities, Competencies and Postmodernism, in *British Journal of Social Work*, April.

Dominelli, L and Hoogvelt, A (1994) The Taylorisation of Intellectual Labour: The Making of a New Intellectual Class, in *History of European Ideas*, Autumn, 191–212.

Dominelli, L, Jeffers, L, Jones, G, Sibanda, S and Williams, B (1995) *Anti-Racist Probation Practice*. Aldershot: Arena.

Dominelli, L and McLeod, E (1989) *Feminist Social Work*. London: Macmillan.

Dominelli, L, Patel, N and Thomas Bernard, W (1994) *Anti-Racist Social Work Education: Models for Practice*. Sheffield University.

Dominelli, L and Whitehead, A (1994) Masculinity and Crime. Unpublished Paper. Sheffield University.

Doyal, L and Gough, I (1991) *A Theory of Human Need*. London: Macmillan.

Doyal, L, Hunt, G and Mellor, J (1981) Your Life in Their Hands: Migrant workers in the NHS, in *Critical Social Policy*, February.

Driver, E and Droisen, A (eds) (1989) *Child Sexual Abuse: Feminist Perspectives*. London: Macmillan.

Duckworth, B (1994) *The Employment Based Route*. Paper to the Programme Council. Sheffield Hallam University.

Dunant, S (ed.) (1994) *The War of the Words: The Political Correctness Debate*. London: Virago.

Durkheim, E (1964a) *The Rules of Sociological Method*. London: Macmillan.

Durkheim, E (1964b) *The Division of Labour in Society*. London: Macmillan.

Durkheim, E (1969) Individualism and the Intellectuals, in *Political Studies*, **17**:14–30.

Durrant, J (1989) Continuous Agitation, in *Community Care*, 13 July, 23–5.

Dworkin, A (1981) *Pornography: Men Possessing Women*. New York: Perigee.

Ehrenreich, B and English, B (1979) *For Her Own Good: 150 Years of the Experts' Advice to Women*. London: Pluto Press.

Eichler, M (1980) *The Double Standard: A Feminist Critique of Feminist Social Sciences*. London: Croom Helm.

Eichler, M (1983) *Families in Canada.* Toronto: Gage.

Eichler, M (1988) *Non-Sexist Research Methods: A Practical Guide.* London: Allen and Unwin.

Eisenstein, Z (1979) *Capitalist Patriarchy and the Case for Socialist Feminism.* New York: Monthly Review Press.

Eisenstein, Z (1994) *The Color of Gender: Reimaging Democracy.* Berkley, Calif: University of California Press.

Eley, R (1989) Women and Management in Social Work, in *Insight,* July, 10.

Elliott, N (1990) *Practice Teaching and the Art of Social Work.* Norwich: University of East Anglia Monographs.

England, H (1986) *Social Work as Art: Making Sense of Good Practice.* London: Allen and Unwin.

Esping-Andersen, G (1990) *The Three Worlds of Welfare Capitalism.* Cambridge: Polity Press.

Evans, R (1994) Out of their Hands, in *Community Care,* 16–22 June, 18–19.

Fagg, C (1993) Domestic Violence and Probation Practice. Unpublished MA Dissertation. University of Sheffield.

Faith, K (1994) *Unruly Women: The Politics of Confinement and Resistance.* Vancouver: Press Gang Publishers.

Family Policy Studies Centre (1984) *An Ageing Population.* London: FPSC.

Farrah, M (1986) *Black Elders in Leicester.* Leicester: Leicester Social Services Department.

Fernando, S (1988) *Race and Culture in Psychiatry.* London: Croom Helm.

Festeau, M F (1975) *The Male Machine.* New York: Delta Books.

Field, M (1989) *Success and Crisis in National Health Systems: A Comparative Approach.* London: Routledge.

Finch, J (1984) Community Care: Developing Non-Sexist Alternatives, in *Journal of Social Policy,* **9**:6–18.

Finch, J and Groves, D (eds) (1983) *Labour of Love: Women, Work and Caring.* London: Routledge & Kegan Paul.

Finkelhor, D (1984) *Child Sexual Abuse: New Theory and Research.* New York: Free Press.

Firestone, S (1971) *The Dialectics of Sex: The Case for Women's Revolution.* New York: Cape.

Flaherty, M (1995) Freedom of Expression or Freedom of Exploration, in *The Simon Fraser University Social Policy Bulletin,* **8**(1):February, 1–3.

Flexner, A (1915) Is Social Work a Profession?, in *Studies in Social Work,* No 4. New York: New York School of Philanthropy.

Foster, P (1989) Improving the Doctor–Patient Relationship: A Feminist Perspective, in *Journal of Social Policy,* **18**(3):337–62.

Foucault, M (1980) *Power/Knowledge: Selected Interviews and Other Writings 1972–1977.* New York: Pantheon.

Frankfort, E (1972) *Vaginal Politics.* New York: Quadrangle Books.

Freire, P (1972) *The Pedagogy of the Oppressed.* Harmondsworth: Penguin.

Freire, P (1973) *Education: The Practice of Freedom.* London: Writers and Reader Publishing Co-operative.

French, M (1985) *The Power of Women.* Harmondsworth: Penguin.

Friedan, B (1963) *The Feminine Mystique.* New York: Bell.

Frost, N (1992) Implementing the Children Act 1989 in a Hostile Climate, in Carter, P, Jeffs, T and Smith, M K (eds) *Changing Social Work and Social Welfare.* Milton Keynes: Open University Press.

Fryer, P (1987) *Staying Power.* London: Pluto Press.

Gairdner, W D (1992) *The War Against the Family.* Toronto: Stoddart Publishing Ltd.

Galper, J (1973) Personal Politics and Psychoanalysis, in *Social Policy,* **4**, November–December.

Gamarnikov, E, Morgan, D, Purvis, J and Taylorson, D (eds) (1983) *The Public and the Private.* London: Heinemann.

Gavron, H (1966) *The Captive Wife.* London: Routledge & Kegan Paul.

George, M (1995) Hey Big Spender, in *Community Care,* 23–29 June, 18–19.

George, V and Manning, N (1980) *Socialism, Social Welfare, and the Soviet Union.* London; Routledge & Kegan Paul.

Gerth, H H and Mills, C W (1948) *From Max Weber: Essays in Sociology.* London: Routledge & Kegan Paul.

Giddens, A (1982) *Sociology: A Brief But Critical Introduction.* London: Macmillan.

Giddens, A (1984) *The Constitution of Society: Outline of a Theory of Structuration.* Cambridge: Polity Press.

Giddens, A (1987) *Social Theory and Modern Sociology.* Oxford: Blackwell.

Giddens, A (1990) *The Consequences of Modernity.* Cambridge: Polity Press.

Gilder, G (1981) *Wealth and Poverty.* New York: Basic Books.

Gilligan, C (1982) *In a Different Voice.* Cambridge, Mass.: Harvard University Press.

Gilroy, P (1987) *There Ain't No Black in the Union Jack.* London: Hutchinson.

Ginsburg, N (1979) *Class, Capital and Social Policy.* London: Macmillan.

Glazer, N (1988) *The Limits of Social Policy.* London: Harvard University Press.

Goffman, E (1961) *Asylums.* Harmondsworth: Penguin Books.

Gordon, L (1985) Child Abuse, Gender and the Myth of Family Independence: A Historical Critique, in *Child Welfare,* **LXIV**(3):May–June, 213–24.

Gordon, L (1988) *Heroes of their Own Lives: The Politics and History of Family Violence.* Harmondsworth: Penguin.

Gordon, P (1992) *Fortress Europe? The Meaning of 1992.* London: The Runnymede Trust.

Gordon, P and Newnham, A (1985) *Passport to Benefits: Racism in Social Security.* London: Child Poverty Action Group and the Runnymede Trust.

Gottlieb, N (ed) (1980) *Alternative Social Services for Women.* New York: Columbia University Press.

Gough, I (1979) *The Political Economy of the Welfare State.* London: Macmillan.

Gould, J (1977) *The Attack on Higher Education: Marxism and Radical Penetration.* London: Institute for the Study of Conflict.

Graef, R (1992) *Living Dangerously: Young Offenders in Their Own Words.* London: Harper Collins.

Graham, H (1983) Caring: A Labour of Love, in Finch, J and Groves, D (eds) *A Labour of Love: Women, Work and Caring.* London: Routledge & Kegan Paul.

Gramsci, A (1971) *Selections from the Prison Notebooks.* London: Lawrence and Wishart.

Grant, L (1992) *Black Perspectives in Social Work Education.* Unpublished MPhil. Warwick University.

Greenwood, V and Young, J (1976) *Abortion in Demand.* London: Pluto.

Greer, P (1994) *Transforming Central Government: The New Steps Initiative.* London: Open University Press.

Gurnah, A (1984) The Politics of Racism Awareness Training, in *Critical Social Policy*, winter.

Gurnah, A (1989) Translating Race Equality Policies into Practice, in *Critical Social Policy*, **27**:110–24.

Guru, S (1987) An Asian Women's Refuge:, in Ahmed, S *et al.* (eds) *Social Work with Black Children and Their Families.* London: Batsford.

Habermas, J (1963) *Theory and Practice.* London: Heinemann.

Habermas, J (1987) *Theory of Communicative Action.* Cambridge: Polity Press.

Haig-Brown, C (1988) *Resistance and Renewal: Surviving the Indian Residential School.* Vancouver: Tillacum Library, Arsenal Pulp Press.

Hall, S (1989) *The Voluntary Sector Under Attack.* London: Islington Voluntary Action Council.

Hall, S, Held, D and McGrew, T (1992) *Modernity and Its Futures.* Cambridge: Polity Press.

Hall, S and Jacques, M (1983) *The Politics of Thatcherism.* London: Lawrence and Wishart.

Hall, S and Jacques, M (1989) *New Times: The Changing Face of Politics in the 1990s.* London: Lawrence and Wishart.

Hallett, C (1990) *Women in Social Work.* London: Sage.

Halmos, P (1978) *The Personal and the Political.* London: Hutchinson.

Handler, J (1973) *The Co-ercive Social Worker: British Lessons for American Social Services.* London: Rand McNalley.

Hanmer, J (1993) Women and Reproduction, in Richardson, D and Robinson, V (eds) *Introducing Women's Studies.* London: Macmillan.

Hanmer, J and Statham, D (1988) *Women and Social Work: Towards a Woman-Centered Practice.* London: Macmillan.

Hanscombe, G and Forster, J (1982) *Rocking the Cradle: Lesbian Mothers.* London: Sheba Feminist Publishers.

Hanvey, C and Philpot, T (1994) *Practising Social Work.* London: Routledge.

Harbart, W (1985a) Status Professionalism, in *Community Care,* 10 October, 14–15.

Harbart, W (1985b) Crisis in Social Work, in *Community Care,* 21 March, 14–16.

Hatton, K and Nugent, C (1993) *Empowerment: Professionalism's Achilles Hill.* Paper presented at the Facing the European Challenge – the Role of the Professions in a Wider Europe Conference. Leeds University, July.

Hayles, M (1989) Probation and Management: What Choice for Women, in *Probation Journal,* 17 March, 12.

Hearn, J (1987) *The Gender of Oppression: Men, Masculinity and the Critique of Marxism.* Brighton: Wheatsheaf.

Henwood, M (1986) Community Care: Policy, Practice and Prognosis, in Brenton, M and Ungerson, C (eds) *The Yearbook of Social Policy in Britain.* London: Routledge & Kegan Paul.

Heraud, B (1970) *Sociology and Social Work: Perspectives and Problems.* Oxford: Pergamon.

Heraud, B (1979) *Sociology in the Professions.* London: Open Books.

Heraud, B (1981) *Training for Uncertainty: A Sociological Approach to Social Work Education.* London: Routledge & Kegan Paul.

Higgins, J (1989) Caring for the Carers, in *Journal of Social Administration,* summer, 382–99.

Higher Education Funding Council for England (HEFCE) (1995) *Assessment of Applied Social Work.* HEFCE.

Hollis, F (1964) *Casework: A Psychosocial Therapy.* New York: Random House.

Home Office (1986) *The Ethnic Origins of Prisoners.* London: Home Office.

Home Office (1991) *Gender and Crime.* London: Home Office.

hooks, b (1982) *Ain't I a Woman? Black Women and Feminism.* London: Pluto Press.

hooks, b (1984) *Feminist Theory: From Margin to Centre.* Boston: South End Press.

hooks, b (1989) *Talking Back: Thinking Feminist; Thinking Black.* Boston: South End Press.

hooks, b (1990) *Yearning: Race, Gender and Cultural Politics.* Boston, MA: Southend Press.

hooks, b (1992) *Black Looks: Race and Representations.* London: Turnaround.

hooks, b (1993) *Sisters of the Yam: Black Women and Self-Recovery.* Toronto: Between the Lines.

Howe, D (1986) The Segregation of Women and Their Work in the Personal Social Services, in *Critical Social Policy,* **15**:21–36.

Howe, D (1987) *Introduction to Social Work Theory.* Aldershot: Wildwood House.

Hudson, A (1985) Feminism and Social Work: Resistance or Dialogue, in *British Journal of Social Work,* **15**:635–55.

Hudson, A (1987) *Report of a Conference on Women in Social Work.* Manchester. Manchester University.

Hughes, B and Mtezuka, M (1989) Social Work and Older Women: Where have Older Women Gone?, in Langan, M and Day, L (eds) *Women, Oppression and Social Work.* London: Routledge.

Hugman, R (1991a) Organisation and Professionalism: The Social Work Agenda in the 1990s, in *British Journal of Social Work,* **21**:199–216.

Hugman, R (1991b) *Power in the Caring Professions.* London: Macmillan.

Hutton, W (1995) *The State We're In.* London: Jonathan Cape.

Hyde, C (1989) A Feminist Model for Macro-Practice: Promises and Problems, in *Administration in Social Work,* **13**(3/4):145–81.

Ireland, P M (1985) Liberal Education: A Plea for Reconsideration. Unpublished M Ed thesis. University of Sheffield.

Irigary, L (1985) *The Sex Which is Not One.* Translated by Porter, C. Ithaca, N Y: Cornell University Press.

Issitt, M (1994) Competence, Professionalism and Equal Opportunities, in Hodkinson, P and Issitt, M (eds) *The Challenge of Competence.* London: Cassell.

Jacobs, S and Popple, K (eds) (1994) *Community Work in the 1990s.* Nottingham: Spokesman.

Jagger, A M (1983) *Feminist Politics and Human Nature.* Totowa, N. J.: Rowman and Allenheld.

Jaques, E (1975) Social Analysis and the Glacier Project, in Brown, W and Brown, J E *Glacier Project Papers.* London: Heinemann.

Jaques, E (1977) *A General Theory of Bureaucracy.* London: Heinemann.

Jayawardna, K (1986) *Feminism and Nationalism in the Third World.* London: Zed Press.

Jones, C (1979) Social Work Education: 1900–1977, in Parry, N, Rustin, M and Satyamurti, C (eds) *Social Work, Welfare and the State.* London, Edward Arnold, pp. 72–88.

Jones, C (1983) *State Social Work and the Working Class.* London: Macmillan.

Jones, C (1989) The End of the Road? Issues in Social Work Education, in Carter, P, Jeffs, T, and Smith, M (eds) *Social Work and Social Welfare Yearbook, One.* Milton Keynes: Open University Press, pp. 204–16.

Jones, C (1994a) *Dangerous Times for British Social Work Education.* Paper presented at the International Association of Schools of Social Work 27th Congress, Amsterdam, 11–15 July.

Jones, C (1994b) *Anti-Intellectualism and Peculiarities of British Social Work Education.* Paper presented at the Future of Social Work Conference, Sheffield University, 25 November.

Jordan, J (1981) *Civil Wars.* Boston: Beacon.

Joyce, P, Corrigan, P and Hayes, M (1987) *Striking Out: Trade Unionism in Social Work.* London: Macmillan.

Kadushin, A (1959) The Knowledge Base of Social Work, in Kahn, A J (ed.) *Issues in American Social Work.* New York: Columbia University Press.

Kaseke, E (1994) *Social Work and Social Development in Zimbabwe.* Paper presented at the International Association of Schools of Social Work Seminar on Social Development, Sheffield University, 28 February.

Kendall, K (1978) *Reflections on Social Work Education: 1950–1978.* New York: International Association of Schools of Social Work.

Kettle, M (1994) Emerging Findings of the Multi-Departmental Scrutiny on the Government's Use of External Consultants, in the *Guardian,* 30 April.

Kollantai, A M (1971) *Communism and the Family.* London: Pluto Press.

Kristeva, J (1984) *Powers of Horror.* Translated by Roudiez, L. New York: Columbia University Press.

Kulin, T (1970) *The Structure of Scientific Revolution.* Chicago: University of Chicago Press.

Lacan, J (1977) *Ecrits: A Selection.* Translated by Sheridan, A. New York: W W Norton.

Lambeth Social Services Committee (Lambeth) (1981) *Black Children in Care Report.* London: Lambeth Social Services Department.

Lampton, D (1977) *The Politics of Medicine in China, 1947–1977.* Folkstone, USA: Westview Press.

Langan, M and Day, L (eds) (1989) *Women, Oppression and Social Work.* London: Tavistock.

Langan, M and Lee, P (eds) (1989) *Radical Social Work Today.* London: Unwin Hyman, pp. 178–91.

Layton Henry, Z (1985) *The Politics of Race in Britain.* London: George Allen and Unwin.

Lederer, L (ed.) (1980) *Take Back the Night: Women on Pornography.* New York: William Morrow.

Lee, P (1982) Contemporary and Perennial Problems, in Bailey, R and Lee, P (eds) *Theory and Practice in Social Work.* Oxford: Basil Blackwell.

Le Grand, J and Robinson, R (1984) *Privatisation and the Welfare State.* London: Unwin Hyman.

Lenin, V I (1961) *Collected Works.* Moscow: Foreign Language Publishing House.

Lenski, G E (1954) Status Crystallization: A Non-Vertical Dimension of Social Status in American Society, in *American Sociological Review,* **19**:405–14.

Leonard, P (1966) *Sociology in Social Work.* London: Routledge & Keagan Paul.

Leonard, P (1975a) *The Sociology of Community Action. Sociological Review Monograph, 21.* University of Keele.

Leonard, P (1975b) Towards a Paradigm for Radical Practice, in Bailey, R and Brake, M (eds) *Radical Social Work.* London: Edward Arnold.

Leonard, P (1984) *Personality and Ideology: Towards a Materialist Understanding of the Individual.* London: Macmillan.

Levitas, R (ed.) (1986) *The Ideology of the New Right.* Cambridge: Polity Press.

Lewis, R (1952) *Edwin Chadwick and the Public Health Movement, 1832–1854.* London: Longmans.

Linton, R (1936) *The Study of Man.* New York: Appleton.

Lishman, J (ed.) (1991) *Handbook of Theory for Practice Teachers in Social Work.* London: Jessica Kingsley Publishers.

Littlewood, R and Lipsedge, M (1982) *Aliens and Alienists.* London: Unwin Hyman.

Livingstone, K (1987) *If Voting Changed Anything, They'd Abolish It.* London: Collins.

Loney, M (1983) *Community Against Government: The British Community Development Project, 1968–78.* London: Heinemann.

Loney, M (1986) *The Politics of Greed: The New Right and the Welfare State.* London: Pluto Press.

Loney, M (1987) *The State or the Market: Politics and Welfare in Contemporary Britain.* London: Sage.

Longres, J and McLeod, E (1980) Consciousness-Raising and Social Work Practice, in *Social Casework,* **61**(5), May, 267–77.

Lorde, A (1984) *Sister Outsider.* New York: The Crossing Press.

Lorenz, W (1994) *Social Work in a Changing Europe.* London: Routledge.

Lowe, R (1993) *The Welfare State in Britain since 1945.* London: Macmillan.

Lowith, K (1964) *From Hegel to Nietzsche.* London; Constable.

Lukes, S (1974) *Power: A Radical View.* London: Macmillan.

Luxemburg, R (1951) *The Accummulation of Capital.* Translated by Schwarzschild, A. London: Routledge & Kegan Paul.

Lyndon, J. (1992) *Men In Danger.* New York: Random House.

MacKinnon, C (1977) *Feminism Unmodified: Discourses on Life and the Law.* Cambridge, Mass.: Harvard University Press.

MacKinnon, C (1983) Feminism, Marxism, Method and the State: Towards Feminist Jurisprudence, in *Signs: Journal of Women in Culture and Society,* **8**(4):635–58.

MacPherson, S (1982) *Social Policy in the Third World: The Social Dilemmas of Underdevelopment.* Brighton: Wheatsheaf.

MacPherson, S and Midgley, J (1987) *Comparative Social Policy and the Third World.* London: Wheatsheaf.

Mainframe (1994) *Review of the Diploma in Social Work: Functional Outline.* Communication to External Assessors. May, July and August versions. London: CCETSW.

Mama, A (1989) *Hidden Struggle: Statutory and Voluntary Responses to Violence Against Black Women in the Home.* London: London Race and Housing Unit.

Marchant, C (1994) Fist of Fear, in *Community Care,* 8–14 December, 16–17.

Marchant, H and Wearing, B (eds) (1986) *Gender Reclaimed.* Sydney: Hale and Iremonger.

Marcuse, H (1968) Negations, in *Essays in Critical Theory.* London: Allen Lane.

Marshall, T (1950) *Citizenship and Social Class.* Cambridge: Cambridge University Press.

Martin, G (1978) *Socialist Feminism: The First Decade, 1966–1976.* Seattle: Freedom Socialist Publishers.

Marx, K (1965) *A Critical Analysis of Capitalist Production.* Vols I, II, III. Moscow: Progressive Publishers.

Marx, K and Engels, F (1985) *The Communist Manifesto.* Harmondsworth: Penguin.

Mathiesen, T (1974) *The Politics of Abolition.* London: Martin Robertson.

Matza, D (1964) *Delinquency and Drift.* New York: Wiley.

May, L and Strikwerda, R (1992) *Rethinking Masculinity: Philosophical Explorations in Light of Feminism.* Lantham: Littlefield Adams Quality Paperbacks.

Mayhew, P and Hough, M (1990) *The British Crime Survey.* London: HMSO.

McIntosh, P (1989) White Privilege: Unpacking the Invisible Knapsack, in *Peace and Freedom*, July–August, 10–12.

McLeod, E and Dominelli, L (1982) The Personal and the Apolitical: Feminism and Moving Beyond Integrated Methods Approach, in Bailey, R and Lee, P (eds) *Theory and Practice in Social Work*. Oxford: Basil Blackwell, pp. 112–27.

Mead, G (1936) *Mind, Self and Society*. Chicago: University of Chicago Press.

Merton, R K (1957) *Social Theory and Social Structures*. New York: Free Press.

Michels, R (1962) *Political Parties: A Sociological Study of the Oligarchical Tendencies of Modern Democracy*. New York: Collier-Macmillan.

Midgley, J (1981) *Professional Imperialism: Social Work in the Third World*. London: Heinemann.

Millett, K (1970) *Sexual Politics*. Garden City, N Y: Doubleday.

Mills, C W (1957) *The Power Elite*. Oxford: Oxford University Press.

Mills, C W (1970) *The Sociological Imagination*. London: Pelican Books.

Minford, P (1984) State Expenditure: A Study in Waste, *Economic Affairs, Special Supplement*, **1**(3):i–xix.

Moraga, C and Azaldna, G (eds) (1981) *This Bridge Called My Back: Writings by Radical Women of Colour*. Watertown, Mass.: Persephone Press.

Moreau, M (1979) A Structural Approach to Social Work Practice, in *Canadian Journal of Social Work Education*, **5**(1):78–94.

Morgan, R (1970) *Sisterhood is Powerful*. New York: Vintage Books.

Morris, C (ed.) (1975) *Literature and the Social Workers: A Reading List for Practitioners, Teachers, Students and Voluntary Workers*. Second Edition. London: The Library Association.

Morris, J (1991) *Pride Against Prejudice: Transforming Attitudes to Disability*. London: The Women's Press.

Morris, L (1994) *Dangerous Classes: The Underclass and Social Citizenship*. London: Routledge.

Morrison, T (1992) *Race-ing Justice, Engendering Power: Essays on Anita Hill, Clarence Thomas and the Construction of Social Reality*. New York: Pantheon.

Mount, F (1982) *The Subversive Family: An Alternative History of Love and Marriage*. New York: Jonathan Cape.

Mowatt, C L and Loch, C (1961) *The Charity Organisation Society, 1869–1913*. London: Methuen.

Moynihan, D P (1965) *The Negro Family: The Case for National Action*. Washington DC: Office of Policy Planning and Research, US Department of Labour.

Mullaly, R (1993) *Structural Social Work*. Toronto: McClelland and Stewart.

Munday, B (1972) What is Happening to Social Work Students?, in *Social Work Today*, 15 June, 4–5.

Murray, C (1984) *Losing Ground: American Social Policy, 1950–80*. New York: Basic Books.

Murray, C (1990) *The Emerging British Underclass. Choice in Welfare Series No. 2*. London: Health and Welfare Unit, Institute of Economic Affairs.

Murray, C (1994) *Underclass: The Crisis Deepens*. London: Health and Welfare Unit, Institute for Economic Affairs.

Murray, P (1970) The Liberation of Black Women, in Tompson, M L (ed.) *Voices of the New Feminism*. Boston Beacon Press, pp. 87–102.

Narayan, U (1988) Working Together Across Difference: Some Considera-tion on Emotions and Political Practice, in *Hypation*, **3**(2):summer, 31–47.

National Association for the Care and Rehabilitation of Offenders (NACRO) (1992) *Statistics on Black People Working in the Criminal Justice System: NACRO Briefing 109*. London: NACRO.

National Association of Social Workers (NASW) (1992) Social Workers' *Code of Practice*. Washington D.C.: NASW.

National Institute of Social Work (1994) *The Black Students' Handbook*. London: NISW.

Navarro, V (1979) *Medicine Under Capitalism*. London: Croom Helm.

Newburn, T and Hagell, A (1994) Arrested Development, in *Community Care*, 2–8 June, 24–5.

Nicholson, L (ed.) (1990) *Postmodernism/Feminism*. London: Routledge.

Nicolaus, M (1966) *The Fat Cat Sociologist*. Paper delivered at the American Sociological Association Annual Conference. Berkley, California.

Nicolaus, M (1973) Foreword to the *Grundrisse* by Marx, K. Harmondsworth: Penguin.

Nieman, L J and Hughes, J W (1961) The Problem of the Concept of Role – A Resurvey of the Literature, in Stein, H D and Cloward, R A (eds) *Social Perspectives on Behaviour*. Glencoe: The Free Press.

Nissel, M and Bonnerjea, L (1982) *Family Care of the Handicapped Elderly: Who Pays?* London: Policy Studies Institute.

Oakley, A (1974) *The Sociology of Housework*. London: Martin Robertson.

Oakley, A (1980) *Women Confined: Towards a Sociology of Childbirth*. Oxford: Martin Robertson.

Oakley, A and Williams, S A (1994) *The Politics of the Welfare State*. London: University College London Press.

Offe, C (1984) *Contradictions of the Welfare State*. London: Hutchinson.

Ohri, A, Manning, B and Curno, P (1982) *Community Work and Racism*. London: Routledge & Kegan Paul.

Oliver, P (1990) *The Politics of Disablement*. London: Macmillan.

Omi, M and Winant, H (1986) *Racial Formation in the United States from the 1960s to the 1980s.* London: Routledge & Kegan Paul.

Orme, J and Glastonbury, B (1993) *Care Management.* London: Macmillan.

Pahl, J (1985) *Private Violence and Public Policy.* London: Routledge & Kegan Paul.

Palmer, S E (1983) Authority: An Essential Part of Practice, in *Social Work*, March–April, 120–5.

Parker, R *et al.*, (1990) *The Arguments for a General Council in Social Care.* London: National Institute for Social Work.

Parmar, P (1982) Gender, Race and Class: Asian Women in Resistance, in Centre for Contemporary Culture Studies, *The Empire Strikes Back.* London: Hutchinson, pp. 236–75.

Parmar, P (1986) Can Black and White Women Work Together?, in *Spare Rib*, **168**, July, 20.

Parry, N, Rustin, M and Satyamurti, C (eds) (1979) *Social Work, Welfare and the State.* London: Edward Arnold.

Parsloe, P (1984) The Review of Quality Training: A Comment from Phylida Parsloe, in *Issues in Social Work Education*, 4(2):107–17.

Parsons, T (1957) The Professions and Social Structure, in *Essays in Sociological Theory*, New York: Free Press.

Parsons, T (1968) Professions, in Sills, D (ed.) *International Encyclopaedia of the Social Sciences.* London: Macmillan.

Pascall, G (1986) *Social Policy: A Feminist Analysis.* London: Tavistock.

Patel, N (1990) *Race Against Time: Ethnic Elders.* London: Runnymede Trust.

Patel, N (1994) *Establishing a Framework for Anti-Racist Social Work Education in a Multi-Racial Society – the UK Experience from a Statutory Body, CCETSW.* Paper given at the 27th Congress of International Association of Schools of Social Work. Amsterdam, July.

Payne, M (1991) *Modern Social Work Theory: a Critical Introduction.* London: Macmillan.

Perlman, H (1957) *Social Casework: A Problem Solving Process.* Chicago: University of Chicago Press.

Perry, L (1989) *Racism and Black Resistance.* London: Pluto Press.

Phillips, D (1993) New Technology and the Human Services: Implications for Social Justice, in Leiderman, M, Guzetta, C, Struminger, L and Monnickendam, M (eds) *Technology in People Services: Research, Theory and Applications.* London: The Haworth Press.

Phillips, D and Berman, Y (1995) *Human Services in the Age of New Technology: Harmonising Social Work and Computerisation.* Aldershot: Avebury.

Phillips, M (1993) Oppressive Urge to End Oppression, in the *Observer*, 1 August.

Phillips, M (1994) Illiberal Liberalism, in Dunant, S (ed.) *The War of the Words: The Political Correctness Debate*. London: Virago.

Phillipson, C (1982) *Capitalism and the Construction of Old Age*. London: Macmillan.

Phillipson, C and Walker, A (eds) (1986) *Ageing and Social Policy*. Aldershot: Gower.

Phillipson, J (ed.) (1988) *Towards a Practice Led Curriculum*. London: National Institute of Social Work.

Phillipson, J (1992) *Practising Equality: Men and Women in Social Work*. London: CCETSW.

Philpott, T (1990) Forward to the Future, in *Community Care*, 18 Jan, 27.

Pierce, R (1994) *Communication to External Assessors*. London: CCETSW. August.

Pincus, A and Minahan, A (1973) *Social Work Practice: Model and Method*. Itasca, Ill.: F E Peacock.

Pinker, R (1979) Slimline Social Work, in *New Society*, 13 December.

Pinker, R (1984) The Threat to Professional Standards in Social Work Education: A Response to Some Recent Proposals, in *Issues in Social Work Education*, 4(1):5–15.

Pinker, R (1986) Time to Stop CCETSW in Its Tracks, in *Community Care*, 18 September, 21–2.

Pinker, R (1993) A Lethal Kind of Looniness, in *The Times Higher Educational Supplement*, 10 September.

Pinker, R (1994) Playing Devil's Advocate, in *Community Care*, 24–30 November, 18–19.

Popplestone, J (1971) The Ideology of Professional Community Workers, in *British Journal of Social Work* 1(1): April, 85–104.

Poulantzas, N (1978) *State, Power and Socialism*. London: New Left Review.

Price-Waterhouse (1990) *Implementing Community Care: Purchaser/Commissioner and Provider Roles*. London: HMSO.

Ramazanoglu, C (1989) Improving on Sociology: Problems in Taking a Feminist Viewpoint, in *Sociology*, 23(3):427–42.

Rees, S (1991) *Achieving Power: Practice and Policy in Social Welfare*. London: Allen and Unwin.

Reinharz, S (1992) *Feminist Methods in Social Research*. Oxford: Oxford University Press.

Remfry, P (1979) North Tyneside Community Development Project, in *Journal of Community Development*, 14(3):186–9.

Rich, A (1976) *Of Woman Born: Motherhood as Experience and Institution*. New York: W W Norton and Company.

Richards, M (1987) Developing the Content of Practice Teaching, in *Social Work Education* **6**(2).

Richardson, D (1992) *Women, Motherhood and Childrearing*. London: Macmillan.

Richardson, D and Hart, J (1981) *The Theory and Practice of Homosexuality*. London: Routledge & Kegan Paul.

Richardson, D and Robinson, V (1993) *Introducing Women's Studies*. London: Macmillan.

Rickford, F (1995a) Britain Failing to Guarantee Children's Rights, Says UN, in *Community Care*, 2–8 February, 4.

Rickford, F (1995b) Losing More Than Liberty, in *Community Care*, 19–25 January, 18–19.

Roberts, H (1981) *Women, Health and Reproduction*. London: Routledge & Kegan Paul.

Rogaly, J (1977) *Grunwick*. Harmondsworth: Penguin.

Rooney, B (1987) *Resistance and Change*. Liverpool: Liverpool University.

Rowbotham, S (1986) More than Just a Memory: Some Political Implication of Women's Involvement in the Miner's Strike, 1984–85, in *Feminist Review*, (23), summer, 109–25.

Rowbotham, S (1994) Interpretations of Welfare and Approaches to the State, in Oakley, A and Williams, S A (eds) *The Politics of the Welfare State*. London: University College London Press.

Rowe, D (1983) *Depression: The Way Out of Your Prison*. London: Routledge.

Rush, F (1980) *The Best Kept Secret: Sexual Abuse of Children*. New York: McGraw-Hill.

Ruth, S (1989) A Feminist Analysis of the New Right, in Klein, R E and Steinberg, D L (eds) *Radical Voices: A Decade of Feminist Resistance*. Oxford: Pergammon Press, pp. 93–106.

Ruzek, S B (1978) *The Woman's Health Movement: Feminist Alternatives to Medical Control*. New York: Praeger.

Ruzek, S B (1986) Feminist Visions of Health: An International Perspective, in Mitchell, J and Oakley, A (eds) *What is Feminist?* Oxford: Basil Blackwell.

Sainsbury, E (1982) Knowledge, Skills and Values in Social Work Education, in Bailey, R and Lee, P (eds) *Theory and Practice in Social Work*. Oxford: Basil Blackwell.

Sainsbury, E (1985) Diversity in Social Work Practice: An Overview of the Problem, in *Issues in Social Work Education*, **5**(1):3–12.

Sawyer, J (1989) Internalised Dominance, in *Quarterly Change*, **1**(4):16–23.

Schlaffy, P (1977) *The Power of the Positive Woman*. New York: Jove Books.

Schur, E (1973) *Radical Non-Intervention: Rethinking the Delinquency Problem.* Englewood Cliffs, N J: Prentice-Hall.

Scott, H (1984) *Working Your Way to the Bottom: The Feminisation of Poverty.* London: Pandora Press.

Scrutton, S (1990) *Counselling Older People.* London: Edward Arnold.

Seebohm Report, (1968) *Reports of the Committee on Local Authority and Allied Personal Social Services.* Cmnd 3703. London HMSO.

Segal, L (1983) *What is to be Done about the Family?* Harmondsworth: Penguin.

Segal, L (1987) *Is the Future Female? Troubled Thoughts on Contemporary Feminism.* London: Virago.

Seidler, V (1992) *Men, Sex and Relationships: Writings from Achilles Heel.* London: Routledge.

Showstack-Sassoon, A (ed.) (1987) *Women and the State.* London: Unwin Hyman Ltd.

Sibeon, R (1989) The Sociology of Social Work, in *British Social Policy Association Conference,* Plymouth University, July.

Sibeon, R (1991) *Towards a New Sociology of Social Work.* Aldershot: Avebury.

Sidel, R (1986) *Women and Children Last: The Plight of Poor Women in Affluent America.* New York: Viking Books.

Sidel, R and Sidel, V (1977) *A Healthy State: An International Perspective on the Crisis in United States Medical Care.* New York: Pantheon Books.

Sidel, R and Sidel, V (1982) *The Health of China: Conflicts in Medical and Human Services for 1 Billion People.* Boston: Beacon Press.

Simpkin, M (1979) *Trapped Within Welfare: Surviving Social Work.* London: Macmillan.

Simpkin, M (1989) Holistic Health Care and Professional Values, in Shardlow, S (ed.) *The Values of Change in Social Work.* London: Tavistock.

Sivanandan, A (1982) *A Different Hunger: Writings on Black Resistance.* London: PLuto Press.

Sivanandan, A (1976) Race, Class and the State: The Black Experience in Britain, in *Race and Class,* **17**(4):437–68.

Sklair, L (1991) *Sociology of the Global System.* London: Harvester/ Wheatsheaf.

Small, J (1984) The Crisis in Adoption, in *International Journal of Psychiatry,* **30**: Spring, 129–41.

Small, J (1994) *Management Issues from a Black Perspective.* Paper presented at the International Association of Schools of Social Work, Amsterdam, July.

Small, S (1994) *Racialised Barriers: The Black Experience in the United States and England in the 1980s.* London: Routledge.

Smart, C (1976) *Women, Crime and Criminology – A Feminist Critique.* London: Routledge & Kegan Paul.

Smart. C (1984) *The Ties that Bind: Law, Marriage and the Reproduction of Patriarchal Relations.* London: Routledge & Kegan Paul.

Smith, D (1976) *The Facts of Racial Disadvantage: PEP Report.* Harmondsworth: Penguin.

Smith, D E (1979) A Peculiar Eclipse: Women's Exclusion from Men's Culture, in *Women's Studies International Quarterly*, **1**:281–95.

Smith, D E (1987) *The Everyday World as Problematic: A Feminist Sociology.* Milton Keynes: Open University Press.

Social Services Inspectorate (SSI) (1991a) *Purchase of Service: Practice Guidance and Practice Material for Social Services Departments and Other Agencies.* London: HMSO.

Social Services Inspectorate (SSI) (1991b) *Women in Social Services.* London: SSI.

Social Work Today: Special Issue on Social Work with Ethnic Minorities. 20 February 1979.

Solanas, V (1971) *Society for Cutting Up Men.* New York: Olympia Press.

Solomon, B (1976) *Black Empowerment: Social Work in Oppressed Communities.* New York: Columbia University Press.

Sone, K (1995) Get Tough, in *Community Care.* 16–22 March, 16–18.

Spencer, H (1877) *Principles of Sociology.* London: Williams and Worgate.

Spender, D (1980) *Man Made Language.* London: Routledge & Kegan Paul.

Stack, C (1975) *All Our Kin: Strategies for Survival in a Black Community.* New York: Harper and Row.

Stalker, J (1961) *Readings in Organisational Change.* New York: Random House.

Stanley, L (ed.) (1990) *Feminist Praxis.* London: Routledge.

Stanley, L and Wise, S (1983) *Breaking Out: Feminist Consciousness and Feminist Research.* London: Routledge & Kegan Paul.

Staples, R (1988) *Black Masculinity: The Black Male's Role in American Society.* San Fransisco: Black Scholar Press.

Stedman Jones, G (1971) *Outcast London.* Oxford: Clarendon Press.

Steele, S (1990) *The Content of Our Character: An Alternative Vision of Race in America.* New York: Harper Collins.

Steinem, G (1990) *The Revolution Within: A Book of Self-Esteem.* New York: Harper Collins.

Swann, L (1985) *Education for All: The Report of the Committee of Enquiry into the Education of Children from Ethnic Minority Groups.* Cmnd 9453. London: HMSO.

Tannen, D (1992) *You Just Don't Understand: Women and Men in Conversation.* London: Virago.

Taylor, W (1981) *Probation and After-Care in a Multi-Racial Society.* London: CRE.

Thomas, Bernard, W (1994) Black Masculinity: Survival and Success. Unpublished Ph D. Sheffield University.

Thompson, J (1993) Developing a Value Base for Work With Sex Offenders, in Senior, P and Williams, B (eds) *Values, Gender and Offending.* Sheffield: PAVIC Publications, 35–41.

Tissier, G (1994a) Social Police, in *Community Care,* 3–9 November, 25.

Tissier, G (1994b) Situations Vacant, in *Community Care,* 22 December– 5 January, 28–19.

Titmuss, R (1968) Community Care: Fact or Fiction?, in Titmuss, R, *Commitment to Welfare.* London: Allen and Unwin.

Titmuss, R (1970) *The Gift Relationship.* London: Allen and Unwin.

Tolson, A (1977) *The Limits of Masculinity.* London: Tavistock.

Tong, R (1989) *Feminist Thought: A Comprehensive Introduction.* San Francisco: Westview Press.

Toren, N (1972) *Social Work: The Case of a Semi-Profession.* London: Sage.

Torkington, C (1981) Women in Action: Preservers of the Status Quo or a Force for Change? Unpublished MA dissertation. University of Warwick.

Trotsky, L (1963) *The Essential Trotsky.* London: Unwin Books.

Ungerson, C (1987) *Policy is Personal: Sex, Gender and Informal Care.* London: Tavistock.

Walby, S (1990) *Theorizing Patriarchy.* Oxford: Basil Blackwell.

Walker, A and Walker, C (1987) *The Growing Divide: A Social Audit.* London: CPAG.

Walton, R (1975) *Women in Social Work.* London: Routledge & Kegan Paul.

Ward, D and Spencer, J (1994) The Future of Probation Qualifying Training, in *Probation Journal,* **41**(2).

Warner, N (1994) *Community Care: Just a Fairytale?* London: Carers National Association.

Warwick Course Handbook (1976) Course handbook for the MA/CQSW Course at Warwick Univeristy.

Warwick Feminist Social Work Practice Conference Group (Warwick) (1978) *Feminist Social Work Practice: Notes on the Conference.* Warwick University.

Weber, M (1949) *Methodology of Social Sciences.* New York: Free Press.

Weber, M (1968) *Economy and Society.* Vol 1. New York: Bodminster Press.

Weber, M (1978) *Selections from Max Weber.* Translated by Runciman, W C. Berkeley: Univeristy of California Press.

Weeks, J (1981) Discourse, Desire and Sexual Deviance: Some Problems in the History of Homosexuality, in Plummer, K (ed.) *The Making of the Modern Homosexual.* London: Hutchinson, pp. 76–111.

Whitlock, M J (1987) Five More Years of Desolation, in *Spare Rib*, **180**:15, July.

Whyte, W F (1961) *Street Corner Society: The Social Structure of an Italian Slum*. Chicago: Chicago University Press.

Wilson, A (1978) *Finding a Voice*. London: Virago.

Wilson, D (1974) Uneasy Bedfellows, in *Social Work Today*, **5**(1):9–12.

Wilson, E (1977) *Women and the Welfare State*. London: Tavistock.

Wilson, M (1993) *Crossing the Boundary: Black Women Survive Incest*. London: Virago.

Winant, H (1994) *Racial Conditions: Politics, Theory, Comparisons*. Minneapolis: University of Minnesota Press.

Wistow, G, Knapp, M, Hardy, B and Allen, C (1994) *Social Care in a Mixed Economy*. Buckingham: Open University Press.

Worrall, A (1990) *Women Offending: Female Lawbreakers and the Criminal Justice System*. London: Routledge.

Worsley, P (1987) *The New Introducing Sociology*. 3rd edn. Harmondsworth: Pelican Books.

Wright, R (1977) *Expectations of the Teaching of Social Work on Courses Leading to the CQSW. Consultative Document 3*. London: Central Council for Education and Training in Social Work.

Younghusband, E (1964) *Social Work with Families: Readings in Social Work*. London: Allen and Unwin.

Younghusband, E (1978) *Social Work in Britain: 1950–1975*. 2 Vols. London: Allen and Unwin.

Zaretsky, E (1976) *Capitalism, the Family and Personal Life*. London: Pluto Press.

AUTHOR INDEX

SUBJECT INDEX

Index

values 3, 11, 14, 62, 66–7, 83, 98, 100,
121–2, 151, 174, 179–80, 195–6, 207,
215, 218, 234
valuing difference 15, 29–30, 40–1, 91, 153,
179, 229
valuing women 29
variables 12–18
verification 13–14
viability of relations of domination 100,
122
vicarious knowledge 238
vice-chancellor 159
victim 24, 95, 133, 140, 166, 207, 210–11,
232–4
victim blaming 210–11
victim-survivor 133, 140, 211
Victorian England 153, 209
Victorian morality 198
violence against social workers 95
violence against women 112
violent men 35, 90, 95, 110
vision 47, 71, 86, 104, 153, 211, 223,
240–1, 248
voice 28–9, 32, 58, 158, 175, 222, 227
voluntary organisations, nationalisation and
internationalisation of 204
voluntary sector 5, 57, 71, 79, 175, 184,
195, 201
vulnerable women 148

Waged work 35, 67, 93, 116, 132, 206
waiting list 119, 147, 243
War on Poverty 21, 74
Warwick University 21, 121, 160
Warwickshire Social Services 142
wealth 23, 67, 220, 241
wealthy black woman 79
wealthy white men 88
Weberian formulations 127
welfare credits 132
welfare dependency 23, 72, 133, 211
welfare dilemmas 204
welfare experience 17–18, 25–30, 32, 35–6,
48, 52, 56, 60, 65, 88, 91–4, 99–109,
112, 126–9, 132, 135, 176, 180–7, 206,
208, 217–20, 228, 234, 238, 241, 248
welfare needs 15, 22, 131, 239–40
welfare provisions 15, 43, 56, 88, 132–5,
142, 194, 202, 212, 224, 239
welfare rights 46, 51, 64, 77, 93, 134–5
portability 239
welfare roles 72, 211
welfare scroungers 133–5
welfare state 54–6, 70–2, 77, 88, 93, 96,
100–1, 115, 120, 132, 135–6, 139,
142–3, 160–2, 170, 193–5, 201–5, 210,
212

British 70, 88, 135, 136
Well Women Clinics 92
western democracies 36–7, 67, 134–5, 209
white academics 158, 163–5
White Collective for Anti-Racist Social
Work 163
white English neighbours 243
white environment 226
white feminism 29, 34–8, 86, 91, 103, 233,
238
white feminist refuges 233
white ghetto 217
white ideological positions 17, 74
white male orderly 147
white male probation officer 36, 110, 146
white male student 215
white male supervisor 109
white man of Polish descent 242
white Marxist feminists 36, 74
white men 36, 60, 71–2, 88–98, 100, 103,
109–11, 126–9, 145–6, 176, 204–7, 242
white men's backlash 205–6
white men's needs 126, 207
white middle class 13, 29, 36–7, 71–2, 100,
102, 116, 153, 196–7, 202, 208, 210,
213–17
white middle-class Victorians 153
white organisations 159
white practitioners 146, 163–5
white supremacy 201, 229
white values 234
white woman 60, 90, 94–5, 144, 147, 168,
215–17, 231, 234
white working class 37, 43, 79–80, 90, 99,
101, 105–6, 132, 173, 199, 208–9,
216–17, 244
white working-class man 43, 79–80, 209,
217, 244
white working-class women 27, 90, 99,
101, 105, 173, 199, 208
widows 198
women social workers 44, 144–5
woman-centred provisions 30–3, 57, 104,
128
womanist 38
women 9, 17–18, 22–47, 53, 56–7, 60–4,
67, 71–6, 79, 85–104, 107–12, 122–34,
139–48, 153, 156–7, 163, 173, 186,
195, 197–218, 224–7, 231–7, 241
women as equals 90, 233–5
women carers 140, 224
women community workers 76
women managers 91–4, 110, 126–9, 224
women offenders 24
women social workers 25, 97–8, 197–9,
201
women with disabilities 147–8